The Intersection of Class and Space in British Postwar Writing

The Intersection of Class and Space in British Postwar Writing

Kitchen Sink Aesthetics

Simon Lee

BLOOMSBURY ACADEMIC
LONDON • NEW YORK • OXFORD • NEW DELHI • SYDNEY

BLOOMSBURY ACADEMIC
Bloomsbury Publishing Plc
50 Bedford Square, London, WC1B 3DP, UK
1385 Broadway, New York, NY 10018, USA
29 Earlsfort Terrace, Dublin 2, Ireland

BLOOMSBURY, BLOOMSBURY ACADEMIC and the Diana logo
are trademarks of Bloomsbury Publishing Plc

First published in Great Britain 2023
Paperback edition published 2024

Copyright © Simon Lee, 2023, 2024

Simon Lee has asserted his right under the Copyright,
Designs and Patents Act, 1988, to be identified as Author of this work.

For legal purposes the Acknowledgments on pp. ix–xi constitute
an extension of this copyright page.

Cover design: Rebecca Heselton
Cover image © Courtyard with Washing, 1956 (oil on masonite board),
Birmingham Museums Trust/Purchased with the assistance of the Friends of
Birmingham Museums & Art Gallery, the National Art Collections Fund and the
Victoria & Albert Purchase Grant Fund, 2001/Bridgeman Images

All rights reserved. No part of this publication may be reproduced or transmitted
in any form or by any means, electronic or mechanical, including photocopying,
recording, or any information storage or retrieval system, without prior
permission in writing from the publishers.

Bloomsbury Publishing Plc does not have any control over, or responsibility for,
any third-party websites referred to or in this book. All internet addresses given in this book were correct
at the time of going to press. The author and publisher regret any inconvenience caused if addresses
have changed or sites have ceased to exist,
but can accept no responsibility for any such changes.

A catalogue record for this book is available from the British Library.

Library of Congress Cataloging-in-Publication Data
Names: Lee, Simon, 1976- author.
Title: The intersection of class and space in British post-war writing : kitchen sink
aesthetics / Simon Lee.
Description: London ; New York : Bloomsbury Academic, 2023. | Includes
bibliographical references and index. |
Summary: "Centering on the British kitchen sink realism movement of the late 1950s and early 1960s,
specifically its documentation of the built environment's influence on class consciousness,
this book highlights the settings of a variety of novels, plays, and films, turning to archival research to
offer new ways of thinking about how spatial representation in cultural production sustains or
intervenes in the process of social stratification. As a movement that used gritty, documentary-style
depictions of space to highlight the complexities of working-class life, the period's texts chronicled
shifts in the social and topographic landscape while advancing new articulations of citizenship in
response to the failures of post-war reconstruction. By exploring the impact of space on class,
this book addresses the contention that critical discourse has overlooked the way the
built environment informs class identity"– Provided by publisher.
Identifiers: LCCN 2022031301 | ISBN 9781350193093 (hardback) | ISBN 9781350193154
(paperback) | ISBN 9781350193109 (ebook) | ISBN 9781350193116 (epub) | ISBN 9781350193123
Subjects: LCSH: English literature–20th century–History and criticism. | Working class in literature. |
Social classes in literature. | Space and time in literature. | Motion pictures and literature–Great Britain. |
Literature and society–Great Britain–History–20th century.
Classification: LCC PR120.L33 L44 2023 | DDC 820.9/08623–dc23/eng/20220829
LC record available at https://lccn.loc.gov/2022031301

ISBN:	HB:	978-1-3501-9309-3
	PB:	978-1-3501-9315-4
	ePDF:	978-1-3501-9310-9
	eBook:	978-1-3501-9311-6

Typeset by Integra Software Services Pvt. Ltd.

To find out more about our authors and books visit www.bloomsbury.com
and sign up for our newsletters.

If you are going to write about the people, then one must do them justice, by writing about them in such a way that you hold their voice with yours, so that no one can detect the seams of such an amalgamation.

—Alan Sillitoe, *unpublished essay*[1]

---

[1] While the catalog title lists this document as "Under Spiritual Horizons," the typescript is titled "Wider Spiritual Horisons" [*sic*]. It is a brief meditation on "the proletarian man, the working class hero"—one that Sillitoe considers "a material man, whose happiness will be sufficient to hold in chec [*sic*] check the spiritual man which in past times led him into subjection." Mss. II, Box 22, The Sillitoe Mss. II, 1950–1996, The Lilly Library, Indiana University, Bloomington, IN.

Contents

Acknowledgments	ix
About the Author	xii
Introduction	1

1 "Look at the State of This Place!"—The Impact of Domestic Space
    on Postwar Class Consciousness   23
    New Domestic Forms   25
    Postwar Housing and Classed Space   28
    Writing Home   38
    Theorizing Domestic Space and Classed Identity   43
    Domestic Anxiety in *Look Back in Anger*   51
    Renegotiations of Identity in *Saturday Night and Sunday Morning*   55
    Queering the Domestic in *A Taste of Honey*   60

2 "Off Down the Local"—Institutional Borders in Working-Class
    Communities   71
    Shared Space and Working-Class Institutions   73
    The Pub   75
    Schools and Education   80
    The Factory   85
    Collective Consciousness and Shared Experience   91
    Shared Space and Identity Formation in *Saturday Night and
    Sunday Morning*   93
    Class Migration and Social Stasis in *This Sporting Life*   99
    Contours of Class and Mobility in *Up the Junction*   105

3 Spatial Transgression and the Working-Class Imaginary   114
    Theorizing Spatial Transgression: From the Production of
    Space to the Non-Place   116
    Transgressive Space and Postwar Potentiality   124

Spatial Transgression and the Working-Class Imaginary
in *Up the Junction*   135
Subterranean Space and Diasporic Demimondes in *City of Spades*   141
Differential Space and Inversion in *The Loneliness of the Long
Distance Runner*   147

4   Against Class Fetishism: The Legacy of Kitchen Sink Realism   156
    A Genealogy of the Realist Mode: Form versus Function   157
    Critical Approaches to Kitchen Sink Aesthetics   161
    Multimedia Motifs and Kitchen Sink Thematics   164
    Toward a Spatial Aesthetics of Class   169
    Coronation Street as Commodified "Kitsch-en" Sink   173
    Channel 4 and Commodified Class Aesthetics   179
    Theaters of Anger and Aggression   188
    Class and Space in Contemporary Fiction   191

References   199
Index   211

Acknowledgments

Sherry Lee Linkon has discussed the value of scholarly personal narratives, noting in particular how identification validates one's motivation, adds ethos to one's argument, and celebrates the role of lived experience as it pertains to class articulation. She writes, "In the context of a contested, diverse, and emerging field, scholarly personal narratives have defined core concepts, modeled scholarly practices, and helped to define working-class studies as an interdisciplinary academic field" (2021, 21). Narratives of identification matter, Linkon insists, in that "By foregrounding working-class perspectives, these narratives also challenge academic analyses of the working class, which often misread class culture because they begin with theoretical assumptions rather than with experience" (22). Identification, though, is a slippery notion, and today's definitions of "working-class" are less stable than they once were in the past. As such, Linkon adds how scholarly work in this area is often about personal reconciliation as much as it is about the production of scholarship: "Most working-class studies scholars identify themselves either as professionals who come from working-class backgrounds or as straddlers with dual affiliations and identities" (25). This text—and much of my scholarly work—originates from a 2013 graduate seminar, "The Long 1960s in Fiction and Film." The course helped me plot my academic trajectory in that it granted legitimacy to my own lived experience. I am indebted to the faculty members at UCR who recognized this trajectory, who helped refine and tailor my work, and who always treated me as a colleague rather than as a student.

First and foremost, my thanks go to David Lloyd who chaired this project in its early form as a dissertation. David's willingness to regularly meet and discuss my research helped keep me on track and stay engaged. Above all, David taught me how to treat graduate students with kindness and care. I try to model much of his demeanor in my own scholarly life and I strive to treat the students with whom I work in a manner that honors his guidance. Similarly, the members of my committee—Kim Devlin and Pat Morton—supported me in the same manner, going above and beyond to help. Their dedication to my project and their attentive close reading and thoughtful feedback were instrumental in the project's success. At-large committee members Erika Suderburg and

Carole-Anne Tyler were equally supportive resources throughout the process, offering perspectives and suggestions as to where the project might turn next. I have fond memories of all involved, and of many other faculty members at both UCR and The Claremont Colleges who demonstrated academic gregariousness over and over. This includes (but is certainly not limited to) Steven Axelrod, John Briggs, Jennifer Doyle, John Ganim, Weihsin Gui, Katherine Kinney, Jeanette Kohl, Rob Latham, James Tobias, Sherryl Vint, Traise Yamamoto, and Susan Zieger. From the 5Cs, Bill Anthes, Brent Armendinger, Sumangala Bhattacharya, John Farrell, Patrick Frank, Ken Gonzales-Day, Judith Grabiner, Nancy Macko, Nina Revoyr, Ron Rubin, Rudi Volti, Al Wachtel, Cheryl Walker, Keri Walsh, and Phil Zuckerman.

Thanks also to Nick Bentley, Ben Clarke, and Nick Hubble. Not long after I learned that writing about working-class culture in England was permissible, I reached out to these scholars to express interest in their work. Their response was to invite me to contribute an essay—an adapted version of the first chapter of this book—for one of their collections. Their benevolence led to a continued working relationship with all three. I have adopted their practice of "paying it forward" by making sure I reach my hand out to graduate students in the early stages of their careers. Thanks to the Working-Class Studies Association, which not only has supported my work but also has proven that academic organizations and conferences can actually be joyful and encouraging. In particular, thanks to Sarah Attfield, Nathan Bryant, Marc DiPaolo, Michele Fazio, Scott Henkel, Lisa Kirby, Christie Launius, John Lennon, Sherry Linkon, Magnus Nilsson, John Russo, Tim Strangleman, Valerie Walkerdine, and Joe Varga. Similarly, thanks to Ben Doyle for his support—not just of this project, but of my work in general. I am also indebted to Chris Freeberg and Dave Wallace, two much-missed figures instrumental in my return to academia—figures whose spirits I still bring into my own classroom with regularity.

Thanks to the Lilly Library at the University of Indiana and the River Campus Libraries at the University of Rochester for their assistance with the Sillitoe and MacInnes archives. Thanks also to Sussex's Mass Observation archive and—in particular—to the Adam Matthew Digital sales rep who renewed my thirty-day trial subscription over and over and over and over. Although this project would have benefitted from the Harry Ransom Center's Osborne and Wesker archives, the pandemic put an end to that. Hopefully my next book will warrant access to those particular holdings.

Thanks also to the Texas State University English Department for all of their help and support of my work and this project in particular. Special thanks go to

Suparno Banerjee, Rebecca Bell-Metereau, Mary Brennan, drea brown, Ruben Zecena Cartagena, Chris Dayley, Geneva Gano, Tom Grimes, Katie Kapurch, Eric Leake, Dan Lochman, Whitney May, Kate McClancy, Susan Morrison, Cecily Parks, Francine Pilkington, Teya Rosenberg, Aimee Roundtree, Leah Schwebel, Nithya Sivashankar, Elizabeth Skerpan-Wheeler, Vicki Smith, Rob Tally, Louie Dean Valencia, Graeme Wend-Walker, and Nancy and Steve Wilson. Thanks to Taylor Cortesi, Deanna Voigt, Paivi Rentz, Brian Solis, Danny Williams, Corey Weber, and everyone else who keeps the place running. Extra-special thanks go to Sara Ramírez, James Reeves, and Julie McCormick Weng—who quickly became a cohort of colleagues and friends. It seems impossible to operate in higher education without drama and tension, but our department is an exception in that regard.

Since academia is only a part of my life, there are many folks to thank who have supported my scholarly pursuits while helping to keep me level-headed. First, thanks to all my family in the UK. Second, thanks to my friends and family in California. Third, thanks to my friends in Austin who, at this point, might as well be family. I would name names, but it would take up too much space. This book is dedicated to my parents who know the world I write about all too well. Much love to them and all who supported me along the way.

The project was made possible by grants, fellowships, awards, and general support from UCR's Center for Ideas and Society, the UC Dissertation Year Program, the Alkek Library at Texas State University, the University of La Verne, and various other academic organizations. Material in this text is reproduced with permission of Curtis Brown, London on behalf of The Trustees of the Mass Observation Archive © The Trustees of the Mass Observation Archive. Other material appears Courtesy of the Lilly Library, Indiana University, Bloomington, Indiana. A portion of Chapter 1 is reprinted/adapted with permission from Palgrave Macmillan's *Working-Class Writing: Theory and Practice* (2018), eds. Ben Clarke and Nick Hubble.

About the Author

Simon Lee is Assistant Professor of English at Texas State University, USA, where he researches and teaches postwar British Literature with a particular focus on working-class writing and culture. He has published a range of scholarship on British life.

Introduction

Concerns about class and class culture are at a boiling point. Few would question recent years' uptick in political disruption, much of which is underwritten by forms of class anxiety exacerbated by individuals seeking to exploit social division for personal and political gain. The result is the increased scapegoating of minorities as well as the demonization of immigrant refugees—an effect accelerated by populist and xenophobic rhetoric. However, the manipulation of class anxieties has a historical lineage in British culture, and today's concerns echo concerns of the past. For example, Conservative MP Enoch Powell's "Rivers of Blood" speech, delivered in April of 1968, rallied working-class people as part of a nationalist effort to prohibit immigration under the auspices of "preserving heritage." Powell's message was that Commonwealth immigration posed a decisive threat to British culture and was responsible, he claimed, for an increase in violent crime in urban centers. As Paul Gilroy remarked, Powell's stance on immigration policy—and his vocal opposition to the 1965 Race Relations Act[1]—insinuated that such an approach would "assist[s] in the process of making Britain great again" in that it "restores an ethnic symmetry to a world distorted by imperial adventure and migration" (1987: 46). The speech tied British working-class culture to nationalist tumult, suggesting that issues such as unemployment were the fault of non-white immigrants. This led to a sequence of hate crimes carried out together with chants of Powell's name. Yet, the speech found surprising support from white dock workers, miners, and laborers who, as Camilla Schofield proposes, lacked the critical skills required to identify such calculated rhetoric (2013: 241). As Gilroy adds, it was not until the 1980s that Powell's working-class supporters fully comprehended their mistreatment as political pawns in that, concerning policy, they came to find that they were viewed no differently from the racial and ethnic minorities Powell's message condemned. Following the unequivocally racist speech, Powell was relieved of his position by Edward Heath and his claims were denounced by his peers.

Although Margaret Thatcher, MP for the North London region of Finchley at the time, conceded that aspects of Powell's speech were incendiary, his political influence resonated through her subsequent politics of disenfranchisement, deindustrialization, nationalism, and tendency toward retrograde cultural nostalgia, euphemistically packaged and sold as "preserving heritage."

Today's class anxieties parrot much of what Powell championed in 1968, only the populist rhetoric employed is disseminated through more complex streams. Having said that, working-class people—figured as obligatory components of political disruption—have legitimate reasons for their frustration. Policies of social mobility implemented in the years following WWII only went so far, and, to this day, working-class people—broadly defined—experience inordinate barriers in life and their struggles are often weoponized for political gain. In a 2022 article for Jacobin, Alberto Prunetti comments how

> The Right has played its hand well: it has captured the desperation of the common people and tried to divert it toward its own goals, in defense of the rich. The institutional, gentrified left doesn't give a shit about people's desperation; it has become a party of educated people making enlightened consumer choices. Increasingly, this only fuels the resentment of the oppressed.
>
> (2022)

Fifty-four years after Powell's speech, little has changed. The working class—a category that, today, requires comprehension through the prism of intersectionality—continues to face alienation and calculated exploitation. Furthermore, the reiteration and proliferation of class stereotypes have led to increased intra-class divisions. In the revised preface to the new edition of *Chavs: The Demonization of the Working Class*, Owen Jones (2011) discusses the reasons why working-class people in twenty-first-century Britain are viewed so poorly. In addition, Jones also underscores the impact of cultural production, noting how tabloids and media-driven representations of working-class people tend to amplify social anxiety. The result is broadly felt alienation in search of an uprising—the kind of feelings susceptible to the machinations of figures like Powell and others who capitalize on such concerns. To that end, working-class identities have grown increasingly lucrative, and cultural production has taken note. The rise of popular television shows like *Shameless* and *Benefits Street*, that foreground classed lives in a manner sometimes described as "poverty porn," behooves us to pay careful attention to the way class is understood and reiterated through media forms—especially in a moment in which a nostalgic and romanticized notion of a monolithic working-class culture is commodified despite its phantasmagoric state. With working-class representation on the rise, interpretation across a range of media forms proves increasingly challenging yet absolutely vital. Discussing writing, Prunetti adds: "In short, we're going through an interesting time for working-class literature, but it's hardly plain sailing. Working-class stories are having a growing impact on the mainstream culture industry" (2022). Referencing recent texts by French writers such as Didier Eribon and Édouard Louis, he notes that "I imagine these French authors fighting for a new working class that can be enlightened by their biographical trajectories, without feeling crushed by them. That they see in these works the possibility of reconstructing a new imaginary" (2022). Reading Prunetti's recent claims is remarkably illuminating since his emphasis on narratives as a path to construct a new imaginary is precisely what this book is about.

This text centers on postwar British writing, chiefly writing associated with what is commonly known as the kitchen sink realism movement—a short-lived body of British cultural production existing from the late 1950s to the early 1960s.[2] It does so under the pretense that this period of British writing reflects a unique moment in which representations of working-class life documented and challenged the exploitative representations referenced by Jones above. Encompassing novels, plays, television, and films, the movement made a lasting impression on the arts with contemporary working-class texts routinely referencing work produced during this time. Be that as it may, the texts of this period are somewhat discounted in terms of recognition, registered largely as cult classics that denote a certain aesthetic style and sensibility. This book argues that kitchen sink realism's contribution to working-class representation is far more significant in that it builds on principles of social realism—specifically through a documentary-style allegiance to verisimilitude that sought neither to glamorize nor to hyperbolize class representation. It is a moment in which those associated gave voice to members of the British public historically marginalized from the stage, the page, and the screen—at least in regard to mimetic fidelity. The movement, in part, advanced a corrective to representational problems of the past, rejecting the stereotypical characterizations of working-class people frequently associated with the "social novel" and drawing-room comedies while also testing the limits of realist aesthetics. The "kitchen sink" of the title refers to David Sylvester's 1954 discussion of social realist art such as that of John Bratby, Jack Smith, and Derrick Greaves. Delivered as a pejorative, Sylvester's term addressed an artistic style characterized by morose intemperance, with the critic arguing that "The post-war generation takes us back from the studio to the kitchen" in which "every kind of food and drink, every kind of utensil and implement … the kitchen sink too" is on display (1954: 62). But Sylvester's main contention was that such images lack thematic flair: "The point is that it is a very ordinary kitchen, lived in by a very ordinary family. There is nothing to hint that the man about the house is an artist or anything but a very ordinary bloke" (1954: 62). While Sylvester's invective addressed a specific group of painters, the name is aptly suited for a movement best recognized by its fascination with the conventional as well as a preoccupation with space and environment.

In addition to the kitchen sink label, the movement is also sometimes known by the equally inelegant moniker, "The Angry Young Men," with associated writers granted the shorthand title of "The Angries." This reference grew out of a press agent's promotional material accompanying the Royal Court Theater's 1956 premiere of John Osborne's *Look Back in Anger*. The intent was to align Osborne's incensed protagonist with the author himself in ways that convey the sort of sensational fetishism linked to "gritty" working-class identities. Despite a swift rejection of the label by all involved, the description does call to mind a key motif that runs throughout the texts of the period: that of disaffected, alienated youth, failed by a state that vowed to address social issues in the postwar years. Anger and frustration certainly characterize a number of the movement's more notorious protagonists, like *Look Back in Anger's* Jimmy Porter, and Arthur Seaton from Alan Sillitoe's novel, *Saturday Night and Sunday Morning*. And, as Enoch Powell and others have shown, such powerful and perceptible emotional states are ignited in both the political and the commercial realm. Jim Dixon, the bumbling protagonist of Kingsley Amis's 1954 novel *Lucky Jim* is sometimes declared the original "Angry." However, it was not until the release of Osborne's play that critics chose to look back on *Lucky Jim* and claim Dixon as the blueprint. Amis's text certainly demonstrates aspects of the characteristic alienation expressed in the work of later "Angry" writers, but the similarity stops there. In fact, it can be argued that Keith Waterhouse's 1959 novel *Billy Liar* acts as a corrective by placing a similarly bumbling character into a more fitting working-class context.

While the "angry" label was ill-suited for many of the writers, such a characterization does facilitate understanding of one of the movement's more innovative social observations: the dissolution of a semi-mythical working-class identity into a more disaggregated class consciousness, anticipating an incipient subculture that would galvanize during the 1960s. Texts such as 1958's *Saturday Night and Sunday Morning* and *A Taste of Honey* from the same year provide clear-cut examples of working-class individuals' renegotiation of class identity in relation to local conditions, echoed in Colin Wilson's 1956 nonfiction text, *The Outsider*—a text that anticipates subcultural identities as well as providing a theoretical framework for the "Angry" motif. This disarticulation of classed identity is never fully enunciated, per se, but it is made known through kitchen sink texts' heightened emphasis on individuals who deliberate on whether or not to remove themselves from their local community. Given that communities represented in such texts are intensely classed, the novels, plays, and films of the time question the value of sustaining working-class traditions in light of new modes of class articulation and self-definition.

Aleks Sierz has claimed that kitchen sink aesthetics fundamentally transformed postwar theater by upending elite motifs of traditional British life, replacing country homes and mansions with dingy working-class flats in industrial regions, thus "introducing an urgent contemporary voice" (2008: 3). This is fundamentally true, but it also possible to read the period's texts as a knowing realignment of realist aesthetics rather than as a radical break. Although the writers affiliated with kitchen sink realism certainly subscribed to motifs of local color and tend to rely upon narrative archetypes, their focus is less of an appeal to social justice and more of a highlighting of a cultural sentiment of frustration surrounding the Welfare State's failure to eradicate the class concerns identified in the Beveridge Report.[3] Much of the work produced during this time is deeply testimonial with writers like Sillitoe and Delaney recreating the worlds in which they themselves were raised, lending the texts heightened validity, and speaking directly to a working-class reader who shared their world. While seminal nonfiction works like George Orwell's *The Road to Wigan Pier* (1937) and Richard Hoggart's *The Uses of Literacy* (1957) rely on the same kind of ethos, such texts tend toward sepia-tinged nostalgia more commonly tied to conventional representations of working-class life. The texts of the kitchen sink sequence circumvent nostalgia by presenting lived experience and the struggles unique to working-class people in a markedly visceral manner. As the result, the period in which Britain moved from postwar austerity to postwar affluence marks perhaps the most expressive and vibrant example of proletarian writing to date.

While Kingsley Amis's supposed role as the precursor to the movement is known as an afterthought, the initial key players included playwrights like John Osborne, Michael Hastings, Shelagh Delaney, Bill Hopkins, Arnold Wesker, Bernard Kops, and Edward Bond in addition to novelists like Alan Sillitoe, John Braine, Stan Barstow, John Wain, Keith Waterhouse, David Storey, and Nell Dunn. Peripheral writers include the critic Kenneth Tynan as well as nonfiction writers such as Colin Wilson and Stuart Holroyd. The films that came about as part of the New Wave were directed by Lindsay Anderson, Tony Richardson, Karel Reisz, Peter Collinson, John Schlesinger, and Jack Clayton with repeat performances from actors like Tom Courtenay, Richard Harris, Albert Finney, and Alan Bates. The "Movement," a group of mid-century poets such as Philip Larkin, Elizabeth Jennings, and Thom Gunn, was also prominent at the time, but the general sentiments differed. Even though figures like Harold Pinter and Ken Loach are occasionally mentioned, Pinter's theater had other goals in mind and Loach's films arrived several years later. Yet, writers like Colin MacInnes are rarely mentioned despite aesthetic parallels and similar political motivations—which, among other things, highlights the arbitrary nature of the grouping itself. MacInnes's work focused on intersectional concerns related to postcolonial London, and a number of postcolonial writers addressing issues of class—Sam Selvon, E.R. Braithewaite, and Buchi Emecheta, for example—are rarely discussed in relation to the movement. This is, of course, the upshot of categorization associated with cultural production. But as this book will argue, the ideas accompanying the kitchen sink movement are better analyzed as portable motifs rather than as clearly demarcated and rigid genre contours.

A number of the individuals involved collaborated freely yet tended to reject the labels applied. No formal manifesto exists and, although working-class sensibilities are centered, not all involved were from working-class backgrounds. In his introduction to Dale Salwak's 1984 text *Interviews with Britain's Angry Young Men*, Colin Wilson notes the parallel between the period and the rise of the Beats in America, noting that "there was probably more sense in grouping together writers like Kerouac, Ginsberg, Rexroth, Clellon Holmes, Corso, Ferlinghetti, Snyder, and the rest than in linking writers with as little in common as Amis, Osborne, and myself" (Salwak 1984: 9). Bill Hopkins, in the same volume, underscores the concerns of being aligned with a group of literary bad boys: "the phrase ['Angry Young Men'] began to take on sinister meaning: the Angry Young Men weren't an innocent group of writers and dreamers, but were enemies of society. This gave license for stupid and uninformed attacks and eventually brainwashed the public into a murderous hostility that destroyed all hopes of effecting a change in public thinking" (Salwak 1984: 61). For John Braine, if there was a group, it was informal at best: "The fact is, the whole Angry Young Men business is nonsense. It's entirely nonsense because in England there haven't been for a long time any real literary groups" with him adding how "British writers just aren't like that. They just don't work that way … England being a small country, I know most of them … There wasn't any formal organization, any committee, meetings, anything like that" (Salwak 1984: 51–2). A caustic, handwritten note found in Alan Sillitoe's archive at the Lilly Library reads "AYM. It enabled them—us, if you like—to make more money than might usually have been the case" (Sillitoe, "A.Y.M. Note"). In his own recollections, Colin Wilson registers sadness over "the wreckage of so many of my contemporaries scattered over the literary battlefield" (2007: 192), referring primarily to the collapse into alcoholism seen with figures like Osborne. What emerges is a sense that not only did the writers of the period attempt to undermine the notion of a group, they also sought to undermine any impact that might have resulted in the context of shared ideas or approaches. What was shared, then, was concern over the state of postwar England and the failure of the Welfare State to adequately solve working-class problems. In spite of the challenges associated with aligning a disparate writers and attitudes, parallels emerge through intent and motif in which collective frustration and disenfranchisement are depicted and processed through spatial negotiations and interactions.

Michael and Steffen Skovmand's 1975 edited collection, *The Angry Young Men*, surveys kitchen sink realism with entries on writers like Osborne, Sillitoe, and Braine, acting largely as an overview of the themes and motifs and situating the movement within a lineage of working-class cultural production. Wilson's *The Angry Years: The Rise and Fall of the Angry Young Men* from 2007 provides an insider perspective, granting a play-by-play look at the movement's beginning, its rise to prominence, and the self-destructive nature of key figures mirrored in its apparent collapse. Also noted above, Salwak's 1984 text, *Interviews with Britain's Angry Young Men*, lives up to its name by providing insightful discussions with luminaries like Braine, Hopkins, and Wilson, all of whom respond to general questions about the field as well as their own connection to the movement and label. Brady et al.'s *Four Fits of Anger: Essays on the Angry Young Men* from 1984 provides a more detailed look at the work of Braine, Amis, Sillitoe, and Osborne in sequence, focusing on their contributions to literary genres as well as the value of vernacular and abrasive dialog. British biographer Humphrey Carpenter's 2009 text, *The Angry Young Men: A Literary Comedy of the 1950s*, marks the most recent return to the movement, drawing on Wilson's approach of using a more subjective voice to relay tales about the writers themselves rather than dispensing analysis or interpretation. Like Carpenter's text, David Castronovo's 2009 *Blokes: The Bad Boys of English Literature* emphasizes the writers and their contexts, expanding the general boundaries of the movement to include peripheral but important figures like Philip Larkin and Kenneth Tynan. Women writers like Shelagh Delaney and Nell Dunn, as well as queer writers like Colin

MacInnes, still see little coverage in these surveys, emphasizing the masculinist nature of the movement in addition to illuminating the sort of cult of personality it created. Gene Feldman and Max Gardenburg's *The Beat Generation and the Angry Young Men* from 1958, reprinted in 2012, builds on the label's titular androcentrism, aligning key figures from both sides of the Atlantic with the antiestablishment identity seen in Wilson's *The Outsider*. Tom Maschler's 1958 collection *Declaration* stands out in that the text is curated more as a loose statement of purpose and is somewhat resistant to the labels applied. Assembling essays from figures like Osborne, Wain, and Hopkins, Maschler also addresses the multimodal nature of the period with essays from Lindsay Anderson, Kenneth Tynan, and Doris Lessing—the latter having little connection to the tenets of the movement and, as such, acting more as an objective observer. *Declaration* exists less as a study of the movement's key texts and more as a series of positions which define the cultural landscape and allow for a better understanding of the reason why such a movement came about to begin with.

Both drama and film fare well in terms of coverage and criticism, but film dominates. Texts such as Andrew Higson's 1996 edited volume, *Dissolving Views: Key Writings on British Cinema* (2016a), offer commentary on film as a whole while providing instructive chapters on kitchen sink aesthetics. Higson's own essay in the same collection, "Space, Place, Spectacle: Landscape and Townscape in the 'Kitchen Sink' Film" (2016b) is frequently cited for its conceptualization of a single cinematic shot associated with the British New Wave. Samantha Lay's 2002 text, *British Social Realism: From Documentary to Brit Grit*, establishes links between working-class representation in the kitchen sink films and working-class life. Both Lay and Higson's texts help to clarify the nature of kitchen sink realism in general, but their focus is primarily on the filmic and the visual rather than the literary. In terms of theater, texts such as Dorothy Chansky's recent *Kitchen Sink Realisms: Domestic Labor, Dining, and Drama in American Theatre* pair American writers with the British movement, observing how "Arthur Miller considered *Look Back in Anger* [as] the only modern British play worth seeing" (2015: 1). However, in terms of theater, few texts are devoted exclusively to the tenets of kitchen sink realism, veering more toward more general overviews of specific writers or key plays. Texts like Michael Patterson's 2003 text *Strategies of Political Theatre: Post-War British Playwrights* seek to locate mid-century theater within leftist political movements while discussing its lasting impact on the medium as a whole. Stephen Lacey's 1995 text, *British Realist Theatre: The New Wave in Its Context, 1956–1965*, explores how writers of the period sought to redefine past models of realist production by advancing new political and aesthetic agendas while undermining conventions pertinent to the medium. Lacey's text concludes by linking developments in theater with developments in film to show how such "new waves" transformed the media landscape more broadly. Such a perspective also privileges the visual over the literary and, although Lacey offers a wide overview of key figures of the time, it would appear that kitchen sink realism was mainly a theatrical or cinematic endeavor—a gesture that undermines the literary foundation upon which the movement was built.[4]

Contemporary views of kitchen sink realism differ from the initial cultural moment, with the novels and the films of the British New Wave shrouded by a cult-like status. Yet, references to the period persist, showing up in unexpected places and in unexpected ways. As the final chapter of this book argues, the aesthetics and technical devices formulated as part of the movement reverberate in today's cultural production more than the original texts themselves. A subcultural phenomenon in its time that punched through to the mainstream, today's references to the movement are generally relegated to similarly subcultural venues—noncommercial music, underground presses, and documentary films, for example. That said, aforementioned political developments around issues of classed identity have sparked a renewed interest in all things working-class. This has led to a resurgence in kitchen sink references and a revision of how the aesthetics accompanying the movement are mobilized in terms of the contemporary commercialization of classed identity as opposed to the emancipation of alienated social classes.

Perhaps one reason why contemporary references persist is because the movement was a multimedia and multiformat endeavor shaped more by ideas than by individual texts. When referenced today, kitchen sink realism is most often understood through visual forms such as film and TV, but it is important to keep in mind that the texts extended across media formats. As stated, the films of British new wave have had the most lasting impression, but almost all of the films produced during this period were developed with the original authors in tow. In several instances, the author wrote the screenplay; in others, they worked closely with the director to ensure their vision remained intact. This corroborates the notion that kitchen sink aesthetics and devices are somewhat portable, suggesting that the movement is best read as an accumulation of aesthetic impulses across media forms. So, on the one hand, such a multimedia approach can be understood as a united force to cement ideas and approaches dominant at the time. But, on the other, this approach underscores the anarchic nature of the movement in that little concerted effort was made to coordinate beyond the multimedia approach. As the result, the legacy of kitchen sink realism is as scattered as its forms and ideas.

The movement was best received by an audience whose own lives resembled the worlds represented in the texts. According to Christopher Taylor, the initial appeal of these texts to a new audience was their allegiance to authentic representation, with work such as Sillitoe's *Saturday Night and Sunday Morning* drawing comments like "His writing has real experience and an instinctive accuracy" and "Very much the real thing" (1984: 104). Responses from critics were mixed. As Mark Brady shows, John Osborne's *Look Back in Anger* received both praise and condescension. But even the most conservative of critics could not overlook the movement's ability to replicate working-class lives as they were lived in the current moment. Brady recounts a review in the New Statesman that captures the sentiment well, noting how the play is "abounding with life and vitality, and the life it deals with is life as it is lived at this very moment—not a common subject in English theatre" (1984: 51). While the novels were generally accepted without much protest—mostly because their content was hardly subversive when compared to the Lady Chatterley trial underway around the same time—the plays and the films garnered objections from morality figures who deemed them antisocial and rebellious. Despite efforts to warn audiences, such voices of moral condemnation only boosted curiosity and helped sensationalize releases.

Aligned with the renewed significance of class in cultural discourse, criticism has also seen a renewed interest in the way media production addresses issues of inequality—in particular, what class means in the context of lived experience. Although mid-century texts are generally not the focus of such analyses, the kind of topics covered can be interpreted as reverberations of mid-century alienation and frustration. For example, Owen Jones's aforementioned *Chavs* considers how popular television shows like Paul Abbott's *Shameless* (2004–2012) "encourage the viewer to laugh at, rather than understand, the lives of the characters" (2020: 130). *Shameless*, arguably, uses motifs of kitchen sink realism, but adapts the aesthetics for a contemporary viewer. Lynsey Hanley's *Estates: An Intimate History* (2007) merged autobiography with social history to show how spaces related to working-class people inform identity and status. If, as this book argues as its guiding premise, one of the movement's most dominant motifs is its preoccupation with space and environment, then Hanley's analysis reveals similar concerns. Indeed, her emphasis on council housing estates is echoed in a number of mid-century texts that raise questions about postwar housing plans—much of which is addressed in subsequent chapters. Such titles have a broad audience in mind, and so their emphasis tends to be more accessible rather than media-specific. Recent academic studies of class and writing have included Nicola Wilson's *Home in British Working-Class Fiction* (2015) and Roberto del Valle Alcalá's *British Working-Class Fiction: Narratives of Refusal and the Struggle Against Work* (2016). The former considers prior theories about working-class cultural texts, arguing that perspectives from figures such as Richard Hoggart or Raymond Williams are beneficial but limited in their capacity to explore the nuances of lived experience. The latter touches on the kitchen sink era, arguing that the period signals "the convulsive resurgence of antagonistic class subjectivities as the new primary, even necessary, context of capital's maturation" revealing the effect of capital on social spaces and communities (2016: 172). Both texts are fruitful in thinking through the vibrant nature of class as represented in cultural production, and this book aims to build on similar perspectives by further exploring the intersection of class and space in terms of representational strategies.

In fact, it is this book's contention that aside from the notorious "Angry Young Man" figure, the most recurring trope associated with kitchen sink realism is the use of space and setting as an essential component of the movement's aesthetic prowess. Space is no mere backdrop in kitchen sink realism and, as the movement's title insinuates, an emphasis on domestic space in relation to the local community runs throughout. Rather than simply organizing space as a necessity of the narrative, kitchen sink texts explore the way working-class spaces inscribe subjecthood and how postwar working-class subjects might renegotiate identity as the upshot of spatial limitations. These texts allow for a robust understanding of the way environment impacts individuality, demonstrating, in the process, hypothetical models of sidestepping social restrictions through disarticulated class consciousness. Particular figures across the movement approached this trope differently, with writers like John Osborne putting forth a protagonist who fails to fully comprehend the limits reflected in the world he inhabits, and writers like Shelagh Delaney or Nell Dunn offering unambiguous and somewhat radical rejections of domestic norms, transcending social limits as experienced in their depicted worlds. What emerges is a persistent and dominant motif used throughout the movement—an emphasis on the way classed environs shape working-class subjects. As a result, kitchen sink realism is a movement that lends itself well to spatial analysis—analysis that engages with setting to gain new understandings of the way British cultural production proposed hypothetical solutions to a notably dynamic cultural moment.

Space and Place

The shift toward space and place as a viable approach to literary analysis reflects Edward's Soja's discussion of the "spatial turn," representing an interdisciplinary effort to think beyond chronology. As outlined by Michel Foucault (1986) in his discussion of heterotopic space, time is generally subjugated to space in terms of the way history is usually comprehended and indexed. The spatial turn transpired as a way to think more critically about the impact of space as the basis for understanding cultural events rather than simply locating events on a timescale. As Leo Mellor writes, "Conceptualising any aesthetic in terms of locale can be useful, since it gives texture to particularity, specificity and the happenstance juxtapositions of geography that could remain obscured" (2011: 3). Terms like "texture" and "particularity" are commonly used in critical frameworks aligned with the spatial turn, suggesting that a shift from the chronological to the spatial can yield information or details that might otherwise go unrecognized. For instance, it is one thing to discuss the experience of social class as it pertains to chronological events, but it is another to parse the ways in which location plays a role in terms of the way class is structured. Whereas time is universally comprehended as inexorable and persistent, space can be understood as a combination of the material and the socially produced, implying transgression and mutability. Mellor continues, "There has recently been the growth of synoptic area studies, and these trace the relationship between literature and the urban experience: with the city as character or at least shaper of a particular consciousness and the possibility of knowledge" (2011: 3). Similar to the labels applied to postwar British writing, slippery referents run amok, and a number of approaches associated with spatial studies popularized as part of the spatial turn tend to overlap. But what is significant here is that while texts of the kitchen sink era certainly address cultural events underway at the time, they are as—if not more—invested in exploring the resonances of space and environment. In particular, they are attentive to the way social class operates relative to place and identity.

Barney Warf and Santa Arias offer an excellent overview of the spatial turn, building on Foucault's claim of space and place's subjugation to time. Observing how major philosophical contributions to culture were primarily temporal, the authors posit that urban analysis materialized and took shape in the 1920s with the Chicago School's study of patterns of immigration and the rise of ethnic communities (2014: 3). Moreover, Robert T. Tally, in his 2013 text *Spatiality*, registers the rising interest in space and place through an increased use of cartographic terminology noticeable across disciplines. Tally surveys salient figures linked to the spatial turn to better consider Foucault's rationale of deprivileging chronology, underscoring claims made by Bertrand Westphal that connections between temporality and "progress" were impacted by WWII (2013: 12). But despite interjections by groups such as the Situationist International during the 1950s and 1960s, it was not until the 1970s that a coherent trajectory of spatial analysis emerged in contrast to the more regimented and methodical manner practiced in the social sciences. Henri Lefebvre's 1974 work, *The Production of Space*, opened the door to new, revolutionary ways of thinking about the impact of space on cultural development and is mostly responsible for the nature of spatial theory today. The concepts advanced in Lefebvre's text provided the groundwork for writers like Soja and David Harvey who reframed Lefebvre's ideas for greater reach. Put simply, Lefebvre's approach to "spatial production" is a framework for analyzing how certain environments reveal undercurrents of power. This is accomplished by understanding how a space can be read as the composite of planning, material reality, and lived experience. In particular for Lefebvre, what matters most is how these factors exist in tension, and subsequent chapters will explore Lefebvre's ideas in greater detail.

Warf and Arias add that what would become the spatial turn was propelled by the integration of Marxist thought into the field of geography through concepts by figures such as Lefebvre and Harvey (2014: 3). Declaring that the "Marxification of space" offered a new way to think about industrialization and the regionality of industry, the authors also point out how such thinking confronts spaces known to subjugate individuals as part of a process of social stratification. This idea was also explored in Williams's *The Country and the City* (1973) in which the author approaches literary representations of spatial division as an upshot of class demarcations. Moving analysis of space from the objective, cartographic qualities of geography into something more like the field of social theory, literature—as Williams suggests—becomes a valuable tool in this regard. While literary theory previously approached the unification of time and space through concepts such as Mikhail Bakhtin's "chronotope" (1981), the spatial turn was less tethered to a specific scholarly field.

Throughout the 1980s and 1990s, theorists built predominantly on Lefebvre's model, expanding the spatial turn and breathing new life into the field of geography through interdisciplinary pathways. Much of this shift is captured eloquently by Reingard Nethersole who claims that the spatial turn signals expansion in a number of arenas where spatial analysis can challenge standard chronological comprehension. For Nethersole, such shifts represent a move away from traditional conceptions of historicism, subject, and meaning:

> Thus, Foucault's rereading of Nietzsche produced genealogy in the place of Historicism, Lacan's rereading of Freud produced the notion of a forever split subject and Derrida's critique of the linguistic model (de Saussure, Pierce and followers) produced *différance*, indeterminacy and constant deferral of signification. Genealogy traces the exteriority of accidents not along logico-temporal lines but in a force-field, Lacan's work is based upon the so-called *Oedipal triangle*, and Derrida's emphasis upon writing (as opposed to speech) stresses spatiality in the form of graphs, gaps, and traces in texts.
>
> (1990: 63)

For Nethersole, the hope is that these changes continue so that perhaps stories will no longer begin with "Once upon a time ..." but with "Once upon a place ..." (1990: 63).

The use of cultural production as hard scientific data is a dubious endeavor, but the value of considering imaginative portrayals in relation to material realities is outlined in Bertrand Westphal's influential *Geocriticism: Real and Fictional Spaces*. Westphal submits that fictive representations of place are useful when piecing together an overall perspective of a locale and its occupants' conception of spatial relations. Paralogical discourse, Westphal contends—the kinds of narrative and metaphorical representation found in fiction—provides viable data that is comparable to the kinds of empirical data addressed in the social sciences (2011: 14). Westphal adds that data such as cartographic information, census reports, and labor statistics can be merged with literary representations of locales such as pamphlets, news reports, and fictional texts to flesh out comprehension of place and environment. What kitchen sink texts provide is a glimpse at how a combination of ethnographic and imaginative writing, when grounded in the intensified realism of the genre, might reveal nuanced articulations of lived experience within working-class space and make visible the way the environment informs and *transforms* lived experience on a large scale. That is to say, if there exists a body of cultural production well suited for spatial analysis in a manner commensurate with Westphal's thinking, it would undoubtably be kitchen sink realism. As this book argues, spatial representation in the texts of this period is granted a form of tacit approval by the sort of individuals represented, therefore marking it as a relatively sanctioned consensus of lived experience.

That said, Westphal's approach explicitly rejects spaces lacking a pre-existing body of cultural production, or spaces that cannot be recognized as a specific locale (e.g., major cities like London would be applicable, but northern working-class regions are too abstract). Eric Prieto amends Westphal's model by demonstrating how established *types* of space can still fit within his framework. I would argue that the kind of domestic environments that appear in British working-class fiction map accurately onto real, existing spaces, permitting a comprehensive depiction of lived experience ideally suited for deeper analysis. In turn, this reemphasizes the notion of literature's capacity to collate experience as data. In a body of cultural production, in which depicted experiences are tacitly endorsed by those portrayed, it seems that Prieto's "types" of space have moved closer to something more like "types of experience." This is akin to what Williams refers to as "knowable communities" (1973: 165–81) and, I would add, the kind of data that kitchen sink realism specializes in producing.[5]

Space and Class

This project turns on the idea of class as a spatialized concept. In doing so, it proposes that if kitchen sink realism is best understood through its tropes rather than through its questionably applied appellations, one trope worthy of attention is the way texts of the movement intensify space and setting to articulate new modes of class consciousness. In their 1987 volume, *Class and Space*, Nigel Thrift and Peter Williams explore this juncture, hypothesizing social position as the upshot of geographic markers. To that end, they pinpoint the subtleties of socially produced identities, moving away from economics and abstraction toward a mode of analysis that honors lived experience more readily. Lived experience, though, resists objective comprehension, and Thrift and Williams's volume does indeed center on discrete case studies and examples. Yet, the authors suggest that the intersection of class and space remains curiously understudied, emphasizing that "there is much to do" (2014: 22) in terms of advancing connections between the two topics. In this respect, cultural production can be useful in its ability to reinforce and add texture to representations of what Lefebvre calls "lived space" that is otherwise unavailable. In other words, the period's texts use tropes and motifs in ways that reproduce something consonant with generalized experience of working-class environs. Whereas Westphal argued that fictional representations of localities augment tangible comprehension, kitchen sink realism can be said to reproduce experiences of classed space and classed environments endorsed by the kind of individuals depicted.

Pierre Bourdieu's work on class analysis functions similarly in that it attempts to codify patterns of behavior known as part of a shared experience. It should be noted that Bourdieu resists concrete schematizations of class, allowing instead room to account for cultural shifts that alter the boundaries of demarcation. For Bourdieu, Lefebvre's model of spatial production offers a practical starting point due to its emphasis on dialectical tension. But the category of perceived space (in which the individual comprehends the space they navigate) is also informed by the dialectical relationship between the subject and capital. That is to say, the apprehension of represented space is always subjective, making the category mutable. As such, relational dynamics are deeply contextual and contingent, grounded in his conception of habitus outlined in *The Logic of Practice* (1990) in which the actions and behaviors of individuals in space are linked to the spaces they occupy in what Bourdieu calls the "social field." Bourdieu's conception of the social field represents flows of power identifiable as the upshot of capitalism—in this sense, symbolic and cultural as well as economic forms of capitalism. Habitus, then, represents the resources that an individual possesses within a field of interaction. That said, habitus is not merely the result of flows of capital acting on the individual; rather, it is the active interplay of a subject's free will relative to flows of power. Habitus is structured upon the notion of social practices that become normalized or habitual within any given social realm, emphasizing the idea of regionality and behavior as the upshot of space and social status. For Bourdieu, such spaces represent fields of interaction, and habitus forms the blueprint that guides individual subjects to act. Shared interactions—what Bourdieu calls doxa—act as basic social rules defining a particular field of movement. It is doxa that transforms cultural capital into symbolic capitol, illustrating a subjective response to an objective reality, regularly mirrored and critiqued in texts of the era. The existential crisis registered in works by writers such as Osborne, Delaney, and Sillitoe can be understood as the interaction between habitus and doxa, but it is the very nature of the field that allows for a way of thinking about class beyond the objective realm of economics and labor.

As David Harvey notes in response to Marx, "Capitalism does not develop upon a flat plain surface endowed with ubiquitous raw materials and homogenous labour supply with equal transport facility in all directions" (2006b: 415–16). He adds that "The forces unleashed under capitalism attack, erode, dissolve and transform much of the pre-capitalist economy and culture" (2006b: 416). Harvey's point is that while regions may be classed by socioeconomic causes, they are the result of a combination of factors that include the sentimental and the material—the impact of space on identity, but also the way identities are renegotiated within specific environments. He writes that classed space is commonly marked by "deep-seated human sentiments—loyalties to place, 'the land', community and nation that spawned civic pride, regionalism, nationalism, etc.—or of equally deep-seated antipathies between human groups founded in race, language, religion, nationality, etc." (2006b: 419). So, understanding class through spatial means calls to mind discussions of Lefebvre's notion of spatial production in that "The historical geography of capitalism is a social process which rests on the evolution of productive forces and social relations which exist as particular spatial configurations" (2006b: 421–2). Harvey adds how "Countervailing forces are at work which put the spatial mobility of capital and labour power into a tension-packed and contradiction-prone geography" (2006b: 421–2). Clearly, capitalism is grounded and structured along spatial lines. While this is perhaps no great revelation, definitions of class rarely draw on spatial demarcation and territory in such a manner; instead, they often rely on socioeconomic metrics and types of labor to mark distinction. What Thrift and Williams argue in their volume—and what this book seeks to explore—is the way space constitutes classed identities as part of a dialectical engagement with space imposing certain characteristics on classed subjects. The texts of the kitchen sink era posit that classed subjects do indeed have agency in terms of negotiating identity relative to space.

If, as Lefebvre suggests, perceived space—essentially lived experience—is the most challenging aspect of spatial production to pin down, then fiction can perhaps index general states of being and moods felt at a precise moment in time. As mentioned, this reiterates Williams's "knowable communities" as well as the kinds of imaginative material that Westphal and Prieto claim help elucidate the true nature of a space at a given moment. Kitchen sink realism, in its efforts to advance the realist mode, adopts a heightened level of verisimilitude akin to that of documentary-style depiction. Because of this, the period's texts act as manifestations of commonly registered sentiments that, as Kenneth Tynan professed upon viewing *Look Back in Anger*, illuminate an explicit frustration expressed through existential crisis. This move—well represented in the texts of the era through depictions of classed space and renegotiations of identity—reveals an approach to understanding social position that responds to Thrift and Williams's call for "more work" on the intersection of class and space. This book submits that kitchen sink's legacy should be reconsidered. Although this body of work is generally viewed as stylized cult-classics or the kind of work associated with rising youth subculture, its relevance today is that it serves as an apogee of working-class representational strategies. In this regard the texts operate as a kind of barometer of authenticity, their tropes and motifs offering an evaluative model for subsequent texts claiming to represent working-class culture. Given the increased fetishization of cultural identities, their commodification, and their weaponization through political rhetoric, the kitchen sink movement, I suggest, serves as an important benchmark by which to gauge intent.

Book Overview

Many of the concepts and approaches discussed above are fleshed out in subsequent chapters, pertinent to the topics addressed. Chapter 1 weighs the impact of shifts in the domestic sphere on representations of working-class people, showing how the kitchen sink movement narrativized the fragmentation of monolithic class consciousness as a partial consequence of postwar redevelopment. Drawing on recent scholarship as well as my assertion that the period serves as a high point of working-class representation, this chapter recounts postwar writers' confrontation with the erratic state of housing and its impact as a basis by which to advance new expressions of class consciousness. Accordingly, the chapter reveals how concepts of social stratification and spatial restriction are interwoven at the site of the domestic—the province of the titular kitchen sink. Working-class representation of the period denotes the inefficacy of the domestic to meet the needs of the British populace, confirming the Welfare State's inability to fully address the root causes of inequality. Through their adherence to spatial representation, writers affiliated with the movement illuminated such failures while promoting counterhegemonic expressions of class identity. The chapter begins with an overview of postwar housing, arguing that new housing developments were no match for the uprooting of established communities. Referring to John B. Calhoun's notions of "behavioral sink" and "defensible space," the chapter considers the nature of the alienation experienced by working-class people, especially those housed in environments socially encoded as derelict. Turning to three key texts from the period—John Osborne's *Look Back in Anger*, Alan Sillitoe's *Saturday Night and Sunday Morning*, and Shelagh Delaney's *A Taste of Honey*—the chapter explores the way kitchen sink writers employ representations of domestic space as symbolic manifestations of social constraint. In doing so, the chapter shows how texts of the period posed a challenge to the romantic idea of the working-class monolith, advancing instead a posture of autonomous, contingent, and fluid class consciousness to navigate the limits of postwar redevelopment.

Chapter 2 extends the discussion of the previous chapter by shifting the focus from portrayals of domestic space to the community at large, exploring how constraint is negotiated in shared spaces. Identifying a handful of sites linked to working-class environs—sites ubiquitous in working-class communities—this chapter traces both their history and their depiction in kitchen sink texts. To that end, the chapter considers how spaces of assumed social and cultural sustenance—the factory, the school, the pub—not only fail to provide adequate substitutions to futile domestic sanctuary but assume a disciplinary posture that buttresses class boundaries and reinforces social limitation. Returning once more to Alan Sillitoe's *Saturday Night and Sunday Morning* while introducing new case studies of David Storey's 1960 novel, *This Sporting Life*, and Nell Dunn's *Up the Junction* from 1963, the chapter reveals how working-class environs are institutionally contoured and policed to maintain the status quo. As static sites within a progressively dynamic culture, the tedium of working-class environs is showcased by kitchen sink writers in ways that encourage social insurgency grounded in altered class consciousness and fluid states of being. Writers like William Hutchings (1993) have referred to this as "Proletarian Byronism"— an existential crisis in which a compulsion to align oneself to the hegemonic order is contradicted by a drive to transcend social expectations.[6] Consequently, kitchen sink texts modify the notion of the collective in their construction of "outsider" ontologies of resistance. This chapter, accordingly, builds on the first to grant a more comprehensive overview of the way new subjectivities are formed through literary representations of classed space, arguing that kitchen sink texts anticipate subcultural trends through their championing of the individual as simultaneously within and without the community.

Chapter 3 augments the preceding chapters by illustrating how ontologies modified as the upshot of spatial confines allow for the reconceptualization of working-class spaces as sites of potential and opportunity. Revisiting texts analyzed in previous discussions, this chapter elucidates the kitchen sink movement's attention to spatial transformations relative to a site's intended purpose. Resting on concepts like Michel Foucault's heterotopic space, Henri Lefebvre's spatial triad, and subsequent evolutions of both advanced by figures such as David Harvey and Edward Soja, it centers on what Lefebvre calls "differential space"—spaces with the capacity to modify social relations in terms of how classed spaces are established and maintained. As Lefebvre posits, spaces are produced through a combination of the tangible, the conceptual, and the experiential—the latter introducing subjectivity into an otherwise objective framework. By privileging the subjective, kitchen sink writers show how spaces like bomb sites can be recast as centers of ethnic community, prisons as spaces of independence, and factories as hubs of subcultural provenance. Although kitchen sink texts are hardly known for their optimism, texts like Colin MacInnes's *City of Spades* from 1957, Alan Sillitoe's *The Loneliness of the Long Distance Runner* from 1959, and Nell Dunn's *Up the Junction* offer enlightening approaches to spatial production in which power dynamics central to social stratification are undermined and, in some cases, reversed. This practice involves what I refer to as the "working-class imaginary" in which working-class subjects envision their social status as one exceeding narratives of class limitation. I conceive of this term as a state of being that can be identified across a number of kitchen sink texts in which optimistic potentiality is employed, not to transform or dislodge existing models of social stratification, but to evade programmatic class designation. In doing so, the individual reconstructs their social position through a modified subjectivity while reimagining working-class environs as sites that transcend prescriptive constraint. Although unambiguously utopian in nature, the emergence of a working-class imaginary can be understood as the upshot of kitchen sink writers' desire to realign political and aesthetic objectives, underscoring the texts' didactic response to the Welfare State's inability to address social inequality in an adequate manner.

Returning to the premise that the kitchen sink era represents a formal zenith, the final chapter surveys efforts by scholars to codify the movement as a defined genre, questioning the efficacy of doing so given the dynamism and definitional-flexibility of working-class writing. Instead, this chapter advances a spatial aesthetics—a summation of the way kitchen sink texts use environment and settings as part of their political and aesthetic agenda. The aim of this chapter—and the project as a whole—is to advance a hypothetical framework by which to assess and consider the veracity of subsequent working-class representations across media forms—especially, their capacity to present modes of existing understood as counterhegemonic. It should be noted that such an effort is not to affix a definitive schema as doing so would reduce a diverse swathe of texts to a single "type"; instead, the goal is the unpacking of characteristics used in a particular body of work as a point of reference by which to contrast subsequent texts that employ similar strategies. In light of my claim that working-class writing of the late 1950s and early 1960s sought to reconvene political and aesthetic objectives in order to reconsider the basis of British citizenship, such a framework provides a path by which to weigh the efficacy of contemporary working-class representation against the transgressive intentions of the kitchen sink movement. Given the commercial and political incentive to commodify classed identities through the fetishization of "grittiness," this chapter surveys a number of contemporary texts to gauge their proximity to kitchen sink's dedication to advancing realism as opposed to instances of class tourism and egregious exploitation designed to sell a product. To do so, the chapter lays out a series of brief spatial readings of contemporary working-class texts such as novels, plays, films, and television shows to illustrate the value of such comparisons. As such, I reiterate the debt owed to spatial motifs and practices pioneered during the kitchen sink era, noting how the movement's legacy persists even when the movement itself is not acknowledged as the source. What this practice shows is that when tropes do diverge, they tend to do so for reasons of gross commercialization by exploiting classed environments and elevating aesthetic agendas over the ethical through sensationalism. But, as this chapter indicates, for every instance of blatant commodification of class identity, a new form of classed representation appears in protest, certifying working-class cultural production as perennially subversive, contingent, and imminently countercultural.

Notes

1 The Race Relations Act outlawed discrimination on the grounds of ethnicity and race. The first Act, however, only addressed racial discrimination in public spaces; the 1968 Act corrected this oversight by extending the law to housing, employment, and advertising.
2 Although I will use "kitchen sink movement" throughout, the work under discussion is barely part of a "movement" at all and is perhaps better understood as a "moment." But for purposes of clarity and consistency, this book will use "kitchen sink realism" to reflect a particular style and aesthetics, recognizable in what I will refer to as "kitchen sink texts" or in "kitchen sink productions," all part of a "kitchen sink era." The use of scare-quotes here is intentional as a way to acknowledge how such labels are neither productive nor accurate. As the book posits, the chronological frame of reference—1956 to 1963—is also relatively inelegant and the final chapter will show how such aesthetic motifs operate in the present.
3 The Beveridge Report, or 1942's "Social Insurance and Allied Services" act, is discussed in the second chapter. In brief, the report summarized social problems in the immediate postwar years, proposing widespread solutions that would mark the emergence of the Welfare State.

4 A simple example is that Delaney's *A Taste of Honey* was initially intended to be a novel.
5 The idea of "knowable communities" comes from *The Country and the City* (1973) and represents Williams's argument for the value of literature in understanding culture, but also culture's ability to shape our experience of literature. For Williams, a "knowable community" emerges from interactions between individuals and the community in which they exist.
6 Hutchings describes Sillitoe's characters as "modern-day working-class counterparts of the Byronic anti-hero" in that they represent "(1) a heedless disdain for conventions of bourgeois propriety, (2) a willingness to flout society's conventional morality and (particularly) its sexual constraints, and (3) a rebelliousness against government and other forms of repressive authority, regimentation, and dehumanization" (1993: 84).

1

"Look at the State of This Place!"—The Impact of Domestic Space on Postwar Class Consciousness

When, on May 4, 1956, the Royal Court Theatre's curtain first rose to reveal the setting of John Osborne's *Look Back in Anger*—a scruffy attic flat containing derelict furniture and a prominently situated ironing board—critics and theater-goers alike were appalled. In fact, according to one theater-goer named Bernice Coupe, the premiere saw a number of walk-outs because the stage set "was just so depressing" (Blishen 1992). For Coupe and others, this exposure to poverty ran counter to theater production of the time in which the audience might ordinarily expect to "see the drawing room, the rather elegant furniture, and the desk, the windows and so on with the long curtains and the charming furniture and charming people" (Blishen 1992). A number of traditional critics dismissed the play as an "insult" (Gilleman 2014: 46), a response prophesied by younger, more enthusiastic critics such as Kenneth Tynan.[1] But the depiction of squalor was hardly unique, and histrionic griping about the play's set design can be read more as a function of its broader thematics. As Ann Marie Adams describes, the design and details of the supposedly offensive set took the expected features of the realist stage and "revolutionized a form that had become outmoded" (2007: 80) by orienting the action around aspects of domestic life associated with the "kitchen sink" appellation. It seems that the disgust was fueled more by the play's unapologetic centering of working-class realities. This reaction stemmed, in part, from Osborne's scrupulous stage direction and the way the set encoded symbolic markers of working-class life primed for aesthetic detonation. What matters for purposes of this argument is how the play used spatial motifs to upset its middle- and upper-class audience by forcing them to confront working-class alienation in ways that sidestepped the more palatable caricatures of poverty from the Victorian era. The overdetermined setting pressurized the narrative's gestalt shock in a manner that underscores the kitchen sink movement's ethical and aesthetic prowess. Given that the play effectively launched the movement, *Look Back in Anger* set the stage for a heightened emphasis on spatial aesthetics as a motif perceptible across texts associated with the movement. By extension, the play opened the door to spatialized representations of class. At a moment in British culture in which the built environment saw a radical transformation in the wake of WWII, it is telling that writers like Osborne opted to intensify working-class space as a way to compound and cement the movement's larger influence.

This chapter weighs the impact of shifts in the domestic landscape on representations of working-class people, specifically showing how texts aligned with the kitchen sink movement narrativized the transformation of class consciousness as a partial consequence of postwar redevelopment. It is concerned with the phantasmagoric conception of a once-monolithic working-class identity that is sustained, in part, through cultural production's allegiance to romanticized nostalgia. As such, it explores the intersection between postwar housing development, changes in working-class life, and the way texts affiliated with kitchen sink realism advanced new modes of personal expression to reflect the nature of classed identities. Structured on the premise that kitchen sink texts recalibrate ethical and aesthetic principles through an elevated form of verisimilitude, the chapter looks at the way postwar writers addressed the erratic state of housing development and its impact on working-class people. To that end, the chapter considers how notions of stratification and spatial restriction overlap at the site of the domestic—the space of the titular kitchen sink. Working-class representation of the period, it can be argued, registers the inefficacy of the domestic to meet the needs of a postwar British populace, echoing the inability of the Welfare State to fully address social disparities and achieve the goals outlined in the 1942 Beveridge Report. Despite the general admiration for the Welfare State and its significance in contemporary British culture, such lapses and failures speak to a degree of alienation and frustration that cement the binaries that Richard Hoggart denotes as "them and us" (1971: 62). Such binaries, of course, typically perpetuate social and ideological divisions that both reinforce and reinscribe rigid class boundaries. Arguably, kitchen sink texts challenge such formations and introduce a greater degree of complexity and nuance to class articulation. Through their adherence to portrayals of space, writers linked to the movement not only illuminated state-driven shortcomings but also suggested alternative expressions of class identity in response. The chapter begins with a survey of postwar housing, showing how new developments based on technological and architectural advances failed to compensate for the uprooting of established communities and its destabilizing impact on classed identity. Drawing on John B. Calhoun's conceptions of "behavioral sink" and "defensible space," the chapter explores the alienation experienced by working-class people housed in environments socially encoded as derelict. Turning to three texts from the period—John Osborne's *Look Back in Anger* (1956), Alan Sillitoe's *Saturday Night and Sunday Morning* (1958), and Shelagh Delaney's *A Taste of Honey* (1958)—the chapter underlines the way kitchen sink writers used representations of domestic space as symbolic manifestations of social constraint and limitation. It also shows how such portrayals create an arena for the renegotiation of identities that shun the kind of limits experienced by working-class people. In doing so, the texts of the period pose a challenge to traditional conceptions of class solidarity and the romantic idea of a working-class monolith, advancing instead a form of autonomous, contingent, and dynamic class consciousness as a potential way to offset the problems of postwar redevelopment.

New Domestic Forms

The expansion of working-class housing in the twentieth century can be read as an attempt to continue the late nineteenth-century process of slum clearance attenuated by the wars. In the consecutive postwar years, the Ministry of Reconstruction (1943–1945), led by the conservative statesman Lord Woolton, implemented a series of parliamentary acts aimed at addressing housing concerns. This coincided with attempts to recuperate the labor force by focusing on issues such as proximity of housing to place of employment, the relationship between employers and employees, and advances in the domestic sphere as women gained access to adapted forms of employment—the upshot of 1919's Sex Disqualification (Removal) Act. While working-class people were no strangers to instability, the shifting landscape of British culture altered the experience of working-class domestic space which, in turn, altered the way class itself was comprehended.[2] But it was Winston Churchill's Housing (Temporary Accommodation) Act of 1944 that accelerated postwar reconstruction, aiming to solve two problems: the rehousing of people displaced by the Blitz, and the renewal of pre-WWI housing programs set to combat health problems resulting from industrialization. An estimated 750,000 people were in need of housing, so 300,000 new makeshift homes were proposed as an immediate response while simultaneously seeking to elevate the work force to that of pre-WWII levels. Following the postwar austerity period (1945–1950), 1949's

Housing Act—buttressed by government propaganda seeking to appease the war-torn psyche of the country—furthered the possibility of social renewal through the lure of private home ownership and forms of labor promoting a sense of autonomy and dignity.[3] The Housing Act was supported by an increased subsidization of personal loans, increased federal financing for urban renewal, and the steady promise of continued development sufficient enough to house the majority of the displaced populace. Aside from practical necessities of rehousing and growing the labor force, the subtext of postwar reconstruction was to cultivate optimism in a country devastated by the war, one whose patriotism was also threatened by the impending collapse of imperialism.

Despite efforts to instill a new confidence in the state of the nation, hindsight confirms that housing developed during this time exacerbated symptoms of inequality through a disregard for the legitimate and meaningful elevation of the working poor. For example, postwar rehousing programs tended to prioritize economy and efficiency due to immediacy of need. The result was housing of mixed quality with equally mixed responses in terms of satisfaction. Prefab-style housing, for instance, was engineered as a temporary solution to an emergency situation. Yet, many prefab constructs not only lasted beyond their intended lifespan, they are fetishized today through the lens of postwar nostalgia in ways that recall the nostalgia often tied to the indirect fetishization of working-class identities.[4] The sheer rapidity of reconstruction is registered in many of the texts in that they tend to depict older, more recognizable domestic forms as an archetypical working-class backdrop with newer prefabs and estates forming at the periphery and acting as symbolic rungs on the social ladder. Postwar tenement flats, modernized "two-up two-down" terraces, and new-build tower blocks certainly appear in texts by authors like John Osborne, Colin MacInnes, Nell Dunn, and Arnold Wesker in a manner that registers their arrival in the British landscape. That said, the more persistent examples of working-class domestic space featured in texts by writers like Alan Sillitoe and Shelagh Delaney tend to center on pre-WWII housing as a means to amplify and dramatize slum-like conditions as working-class signifiers. In fact, the narrative arc of kitchen sink texts is frequently structured around the premise of escaping pre-WWII slums to settle into new estates beyond the industrial center. As a device, these depictions operate as engines of social commentary and demonstrate enough repetition across the genre to act as a persistent motif central to the movement's political intent. In this regard, kitchen sink texts narrativize fast-moving social processes underway with experiential fidelity; they represent changes in the built environment while also highlighting how social elevation was deemed an aspirational goal that guaranteed a stable labor force. Yet the texts also reveal certain discrepancies between the housing made available, the aspirational fantasies on offer, and the inefficacy of Welfare State plans to elevate working-class people in a manner that surpasses superficial, symbolic gestures.

A range of architectural styles came to fruition during the initial postwar years, but three forms of construction endured throughout the 1950s and the 1960s as demonstrative of Britain's rehousing program. All three, in part, sought to venerate housing styles of the past while also gesturing toward housing of the future. Furthermore, they shared progressive objectives such as nods toward community and community well-being. However, the emphasis placed on economy and efficiency hamstrung postwar reconstruction's utopian ideals in that much of the housing developed was characterized by a dispiriting sameness and, in some cases, an alienating austerity due to the materials involved. As part of a national schedule of redevelopment that coincided with the rise of the Welfare State, it was working-class areas that saw an increase in council developments like mass housing estates and the rise of prefabs—the form of housing most commonly associated with quick, cheap construction. Despite their makeshift nature, the design of prefabs signaled efforts to inaugurate a new British architectural vernacular in which modern, forward-thinking designs were met with a rethinking of traditional construction methods to symbolize the country's capacity to advance and bolster national pride.[5] The result is a form of urban renewal which dominated much of the postwar landscape but failed to elevate spirits through the kinds of autonomy promised, leading instead to a host of social problems not adequately anticipated or prepared for given the time-sensitive pressures of the housing crisis. Prefab materials, combined with simple, utilitarian lines, resulted in housing that many found to be cold and unwelcoming—a consequence compounded by the sense of displacement felt when moving from stable, established communities to the periphery of the urban environment with few resources dedicated to supporting such changes.

Although the nature of rehousing varied from region to region—especially given the broad span of the Blitz's destruction—northern industry towns retained preexisting terraces from the Victorian era as opposed to densely populated cities like London that pressed ahead with multi-story high-rise construction. Instead, the residential terraces prominent in the initial development of industry—miner's cottages and row housing—underwent renovation, maintaining community structures and sustaining the labor force. But the relative stability of such communities was at odds with more modernized development underway in other parts of the nation. This was also compounded by lax turnaround times for mandated renovation, inevitably resulting in occupied homes marked as derelict—a mark that, by proxy, pronounced the occupants as similarly condemned. As discussed, kitchen sink texts often feature such arrangements, positioning new developments on the outskirts of towns as a target of social ascension. This play on the quest archetype—a gesture also expressed by Hutchings in his discussion of "Proletarian Byronism"—is well represented in the texts of the era. In essence, kitchen sink narratives, then, take the pulse of a larger conflict felt in the postwar years: the desire for newness symbolized by rehousing programs contrasted with the desire for tradition and persistence associated with community spirit adapted as a national endeavor of postwar regeneration. This paradox—a wish for the new paired with a proclivity for the same—forms a component of kitchen sink realism and, arguably, a determining factor in what might be understood as an ideological shift in working-class consciousness that the texts themselves attempt to map out.

Postwar Housing and Classed Space

In the wake of the 1666 Great Fire of London, housing designs developing as part of the Georgian rebuild prioritized ornamentation and detail. But Victorian-era terraces in the following century elevated function over form, the kinds of housing best suited to meet the needs of increased industrialization. This later approach would become more synonymous with council housing projects than with the glamorous Georgian terraces of areas like London's Grosvenor Square. Up until WWII, terraces were the most typical form of high-density residential housing, and the format functioned as a marker of social position in that classed regions were discernible through the specifics of terrace design, perhaps most saliently, through their sameness.[6] This has changed somewhat due to the inflation of housing stock across the country in addition to the aforementioned fetishization of postwar models in desirable areas.[7] All the same, the format still serves as an index of status and, by extension, as an engine of classed identity. In the postwar years, terrace designs centered on technological improvements to address public health concerns. This made terraces more habitable but also expanded their ubiquity, relegating large swathes of the working-class to uniform and increasingly homogenized space. Prior to the wars, terraced housing responded to patterns of migration to urban centers but struggled to keep up with the influx resulting in severe plumbing problems leading to cholera and typhoid outbreaks. The Public Health Act of 1875 served as the incentive for upgrades in that new byelaws required terraced housing to address the needs of the populace such as indoor plumbing and other basic necessities. Byelaw terraces would become the housing format that dominated much of twentieth-century Britain's domestic landscape, and approximately 15 percent of today's housing stock can be traced to this change.[8]

Terraced houses intended to support industrial labor were often modeled on a "two-up two-down" design with two main rooms on the ground level with two bedrooms above. To meet the stipulations of new byelaws, remodeled terraces needed indoor plumbing and were required to demonstrate tangible ventilation through the use of distinct window designs that let in requisite natural light. A later byelaw modification called for a designated scullery, reducing yard space but allowing for an indoor toilet plumbed into the main sewerage system. Byelaws helped regulate living conditions but played little role in the aesthetic design, so the face of terraced housing tended to be universally dowdy, bordering on oppressive. Although cosmetic facades were sometimes used, terraced housing designs rarely differed. The result was a sense of community that also signaled class designation through pervasiveness and anonymity. While pre-WWII terraces featured communal areas as holdovers from tenement housing, byelaw terraces sacrificed such spaces for increased privacy and, ultimately, atomization. So, it might be said that the social aspects of terraced living became more conceptual than tangible; what working-class terrace residents lost in shared communal spaces they gained through a degree of standardization that assured them that they were part of a community in that they were considered indistinguishable from their neighbors.[9]

The advent of byelaw regulations shaped the postwar landscape while also reconfiguring identity. Whereas terraced houses saw incremental improvement through byelaw mandates, pre-regulation terraces—particularly buildings marked for demolition as part of slum-clearance projects—remained occupied, and frequently overcrowded due to the housing crisis as well as matters of affordability. Slum-clearance programs designed to remove pre-regulation terraces were halted in 1939 and did not resume until the mid-1950s. The result was that working-class people continued to reside in uninhabitable conditions, spaces proclaimed as condemned. This did little to elevate the spirits of residents, which ran counter to the postwar government's desire to boost said spirits. Due, in part, to the pervasiveness of the design, such pre-regulation terraces with superficial fixes in place remained part of the British landscape well into the 1970s.

The glacial nature of terrace redevelopment was due to bureaucratic hurdles and red tape. This led to a number of communities tagged for slum clearance but without actual clearance dates planned. Independent developers avoided certain areas, deeming them a lost cause. Residents were hesitant to perform internal upgrades themselves due to the threat of possible demolition on a nebulous timeline. Yet, the experience of living in pre-regulation terraces still held appeal for many working-class people who praised community and collectivity over the increased privacy associated with more modern housing and newer developments. However, such feelings began to shift as new homes emerged as part of the reconstruction process. A 1943 text compiled by Mass Observation titled *An Enquiry into People's Homes* devotes a section to "keeping to oneself," confirming that working-class people preferred to have their own private space with their own private yard—the kinds of housing promised as part of postwar redevelopment (1943a: 171–5). That said, the sense of community prevalent within inner-city terraces remained palpable, and Joanna Bourke tells of how working-class people felt that "residents in established inner-city localities were friendlier than those on estates" (1993: 127). What this implies is that the desire to live autonomously was at odds with the appeal of community and collective ideals, indicative of a break in the notion of class solidarity and burgeoning crisis of an identity structured on belonging. Bourke adds that few terrace residents were as friendly with their neighbors as they would have liked, and that the physical environment was responsible for the feeling of belonging more than any perceptible relationship to the community itself (1993: 127). In other words, the sense of community and collectivity tied to terraced living was the result of proximity to individuals of the same social rank rather than through actual interactions with them. Rehousing and urban transformation carried an implicit threat of upheaval, but also a degree of psychological upheaval in that leaving a community meant detaching from the shared ideals that help construct and sustain stable identities. For as uninhabitable as pre-byelaw slums were, they offered a coherent sense of kinship—which, in turn, offered a coherent sense of self. In this regard, life in pre-byelaw terraces contributes to the kind of collective working-class identity linked to the mythical monolith. But this identity, it seems, was structured on spatial negotiations as much as it was structured on the tangible, physical experience of a community. The paradox is that while the pre-byelaw terraces were insufficient for modern life, they granted a sense of solidarity that byelaw terrace developments undermined through their emphasis on increased private space and atomization.

The experience of pre-byelaw solidarity is attributable to a conception of shared struggle and a collective sense of immiseration, a state that Richard Hoggart discusses under the guise of "making do." It is also a state dominant in the lived experience of pre-regulation terraces. Hoggart maintains that "When people feel that they cannot do much about the main elements in their situation, feel it not necessarily with despair or disappointment but simply as a fact of life, they adopt attitudes towards that situation which allows them to have a liveable life under its shadow, a life without a constant and pressing sense of the larger situation" (1971: 77–8). Although Hoggart is referring to a kind of performative stoicism that acts as "a self-defense, against being altogether humbled before men" (1971: 78), such forbearance is collectively shared, compounding the sense of community. This is true even if, as Bourke suggests, the community itself remains somewhat conceptual. Furthermore, the emphasis on "making do" can be understood with regard to a culturally driven bashfulness—a desire to not "make a fuss" about any misfortune associated with class or classed space. Data from a separate Mass Observation report titled "People and Homes" confirm that working-class individuals kept their opinions of their living conditions to themselves in that "A great many people never think in terms of actively liking or disliking their homes. They take them for granted" (1943b: 132–3). This stiff-upper-lip attitude of accepting one's lot, Hoggart contends, stems from a sense of resignation conflated with ordinariness: "we are not asked to be the great doers of this world; our kind of life offers little of splendor or of calls for the more striking heroisms, and its tragedies are not of the dramatic or rhetorical kind" (1971: 77). While the conditions accompanying pre-regulation terraces were certainly dire, for many working-class people, spaces such as these represented a tangible sense of solidarity and connection, unified by a system of subjugation and its attendant alienation.

Post-byelaw housing's emphasis on privacy and atomization can be seen as a challenge to traditional notions of working-class solidarity. With housing renovation and new builds promising a greater sense of individualism and social aspiration, it is not a stretch to see how shifts in the built environment might reflect shifts in class articulation. The "People and Homes" report also compiles perceptions on the difference between pre-1900 terraces and estates constructed with regulations in place, concluding that newer constructions were mostly favored over the old with regard to the nebulous descriptor "convenience" (1943b: 113). Convenience, according to the report, speaks to new technology and the optimization of domestic life. For example, the inclusion of a separate scullery to keep laundry out of the dining room and small-scale upgrades in kitchen design like double draining boards next to the sink and built-in storage (1943b: 115). Such reports reveal how superficial advances in domestic life helped reorient public favor toward new housing designs, assuaging the loss of solidarity with supposed gains in independence and creature comforts. What this indicates is that the appeal of postwar terraced housing had less to do with tangible social ascension and more to do with the perceived level of individual comfort driven by concurrent advances in consumerism. The move from slum to new estate can be read as lateral in that it failed to register as a legitimate elevation of social class. However, new domestic technologies assuaged such concerns by simulating social elevation through creature comforts.

As contemporary housing terraces reiterated their Victorian origins, prefabricated housing—or "prefabs"—ushered in the most notable changes in working-class domestic life. Prefabs were initially conceived of as a temporary placeholder for more substantial accommodations. Despite the ubiquity of material used for fabrication, prefab housing arrived in a variety of formats, breaking the uniformity of the terrace and connoting uniqueness while still sustaining class parameters. A total of 300,000 prefab homes were proposed in the immediate postwar years, yet only half of that number materialized. Furthermore, prefabs were inconsistent in their appeal; some were hospitable, warm spaces resembling a traditional home whereas others were considered less favorable due to their shed-like appearance. Prefabs that outlived their designated ten-year lifespan tended to suffer from the same class stigma as other postwar mass-housing schemes, due in part to their uninspired finish, their limited interiors, and their tendency toward shoddy construction. In essence, prefab housing was sold to the public as a necessary fix but also as a symbol of modernity. In tandem with terraces, prefab homes were commonplace for working-class people. And while their presence in kitchen sink realism is less common than that of traditional terraces, prefabs do make a number of appearances as a lure of social elevation.[10] More than twenty different styles of prefabs were produced in the postwar years, but the most known would be the Airey and the AIROH (Aircraft Industries Research Organization on Housing) with the BISF (British Iron and Steel Federation) and the "Wimpey no-fines" providing the most substantive and traditional plans.

The Airey's popularity can be linked to a 1947 propaganda film named *Country Homes* commissioned by the Central Office of Information and directed by Paul Dickson that promoted new construction in rural parts of the country. Designed by Leeds-based architect Sir Edmund Airey, the majority of Airey construction occurred between 1946 and 1955. The design was composed of concrete posts reinforced with steel tubing and external walls made from precast slabs of concrete resembling pebble-dashed planks of wood. Small windows and a traditional sloped roof with chimney system offered a quasi-farmhouse look to complement rural settings. Compliant with the standards required by the Ministry of Works, around 26,000 houses were constructed based on the Airey design. By 1984, however, the Housing Defects Act registered the design as uninhabitable due to issues of corrosion in the steel reinforcement that produced cracking and splitting of the concrete panels. Although a number of Airey homes still stand, they now require a licensed series of repairs that includes replacing the support columns with brick. As the result, many remaining Airey houses are unsaleable similar to pre-regulation terraces listed for renovation—totems of condemned postwar working-class space.

Distinct in design yet assuring a similar sense of independence was the AIROH, named after a model home produced by the Aircraft Industries Research Organization on Housing. While the Airey offered a relatively economic assembly, the AIROH was a mass-produced kit-build product. According to Colin Davies, the same assembly lines that produced Spitfire fighter jets were responsible for the fast throughput, with a single home kit prepared in twelve minutes (2005: 61). The design was rudimentary: four walls of aluminum sheeting packed with aerated cement, lined with insulation and plasterboard. The floors were timber, but the structure relied on aluminum trusses, shipped in flat packs, and bolted together on site. Although high tech in production method and material choice, the assembled homes appeared far more functional than homely. Stripped of domestic ornament, AIROH prefabs resembled industrial sheds, yet they maintained popularity due to the efficiency of the design and modernized production that leant them a hi-tech edge. In addition, their popularity stemmed from the fact that they were free-standing and often featured a sizeable garden space.[11] In this regard, the design promised independence and autonomy while simulating the communal spirit of terraced housing through proximal placement. Despite their economic production and assembly, AIROH homes were more costly than other prefabs at the time. Furthermore, as Brian Finnimore reports, prices elevated further following postwar military budget cuts. As lighter metals were introduced into military armament, the aluminum industry declined, thus boosting AIROH production costs even more (1985: 60). Given the heightened cost of ownership, it might be said that the military-grade production spoke to the desire for security in the immediate postwar years as national security remained at the forefront of people's minds.

Whereas the AIROH used military-grade aluminum, the BISF house relied on steel, also produced through a subsidiary operation of the British Iron and Steel Foundation. The BISF house grew from research conducted by the Burt

Committee—a think tank established in 1942 to provide guidance on the British housing problem. Seeking to address stalled slum-clearance projects, the group helped pass the Housing (Temporary Accommodation) Act of 1944 responsible for green-lighting mass prefab construction. The BISF house came about from early research by the committee on systematic production, specifically cost and manufacturing efficiency. Similar to AIROH, the BISF house was a by-product of postwar military production, but the BISF house was designed with a more substantial and sustained lifespan in mind. Tubular steel struts served as the basic foundations with windows suspended between. Traditional housing materials like brick or wood were combined with prefabricated panels, lending the structure the appearance of permanence. The standard BISF floor plan followed a conventional design of two rooms and a kitchen on the ground floor and three bedrooms and a bath on the first floor. What distinguished it from the "two-up-two-down" terrace, though, was the increased proportions due to the square-shaped plan, offering a total coverage of approximately 1,000 square feet. A total of 36,000 were produced between 1944 and 1950, 30,000 of which were contractually guaranteed in 1941 by the government. Unlike other prefabs of the era, the BISF evaded a defective designation, and many still stand today. Although predating the New Towns Act of 1946, BISF construction was associated with new, make-shift communities of terraced and semi-detached houses found on the periphery of urban centers, affirming the notion of community encoded into rehousing production of the time.

Equally prominent was the Wimpey "No-Fines"—a design that differed from other prefab models in that emphasis centered on the use of concrete with "no fine" aggregates.[12] Proposed by a private contractor named George Wimpey, the structure offered the substance of a brick build while cutting back on assembly. Two- and three-bedroom semi-detached houses and three- to four-bedroom terraces were the norm, granting enough variation to warrant a variety of pricing and size options in addition to bypassing the problem of aesthetic sameness. However, the grey cement exterior was felt to be disaffecting. Today's residual Wimpey constructs tend to rely on pastel paint and cosmetic modifications to counter the drab materials once considered modern. The unadorned Wimpey design became the aesthetic most synonymous with low-rise council estates and the form was adopted in a number of high-rise constructs in the years following its arrival. Housing estates comprised predominantly of no-fines construction still exist in areas of Nottingham, West Yorkshire, and the West Midlands.

Although just a snapshot of the full range of prefab housing tied to the postwar years, these examples help articulate the link between new housing formats and their emotional impact on the psyche of the British working class. A special report by Mass Observation titled "Second Report on the Modern Homes Exhibition" documents a burgeoning set of opinions about proposed postwar prefabs. It centers on overheard commentary and conversations at the exhibit, concluding with a synthesized overview of the public's perception of the postwar constructs on display. The main criticism registered was the lack of light—a problem that commenters blamed on small windows that made the homes feel imprisoning. Furthermore, there were few favorable opinions about aesthetic facades with many commenters reporting that steel-structured houses looked particularly grim. In almost all cases, the houses on display were thought to be constricting and harshly designed. The survey concluded with many of the commenters declaring that they disliked all of the houses on show, with men registering disdain three times as regularly as women (1946: 8). The report also speaks to anxieties of stability in that the most negative comments declared that the houses "looked temporary" (7). In contrast, the Orlit House, a design resembling the Wimpey No-Fines, saw comments that it "Looked more permanent. Had personality" (1946: 8) suggesting how "personality" can be derived from an impression of stability. The Airey house held little visual appeal for commenters, yet some were enamored by its innovations such as a serving hatch that aided domestic operations (1946: 8). The BISF house, however, saw universal condemnation with guests noting that "They look as though they're barracks. You'd feel as though you were in a camp again" (1946: 10). This comment is noteworthy given postwar reconstruction's resolve to simultaneously reconstruct national confidence after the Blitz. That British people aligned postwar housing design with the war itself is ironic in that, on the one hand, the use of military-grade materials and production methods extends the memory of war in the mind of the occupant; on the other, it implies a military-grade security to assuage the feeling of instability stemming from displacement and social upheaval. The report also indicates that repulsion of the cement and steel aesthetics was offset by the desire for such stability, with brick constructs drawing comments such as "The houses would look terrible in a few years" and that "They all look alike" (1946: 10). Despite the desperate need for 750,000 new homes at the time, the report concludes with a conversation heard between two female visitors that sums up the public perception well:

> Honestly, I'm not struck on any of them. I'm not sure I didn't the like LCC one best. The insides of them are all so much better than the outsides. I think it's very important how a house looks from the outside. You know we were offered the

choice of a pre-fab? Well, I wouldn't have it. They're nice inside, but they look dreadful from the orad [sic]. You don't like to feel ashamed every time you get near your own home.

(1946: 11)

Despite the undisputed dislike of the facade, opinions on the internal features—referred to as "the house engine"—were generally more favorable. Tangible concerns about technological and domestic innovation can be discerned in the responses, yet most appear to be irrational. For instance, new appliances such as electric stoves drew feedback such as "it frightened us rather" (1946: 13). This suggests that new domestic attributes both thrilled and alarmed in a manner that indicates more of a resistance to change than the kind of revulsion of exterior aesthetics—an anxiety tied to the break away from an older, more coherent mode of working-class life. Overall, the report denotes that British working-class people wished their homes would appear as substantial as possible such as to recreate the stability of an older, established community—at least psychologically. This desire was at odds with the advent of modernity and industrial mass production. Viewed in this way, prefab construction—one of the most driving forms of rehousing tied to the postwar years—acts as a source of a unique nervousness that not only suspends the individual between the familiar and the unknown, but between their own desire for personal autonomy and their relationship to a community of like-minded individuals.

The initial popularity of tower block construction is attributable to references of progress encoded within the design, but the main appeal for the average citizen was simply the promise of spacious interiors matched with panoramic views. As was true of byelaw terraces, residents in congested urban areas were more than willing to sacrifice outdoor space for an increase in interior comfort. The popularity of high-rise designs was further bolstered by their economic benefit in that construction was often focused on cheap land on the city outskirts with savings passed on to the occupants. Be that as it may, high-rise towers did not fare well in that they quickly earned a poor reputation, mostly due to hasty construction and corner-cutting as they sidestepped the social ethics of better-known modernist housing projects. Increases in crime and delinquency are tied to a dearth of amenities and the steady deterioration of constructs that, while proportionally generous, appeared aesthetically barren and psychologically alienating. The 1968 collapse of the Ronan Point tower foregrounded the disturbing inevitabilities of low-cost, rapid construction which made contractors rich at the expense of working-class lives.[13] Dubious design choices rendered communal areas as socially toxic, and, as many of the basic designs were reproduced across the country, a metaphorical domino effect ensued. By the end of the 1960s, high-rise towers were relatively stigmatized and shunned, losing almost all of their initially optimistic appeal.

Still principally stigmatized as sites of abject poverty, council estate development programs featuring both prefab and high-rise construction were quick to abandon their commitment to elevating the British populace through architectural form. A report from Emily Dugan in *The Independent* labelled such environments as "social concentration camps" (2009), yet more balanced coverage such as Lynsey Hanley's 2007 *Estates* draws similar conclusions. Many of these sites were doomed from the start by their remote locations. Sites chosen by developers, chiefly based on the lowcost of land as a means to maximize profit, led to high degrees of alienation and made inevitable the kind of social problems that ensued. Akin to the prefab concepts, construction materials produced aesthetic alienation. But this effect was further compounded by literal alienation stemming from construction at the margins of urban centers. A lack of basic amenities and connections to transportation recreated the slum-like conditions that new buildings served to eradicate in the first place. Despite the goal of constructing estates around central social hubs intended to form self-reliant communities, the breakup of the original community cemented these concerns even more. Mixed-level estates with both low- and high-rise housing appeared all over the country due to a 1956 subsidy system that sought to combine postwar rehousing with existing slum-clearance projects. As the above suggests, the result was simply a new kind of slum.[14]

It is apparent that changes in the postwar landscape of Britain are matched by tension between tradition and progress, redevelopment and displacement, innovation and familiarity. These tensions played out on the psyche of those most directly affected by changes underway: working-class people. It can be seen how such advances helped destabilize working-class identities in regards to both the individual and the collective, due in part to discrepancies between the proposed function of such spaces and the experience of interacting with them. While blame for social disruption is attributable to the corner-cutting methods used by rehousing contractors, the housing crisis required a timely response. Much of postwar's housing can be understood as a necessary technological fix—one intended as a temporary solution. But as gentrification began in tandem with modifications in political governance, it is no surprise that the more ethical intentions of rehousing were quickly swept aside in favor of profit and greed. As communities were upended, destroying any semblance of stability and security, it was up to the working class to envision new ways of living. Cultural production of the time evidently addresses these challenges. Kitchen sink realism, in particular, foregrounds the significance of domestic space for working-class people, narrativizing and speculating on the impact of changes in the built environment. Given that modern housing's emphasis on autonomy and atomization appeared to undermine traditional sentiments of collectivity, writers linked to the kitchen sink movement explored and offered productive solutions in response. In this regard, the texts of the era articulate models of working-class life that help mediate autonomy and collectivity, chiefly through reinscriptions of space and the disputation of shifts in class consciousness.

Writing Home

Kitchen sink texts' emphasis on space and environment emulates the lived experience of their authors and their commitment to honest portrayals of working-class life. Figures like John Osborne, Alan Sillitoe, and Shelagh Delaney hailed from relatively humble backgrounds, the setting of their narratives somewhat reflective of their own worlds.[15] Sillitoe, for example, was born and raised in Nottingham—the area portrayed in his fictional debut, his personal circumstances and experiences resemble those of his characters.[16] His parents worked as laborers in nearby factories, and the family was poverty-stricken for much of his early life. Early memories of his own home are recounted in a manner comparable to those of his characters: "We lived in a room on Talbot Street whose four walls smelled of leaking gas, stale fat, and layers of mouldering wallpaper" (Hanson 1999: 2). The Great Depression influenced much of Sillitoe's early childhood, but WWII sustained existing industry in the region since Nottingham's proximity to natural resources and transit lines allowed it to function as a hub of wartime manufacturing. Because of this, Nottingham was also a target for airstrikes. This produced a level of uncertainty that Sillitoe chronicles in his discussion of another early family home, one located "only a hundred yards from a vast factory engaged on full war production, which the Germans constantly attempted to bomb and machine-gun" (Hanson 1999: 3). The nature of such domestic instability recalls the public's interest in prefab housing discussed prior. Despite general dissatisfaction in their design and form, the use of military-grade engineering ties perceptions of security to manufacturing, a gesture central to the British government's desire to elevate national spirits.

Sillitoe's father Christopher worked as a tanner until he was made redundant. He then worked a range of jobs intermittently, eventually joining other family members at Nottingham's famous Raleigh factory. At fourteen, Sillitoe began work at the same factory—a move also reproduced in *Saturday Night and Sunday Morning*'s protagonist. Sillitoe's mother, Sabina, had worked in a nearby lace factory from the age of fourteen. Historical records reveal a prominent lace factory at Stanley House on Talbot Street in Nottingham, established in 1784 by Richard Lambert in a former flour mill, one known to employ young laborers from local workhouses while refusing to exploit children under the age of thirteen.[17] The Raleigh factory stood on Faraday Road, a mile from Lambert's lace factory. As such, it is possible to glean a sense of the housing that the Sillitoe family likely inhabited. According to then-local historian J. Holland Walker, Talbot Street was "another rather uninteresting thoroughfare" and the surrounding residences were designed to support workers at Lambert's factory (1928). These surrounding homes, according to Peter Neaverson and Marilyn Palmer, appear to be staggered tenements whose "stark utilitarian facades" contrast sharply against the drama of the factory's clock tower (1994: 111). Today, the area is still defined by terraced housing as well as mid-century prefab estates, suggesting that Sillitoe's childhood domestic environment is emblematic of the slum clearance and postwar rehousing projects discussed.

Sillitoe describes the home he shared with his parents as "an odd kind of house on the edge of some back-to-backs" which consisted of "a living room with scullery attached, a bedroom above, and an attic at the top where we children slept on one bed" (Sillitoe 1995: 19). "Back-to-backs" were Victorian row houses in which outdoor space was sacrificed to link one house to the back of another, or in several cases, to the factory itself. Such designs appear oppressive in that standard Victorian terraces at least granted the worker an iota of private outdoor space as well as more than just one point of access. Back-to-backs, in their original form, circled a shared yard containing communal toilets, a water pump, and an area for domestic tasks such as laundry. Such spaces demonstrate connections between home and work explored in Sillitoe's texts—particularly the notion of acquiescence and resignation to one's lot in life. Neaverson and Palmer note that, by 1840, there were nearly 8,000 back-to-backs in Nottingham that quickly became known as "some of the worst court housing in Britain" (1994: 139). Sillitoe adds that between the ages of fourteen and eighteen, his life consisted of daily labor at the factory and a nightly return to the cramped space that he shared with his family. His only concession to freedom came from weekends spent at his girlfriend's family home in a housing estate on the outskirts of the city. Sillitoe's early life, then, parallels the environments portrayed in his fiction—a space commensurate with the domestic experience of British working-class people at the time. In this sense, *Saturday Night and Sunday Morning* is indicative of the way kitchen sink texts offer a kind of ethnographic snapshot of working-class life in that it depicts the ramifications of living under the ever-present shadow of the factory.

Unlike Sillitoe, Osborne came from the south yet adopted what might be read as a stereotypically northern working-class aesthetic. This is characterized by a stance of insubordination discernible in his characters as well as in his own public persona. Like Sillitoe, however, Osborne recalls his childhood home in Fulham as part of a "dismal district" marked by a "succession of identical streets" lined by Victorian terraces and "strange little gnarled stubs of trees" (1981: 16–17). Osborne's father was notably absent, and much of his early life in Fulham was spent living with his mother whose stress as a single parent led her to a state in which she "had bitten her fingernails to stumps that resembled the trees that lined the streets" (1981: 33). His early years were marked by a sequence of moves from one location to the next—a degree of instability he attributes to his mother's desire for continued upheavals (1981: 57). She regarded their Highdale flat as "'more modern' and less stuffy than a house. Not as chic as a bungalow but a step up from the dead-and-alive cul-de-sac" (1981: 57). Although somewhat distinct from writers whose lives resembled the worlds they created, Osborne's early life was defined by continual displacement and movement through a range of domestic spaces and locales.

His relative instability influenced the style and content of *Look Back in Anger*. But it also contributed to impressions he felt other writers held of him at that moment: "They seem to think I'm a sort of juvenile delinquent, the result of an undesirable background" (Heilpern 2007: 100). Such anxieties—irrational or otherwise—are responsible for stoking Osborne's drive to write class-conscious drama that counters a lack of representation in theater. As Osborne's biographer claims, fully developed representations of working-class characters were unlikely. If they were represented at all, the author notes, they were marked by stereotypes that positioned them as "either a villain or a fool" (2007: 101). While discussing what he refers to as the "Manchester School" of social realism—northern drama from the turn of the century—Heilpern adds that Osborne's exposure to the arts resembled a world distant from his own, one in which the "West End theatre still dressed in dinner jackets and cocktail dresses" (2007: 103).[18] Domestic displacement and continued upheaval, it can be surmised, helped fuel the outsider stance Osborne embraced throughout much of his career. The same attitude is perceptible in his characters, many of which are propelled by restlessness and discontentment as the upshot of instability.

Osborne left London relatively young, sent to boarding school in the west of England only to be expelled for attacking the headmaster. He then took a job as a stage manager and embarked upon a brief career as an actor—a role that neither he nor anybody else, according to his memoir, took seriously (1981: 233). He began work on *Look Back in Anger* in 1951 while living in a cramped houseboat with the actress Pamela Lane—the first of his six wives. Although his childhood was perhaps more culturally cosmopolitan than that of his kitchen sink peers, Osborne's early domestic life corresponded to the instability and precarity experienced by his contemporaries as well as working-class people in general. In a sense, his protagonist—lower-middle class with a noted affinity for working-class culture—mirrors his own lived experience. In this regard, the limited and limiting spaces portrayed in *Look Back in Anger* are informed more by an accumulation of domestic experience crossed with a class-based identity crisis. While Sillitoe and Delaney's work read as autobiographical echoes of their own working-class experience, Osborne's play proposes a more complex and conflicted approach. The result is a text that is perhaps more cerebral and elevated—a play as invested in the psychic interiors of the characters as in the interiors of their working-class homes.

There exists less substantive biographical information on Delaney and the spaces she inhabited as a young person relative to her contemporaries. This may be the result of a career overshadowed by the impact of her first play, but also because she shied away from the spotlight after the 1960s and destroyed much of her own archive. In recent years, Selina Todd's *Tastes of Honey: The Making of Shelagh Delaney and a Cultural Revolution* (2019) helped to fill in some of the blind spots of Delaney's life. However, the lack of a coherent archive alongside her relatively modest creative output continues to sustain Delaney's enigmatic history. Ken Russell's short documentary for the BBC, *Shelagh Delaney's Salford* (1960), reveals a number of beneficial details such as specifics about the author's birth in Broughton with the implicit suggestion that *A Taste of Honey*'s setting replicates the gray, industrial area in which she was raised. The opening scene of the documentary shows her entering a standard-fare Wimpey-style prefab, signifying the kind of domestic spaces Delaney herself was most familiar with. Despite her provincialism—partly a construction of a working-class identity promoted by Joan Littlewood—Delaney informs Russell that she has spent time in Sweden, France, and London, but that she develops "a terrible homesickness" and that Salford is like "a terrible drug" she returns to again and again. She characterizes the town as simultaneously "alive" yet "dying," with much of the region in a state of dereliction—dirty, neglected, and yet romantic "if you can stand the smell." In particular, she highlights the network of "alleyways that go on for miles," that separate houses "that seem to have been built on top of one another." Russell transposes Delaney's own narration over images of Salford's Victorian slum terraces, yet her disembodied voice informs viewers that the cramped confines still manage to generate "a terrific warmth."

Russell's documentary also registers the impact of postwar urban redevelopment. Delaney remarks that when people do leave the area, it is rarely on their own terms—motivated by burgeoning gentrification, moving to places "far away where there's no city." This, of course, is commensurate with postwar rehousing plans of new estates developed in response to the housing crisis. As if to comment on the skepticism of new builds, Russell superimposes images of high-rise construction far removed from the city center that appear ominously carceral. Delaney's superimposed voice states how new housing developments alienate working-class individuals, separating them from their community by placing them into areas that lack basic amenities and, most importantly, cultural influence such as theaters. Tellingly, she adds that "we had the same experience when we moved to this estate"—the referenced estate being one composed of anonymous three-bedroom prefabs responsible for the kinds of alienation she sought to emulate in *A Taste of Honey*.

A 1959 image of a twenty-year-old Delaney, taken during her rise to fame, shows her standing in front of the family home where she lived after their move from Broughton.[19] The house, 77 Duchy Road, appears unchanged today from its original form built in 1946 as part of a slum clearance project. It was here that Delaney composed her famous play. But it was also a space that, despite offering a supposed upgrade, disrupted the sense of community that she had established. This disruption is reflected in the imaginative capacity of the play's protagonist, resulting in one of the foremost examples of kitchen sink realism's spatial negotiation. Today, the Duchy Road house sits amidst identical houses constructed in the same style, but its presence in Delaney's life is curious. For Delaney's protagonist, there exists a tacit rejection of gentrified new builds in lieu of a romantic idealization of slum housing. In a way, *A Taste of Honey* can be viewed as a play that explores the working-class imaginary of the writer whose lived experience differs from the character she constructs; Delaney's own life resembles the life of Sillitoe's Arthur more than that of her character Jo. Yet, an awareness of the kind of domestic spaces Delaney inhabited as a young writer helps elucidate connections between the kitchen sink movement's ethnographic portrayals and the lived experience of its writers. In this regard, Delaney's biography—at least what exists of it—can be mapped against the worlds she creates in her text to better highlight how the movement's authors represented the kind lived experience felt by many postwar working-class British people.

Theorizing Domestic Space and Classed Identity

Environmental psychology is known to increase understanding of the impact of the built environment on lived experience while also providing insights into the way space prescribes class-related behavior. Incidentally, this branch of psychology emerged during the postwar era, branching into specialized fields of architectural psychology, behavioral geography, and urban design research. For example, Humphry Osmond's work on the way institutional buildings impact the human psyche advanced new terminology to discuss social interactions brought forth through spatial design.[20] The objective of environmental psychology was, as Proshansky et al. (1983) suggest, value-oriented; by uncovering problems stemming from spatial design, solutions could be carved out for the betterment of society. The kind of topics the field addresses include large-scale issues of density and overcrowding, pollution, and more general domestic concerns like window placement, interior partitions, and room design's affective capacity. Because the dire nature of postwar housing problems required quick builds with minimal vetting, new housing projects led to environmental problems in need of further solutions. In other words, the expedited nature of postwar housing projects served as an ideal study for the concomitant rise of environmental psychology.

John B. Calhoun's "Population Density and Social Pathology" argued for the value of "defensible space" as a response to what he termed "behavioral sink" (1962: 139). Behavioral sink, as Calhoun would have it, marks a decline in social behavior as the result of overcrowding with defensible space functioning as the antidote. The principle of defensible space refers to the use of comforting elements to create a familiar, territorial sanctuary in an environment felt to be hostile. Whereas Calhoun's primary work centered on the social behavior of lab rats, early environmental psychologists stressed the importance of real-world situations as the basis for accurate socio-psychological research. Calhoun further developed his studies throughout the 1960s, making them more accessible to a general audience as opposed to specialized professionals. Despite the rodent-centered nature of his initial experiments, his results and conjectures were well recognized in the years that followed, largely due to the number of real-world examples that seemed to certify his conclusions.

Additional considerations of the impact of space on consciousness such as "place identity"—a concept outlined by Proshansky et al.—seek to clarify further the way one's environment imparts certain values and beliefs about the world. The concept indicates that an individual's sense of self-worth is contingent upon their environment's ability to meet basic cultural and biological needs. "Place identity" is corroborated by a notion of "space attachment" in which meaningful links are forged between the individual and their built environment based on connections that run deeper than what Lefebvre would refer to as perceived space (1983: 61). For a space to hold such particular meaning, aesthetic evaluation is not required; meaningful ties can be formed to beautiful and ugly spaces in equal measure (1983: 69). Yet, the concept of behavioral sink implies that if an environment fails to provide an aesthetically agreeable experience, then it is liable to register in the mind of the individual as a feeling of abandonment and marginalization. That is to say, if the space that one inhabits is actively deteriorating, and the resulting effect, according to Calhoun, is a form of enacted social deterioration (through delinquency, for example), then place attachment can indeed be comprehended as an aesthetic endeavor—one that reaffirms an individuals' social position and, by extension, their self-worth. In environments rendered inhospitable due to spatial limitations or the kind of condemned states associated with pending slum clearance, it is conceivable how behavioral sink—a hypothetical decline in social behavior—might arise. Furthermore, when adequate defensible space is inaccessible, such limitations imprint themselves on individuals' identity in that their environment operates as an index of their perceived social worth, certifying class associations in the process.

In one of the more extended studies of postwar kitchen sink writing, Ronald Paul declares that the novels of the period offer broader depictions of working-class space than that of the class-conscious texts that came prior. Put differently, such texts suggest a more liberated or evolved working-class experience. Nevertheless, in his discussion of Stan Barstow's 1964 novel *Joby* and Norman Smithson's 1969 novel *The World of Little Foxy*, Paul also notes how kitchen sink texts still tend toward idealized, romanticized depictions of working-class spaces, composed of "limited, light-weight accounts of restricted domestic experiences, without much deeper psychological penetration" (1982: 71). In this regard, Paul seems to overlook the psychological work such representations can provide in terms of their ability to explore spatialized class structures. Arguably, the psychological impact of the movement can be understood in the way the texts present space as both inhibiting and ubiquitous. Such ubiquity—what Paul here considers "limited"—is in the service of representation and recognition, meaning that kitchen sink texts strive to construct a cumulative mimesis of working-class life as it is—an immediately identifiable image of lived experience. By highlighting the ordinary and the grim, kitchen sink writers simulate the conditions central to issues covered by environmental psychology. Paul's critique of kitchen sink's "limited, light-weight" spatialization speaks to Calhoun's concept of behavioral sink—a heightened emphasis on dereliction and marginalization that assist in linking spatial representation to class consciousness. Said differently, environmental psychology helps to show how the aesthetic strategies tied to the movement link to ethical and political impulses.

It is worth noting, also, the distinction between portrayals of space as a mere prop or a narrative device and space depicted through character's responses to working-class environments. This motif is relatively consistent through much of the work of the period, bridging the notion of represented space acting as social marker and space operating as a determinant of social behavior. Kevin Guyan has argued how the physical makeup of the domestic environment is responsible for the mobilization of masculinities that sustain patriarchal norms. Although I would argue that masculinity is, in fact, contested by space in the postwar era—in that masculinity is threatened by advances in equality—Guyan's attention to the impact of domestic space on the individual is instructive. For Guyan, patriarchal norms are the result of patterns of repetition that regularize social structures as quotidian. Drawing on Judith Butler's "Politics in Alliance and the Politics of the Street," Guyan argues for the formation of "place-specific masculinities" (2016: 139) in which men adopt multiple personas that intervene with the more widely accepted assumption of the man as the public figure. He adds that the development of homes in the postwar era posited new freedoms for men in terms of space and creature comforts, inviting them to spend more time at home with the family and sanctioning more domestic performances of masculinity. Although Guyan's analysis stops short of accounting for the long-term failure of these perceived spatial advances—specifically in relation to British postwar housing—his research does indeed point to the way domestic interiors transform how the individual responds to others in a shared space, shifting their sense of identity in regards to the physical world they inhabit.

In *Home Rules*, Denis Wood and Robert J. Beck (1994) examine the way codes of conduct circulate through domestic environments, concluding that attributes of the home not only shape an individual's sense of cultural relation but also police their behavior. Building on work by thinkers like Gaston Bachelard

(1964), their analysis posits what they refer to as an "environmental ethology"—a consideration of domestic interiors and their impact on inhabitants. Whereas Bachelard is concerned with the act of remembering and its ramifications for the individual, Wood and Beck explore how objects and items within a space are emblazoned with meaning that transmits moral codes and values to uphold conduct. Although the authors' focus tends to center on the behavior of infants and young children—especially the way children act as outliers within a space of established rules—a similar circumstance can perhaps be understood regarding multigenerational postwar households in that the housing crisis led to a rise in parents and adult children sharing space. In such cases, objects and artifacts of the older generation conveyed traditional rules and morals that clashed with the advent of consumerism linked to the rise of "the teenager." This is well-represented in the texts of the kitchen sink cycle, most conspicuously in their recounting of the rise of youth subculture and its inherent paradoxes. Texts like *Saturday Night and Sunday Morning* present a younger generation's turn away from the world of their parents but one that curiously clamors to aspects of tradition for a sense of stability. Ultimately, Wood and Beck's analysis denotes how shared spaces produce and reiterate traditional social values and, by extension, class comprehension through the contours of the space itself.

Maria Kaika considers how the spatialized attributes of anxiety are made clear when the apparatus of defensible space is laid bare. Building on principles established by Wood and Beck, Kaika explores the unnerving aspects of domestic comfort—specifically how mundane and ordinary interiors elicit a sensation of the eerie through attempts to perform comfort in response to chaos. For Kaika, the uncanny sensation is most felt in spaces that "show [their] 'guts'" in that "the networks that support its function, can produce a similar uncanny effect, a feeling of discomfort" (2004: 69). Kaika references the externalization of pipelines on structures like Le Centre Pompidou as well as installation art like Rachel Whitread's "House" (1993). But she also suggests that the effect is discernible through the diffusion of commodity products like vacuum cleaners with translucent cylinders that "reveal rather than [hide] away the amount of dirt and grime that has been removed from the home" (2004: 69).[21] Citing Mark Wigley's work on gothic space, Kaika submits that domestic facades aim to assuage the violence of the social forces behind the spaces themselves (2004: 70). Viewed this way, the home—ideally constructed as refuge from the malevolence of the working-world—acts more as a reminder of malevolence in that decor is used as an attempted gesture of defense. As noted in the public's response to the modern amenities of new housing, a certain anxiety around housing persists in the postwar era. Kaika's comments are instructive in this regard, helping to clarify the dichotomy between an optimism for the future that is matched with the unease of leaving the past behind. Arguably, kitchen sink texts operate through an exploration of a wide range of dichotomies. Furthermore, their foregrounding of domestic interactions marks them as uniquely fruitful in terms of understanding postwar anxiety.

As part of his work on the architectural uncanny, Anthony Vidler's conception of "displacement"—most perceptible in cultural production—can help to articulate the alienation felt at the intersection of class and domestic space. In *Warped Space: Art, Architecture, and Anxiety in Modern Culture*, Vidler—like Kaika—also turns to Whitread's "House" project, arguing how the work enunciates the fear of "being trapped inside a space filled so violently, the space and air evacuated around a still-living body" (2000: 145). Commenting on the way writers like E.T.A. Hoffman and Henry James capitalized on sentiments of site-specific discomfort, Vidler discusses how subtle forms of domestic anxiety are reflected in "death stalking through the center of life, the 'unhomeliness' of filled space contrasted with the former homeliness of lived space ... threatening all cherished ideals of domestic harmony" (2000: 145). In this regard, it is possible to consider the way the perceived comfort and familiarity of condemned pre-byelaw housing surpassed the high-tech thrill of new construction and technological advances in creature comforts. Texts such as Osborne's *Look Back in Anger* nod toward impressions of uncanny displacement. The detailed and highly specific stage directions construct a domestic interior that mimics the strange alienation central to Vidler's ideas. The Porter's flat is filled with the kind of books and artifacts that would ordinarily produce a sense of comfort akin to Calhoun's defensible space. Yet the space is porous in that ideological messages breach the boundaries in the form of newspaper stories (that make the characters "feel stupid") and radio signals (that connote "Britishness" through a Vaughan Williams concert), suggesting once more that the home fails to provide sufficient protection against the world outside. Kaika and Vidler clarify how anxiety tied to domestic space—or, the kitchen sink—exceeds the anxiety of displacement and upheaval associated with slum clearance and postwar regeneration efforts. By foregrounding spatial negotiations required by new domestic environments, kitchen sink texts illuminate the value of class articulation that responds to a destabilized identity.

Furthermore, interior design and decor beget an additional degree of class-based stress. Christine Atha shows how attempts to cultivate aesthetic taste in the working class furthered antagonism and alienation in that such efforts suggested that working-class people lacked the style and the cultural savvy necessary to inhabit new forms of British housing. To show this, Atha reviews pamphlets and documents circulated to working-class people between 1937 and 1954. Principally penned by Anthony Bertram and Nicholas Pevsner, such pamphlets inferred that the working classes required a kind of crash course in cultural civility. Declaring that the working classes were "crippled by bad taste" (2012: 207), the pamphlets inferred that access to new forms of British housing would require a new kind of self; establishing a sense of aesthetic discrimination, they felt, was crucial to the performance of social mobility. Since Bertram and Pevsner favored clean, modernist looks, their suggestions were at odds with decor found in working-class homes and defensible space. This led to the use of classist and ableist descriptors of styles to avoid: "vulgar," "common," "crude," "mongrel," and "uncivilized" (2012: 208). As Atha remarks, the pamphlets aimed "to 'heal the social crippledom' of a lack of taste" by assisting the working classes in "learning how to live again once they moved into their new modern homes" (2012: 214). Aside from promoting consumerism as a reversal of wartime austerity, Bertram and Pevsner felt compelled to help working-class people disengage from a style that Atha references as "homely"—decorative choices that act as grounding mechanisms for a destabilized cultural moment. Naturally, such efforts only exacerbated class division further by elevating "experts" as authorities charged with the task of judging and civilizing the "common" lives of working-class subjects. Traditionally British ornamentation—holdovers from Victorian households—was figured as "tasteless" in lieu of stark minimalism, compounding the alienation experienced through geographic dislocation and the effect of modern homes designed with cold, barren sensibilities. From this perspective, the interior space of postwar home developments can be understood as equally alienating to working-class people as the cultural shifts underway.

Atha's study centers on the subsequent postwar years and the attempts to restart slum-clearance efforts. By the late 1950s, though, commodity culture had taken hold with gestures toward aesthetic refinement understood more as the upshot of the shift from the postwar "era of austerity" to the "era of affluence" affiliated with the 1960s. Commodity culture rejected the martial minimalism prescribed by Bertram and Pevsner, but it also moved away from the knick-knack ornamentation that working-class households borrowed from the Victorian era. Instead, a push toward domestic technology took precedence over decor, and the rise of youth subculture championed self-expression through fashion and style. Such a shift can be seen in a character like Sillitoe's Arthur, whose predilection for expensive Italian suits runs counter to the cramped living space he shares with his parents and younger brother. Lacking personal space of his own, Arthur wears his decor as a way to communicate his social elevation. As such, the home he returns to at night is a constant source of anxiety as it clashes with the public-facing image of independence he hopes to portray. Deviations from programmatic, prescriptive styles arose during the 1950s, mainly as the result of the age gap in multigenerational households. The kind of decor declared "mongrel" and "tasteless" served as a bone of contention between a younger generation who looked toward a more American kind of consumerism and that of their parents who clung to Victoriana. So, it can be understood how class fragmentation accompanying generational difference is powered by certain domestic anxieties related to postwar housing development.

The "mongrel" tastes that Bertram and Pevsner railed against can also be understood as a response to expressions of class consciousness. Social status is frequently signaled through material markers, and the baselines of taste established by such pamphlets speak to the importance of conformity. In this regard, "keeping up with the Joneses" is less about competition and more about belonging. Domestic interiors, then, are registered as anchors of class through choices made around shared ideals rather than as individual modes of self-representation. As Andrew Rosen indicates, British homes from all social classes functioned to "protect and conceal domestic life from the world outside" (2003: 131). Yet, whereas upper- and middle-class homes marked distinction, the structure and proximity of working-class housing lent itself well to cohesion and sameness. In a sense, choices made about decor not only signaled belonging and participation within working-class culture, perceptible or intentional deviation was tantamount to self-exile. Even in an atomized postwar era in which privacy was celebrated, it was felt that decor should align with a shared, collective set of acceptable norms.

As Hoggart argues, social shifts identifiable in England's postwar era are commensurate with the proliferation of new media forms. New modes of advertising infiltrated the home via equally new technologies such as TV. The result was a celebration of creature comforts through domestic technology that served to increase atomization while also ensuring the low-hum of perennial dissatisfaction required for the upkeep of consumer culture. Domestic technology, in tandem with new housing developments, complicated prior notions of shared domestic labor and working-class space. For example, the emergence of refrigerators and home freezer systems decreased the need for regular trips to community markets; in-home laundry technology ended what was often a gendered domestic ritual of hanging washing out to dry in shared space. In other words, the influx of technology into the domestic sphere assisted in upsetting the idea of a monolithic working-class experience. Furthermore, traditional domestic arrangements were challenged by changes in gendered relations. Increased opportunities for women to work outside of the home aligned with the rise of second-wave feminism, rendering the domestic organization mapped out by Hoggart as anachronistic. While such transformations were hardly abrupt, kitchen sink texts appear to support such changes through female characters who reject domestic resignation, allowing for new articulations of gendered class consciousness in working-class spaces. The kinds of anxiety identifiable in the "angry young man" are the result of such changes, with kitchen sink texts frequently exploring the space between progress and traditional practices.

Yet the most prominent difference between the way class was once experienced and changes developing during the twentieth century is most apparent in regard to generational divides. There is nothing particularly unusual about the thought that ideological differences exist between one generation and the next, but kitchen sink realism helps consider the way such distinctions play out as a spatial occurrence. The state of the postwar housing crisis ensured that younger people of the 1950s had fewer opportunities to start their own lives than that of their parents. The general shortage of housing followed by the austerity period led to an increase in multigenerational households with adult children sharing space with their parents, even after marriage and starting a family of their own. Kitchen sink texts are especially responsive to such concerns in that the physical proximity of ideologically divided generations highlights how a younger generation's experience of class consciousness mandates new forms of class expression. Texts such as Delaney's *A Taste of Honey* and Sillitoe's *Saturday Night and Sunday Morning* consider this, allowing for a more granular understanding of intergenerational tensions prevalent at the time. Inevitably, they invite exploration of the way domestic interiors and shifts in the built environment exacerbate generation divides and, inevitably, warrant innovative approaches to class expression. Peter Kalliney, in his reading of *Saturday Night and Sunday Morning*, touches on this by exploring Arthur's anxieties and noting how multigenerational spaces tended to aggravate class-based tensions (2006: 129). Kalliney draws on Hoggart's generalized description of the working-class patriarch, a mostly silent "sallow, dark, somewhat unhealthy" individual (2006: 129). He adds that the father's demure presence in the home is understated, but his position has historically been maintained through "tradition and the mutual consent of his spouse but also by economic means: his ownership of the physical structure is both real and metaphorical" (2006: 129).

Sillitoe's Arthur can be interpreted as a paradoxical presence in that he aligns himself with the patriarch's dominance but questions the kind of traditional roles linked to working-class life. In this regard, the text magnifies generational divides, relegating the working-class patriarch to that of an anachronism.

This is all to say that kitchen sink realism constitutes a body of work deeply invested in domestic space—the site of the titular kitchen sink. As a movement, it amplifies setting as a way to explore class dynamics and modes of class expression. As critics have observed, the setting of class-conscious texts of the Victorian era—as well as texts affiliated with 1930s proletarian fiction—veers toward serviceable representations rather than engaging with the idea of space itself. What follows is an analysis of three of the era's most celebrated texts, each demonstrating how an emphasis on domestic space moves beyond mere representation.

Domestic Anxiety in *Look Back in Anger*

John Osborne's 1956 play *Look Back in Anger*—perhaps the defining text of the kitchen sink era—highlights class anxiety as the result of social limitation rendered symbolically through domestic constraint. From the moment of the play's release, the central character—Jimmy Porter—gained a cult-like following in ways comparable to Alan Sillitoe's similarly celebrated Arthur. But whereas Arthur demonstrates a range of emotional states due, in part, to the extended structure of the novel, Osborne's protagonist operates as an assemblage of behavioral ticks and associative responses. These associations, manifested as sociopathic outbursts, stem from a vague sense of persecution just beyond the character's cognition; he experiences a perpetual sense of imprisonment, but the nature of the prison is never fully voiced. Kenneth Tynan registers the ease by which audiences of the time identified with and tacitly sanctioned this vague persecution: "The salient thing about Jimmy Porter was that we—the under-thirty generation in Britain—recognised him on sight. We had met him; we had pub-crawled with him; we had shared bed-sitting-rooms with him. For the first time the theatre was speaking to us in our own language, on our own terms" (1961: 193). Osborne depicted Jimmy as "of the people" in a manner that was uncommon in twentieth-century British theater—largely through his use of realistic dialog, but also in his portrayal of the way working-class people experienced subtle-yet-pernicious social forces that produced a heightened degree of alienation and disenfranchisement.

Critics tend to read the setting of Osborne's play—a "one-room flat in a large Midland town" (Osborne 1956: 9)—as an incidental thumbing of the nose at the affected drawing-room comedies of Terrence Rattigan and Noël Coward. Nevertheless, the kinds of domestic space that Osborne utilizes became more the norm in postwar Britain due to a demographic shift that saw an escalation of smaller households stemming from an increase in early marriages as well as an increase in single-parent families (Hopkins 1991: 139). This, in turn, placed additional strain on housing development resulting in more makeshift arrangements: an increase in maisonettes and local authority flats as well as the need for occupants to compromise by "making do" in less-than-ideal spaces. Osborne's choice of this space—as well as his use of notably-elaborate stage direction—captures this compromise perfectly. That "the furniture is simple, and rather old" (1956: 9) conveys a degree of economic paucity while the piles of books that litter the space signal the intellectual aspirations of the working class following the reform efforts set in place by the Welfare State's postwar education acts. On the one hand, such details communicate the poverty of the space and its inhabitants; on the other, they signal a failure of defensible space in that the artifacts featured as part of the set lack cohesion, representing instead a chaotic mix of floundering identities. The space stands in stark contrast to the "tasteful" spaces outlined by Bertram and Pevsner, locating Jimmy as "mongrel" and "uncivilized" despite his education and cultural capital. Furthermore, Osborne's description of the room's absurd proportions is revealing: the "two small low windows" that look out to the street convey a carceral atmosphere while signaling the theme of myopic perceptions. The opposing wall's window is much longer and more reasonably positioned, yet the view it grants is not of the outdoors but of an internal hallway—essentially one space trapped inside another. The fact that the flat is crammed into the attic of a large Victorian house encapsulates Jimmy's paradoxical state—elevated, yet held captive within his elevation.[22]

The flat where the Porters live is described as large yet crowded in that the three inhabitants (Jimmy, Alison, and Cliff), despite attempts to claim space, struggle to keep from stepping on each other's toes. Movement around the room is minimal to reiterate the limited mobility of the social sphere; even when off-stage, Jimmy's presence registers through the intermittent bursts of his jazz trumpet that discloses his unstable psychic state (1956: 39). The way characters are granted concessions to privacy is by avoiding eye contact and standing behind each other when talking. This is apparent throughout the play, but is noteworthy in moments when Jimmy's facade cracks in the presence of Helena and reveals the nature of his anxiety: "You see, I learned at an early age what it was to be angry—angry and helpless. And I can never forget it" (1956: 58). In this instance, Osborne moves Jimmy's behind Helena to avoid eye contact and to "almost whisper" what can be read as a plea for personal space. The flat— arguably a stand-in for a culture that denies men like Jimmy the opportunity to express such anxieties—challenges autonomy which, in turn, produces a strained attempt at independence that manifests itself as class-subdivision and isolationism. In this sense, the space lacks any of the comforts required that would deem it defensible—a theme that the play embraces by emphasizing the porousness of domestic boundaries in that outside forces continuously penetrate the space, thus increasing Jimmy's paranoia.

Because of this limited mobility, the space is strategically subdivided by gender in that Alison and, later, Helena, both find themselves stationed behind an ironing board while the male figures are generally foregrounded. For Alison, the ironing board serves as a makeshift defense against Jimmy's abuse ("She is used to these carefully rehearsed attacks, and it doesn't look as though he will get his triumph tonight. She carries on with her ironing" [1956: 22]). But, like the walls of the space itself, the ironing board is a frail defense as it is the iron that burns her when Jimmy intentionally collides with it while wrestling with Cliff (1956: 26). As each figure marks his or her own protective space within the room (Jimmy and Cliff are shielded behind newspapers when the play begins), Osborne indexes a rupture in class solidarity as the result of limited mobility. In a way, Jimmy's attacks against Alison can be read as a form of transference from the attacks he believes he experiences at the hands of the state but fails to fully articulate. His lack of self-awareness is what leads him to situate Alison and her upper-class father as the face of manifold cultural anxieties bearing down on him, prompting him to detain her behind the ironing board in retribution for the very existence of class-stratification.[23] Despite this lack of self-awareness, Jimmy seems to understand that the domestic sanctuary has been breached, as the repressive mood inside tends to reflect what he sees outside: "It's started to rain. That's all it needs. This room and the rain" (1956: 21). As noted, Osborne signals this breach throughout via media interferences such as the Sunday papers that usher in "them" through their capacity to "make the lower classes feel ignorant" (1956: 10), and the Vaughan Williams concert on the radio that makes Jimmy pine for what he refers to as a simple, British traditional institution (1956: 17). These moments can be interpreted as cultural and ideological intrusions, increasing the internal anxiety and tension felt by the inhabitants in a way that apes the alienating effects experienced by young working-class people: ideology is perpetual and perpetually crushing, and restricted mobility denies any attempt to shield oneself from its effects.

Kalliney has remarked that Jimmy's anger is too multivalent to be read simply as Osborne's own thinly veiled critique of class demarcation. He proposes that it makes more sense to read the text and texts like it as "ambivalent participants in broader discussions about the changing relationship among the government, the arts, and the public" (2006: 120). In other words, the character of Jimmy can be viewed as a vessel wherein multiple anxieties converge without clear articulation; Jimmy is essentially figured as a lightning rod for nebulous social forces made palpable through Osborne's depiction of repressive, restrictive space, underscoring the importance of setting in postwar British writing. The elevated, yet constrained flat is combined with the cattle-like atmosphere of overcrowding to signal shifts underway in British culture that failed to meet the needs of the populace and only served to further strengthen an awareness of social stratification. For Jimmy, the binary between "them and us" is amplified by such confines, represented in the text through his snide condescension at Alison's aristocratic father. As Hoggart aptly indicates, for the poor working classes, authorities and institutions were felt to be oppositional—abstract bodies that "compose[d] a shadowy but numerous and powerful group affecting their lives at almost every point" (1971: 62). This oppositional carriage toward institutional authority, Hoggart adds, was historically what constituted the more solidarity-oriented, unifying aspects of class consciousness in that "[unanimity] imposes on its members an extensive and sometimes harsh pressure to conform" (1971: 72). But *Look Back in Anger* seems to advance internal fragmentation over solidarity as Osborne brings the "them and us" binary to bear on the play's setting by creating an image of a domestic sanctuary that both stands in for, and fails to shelter from, ideological impositions that inscribe class onto the bodies of the occupants. The former unanimity of class-solidarity, and the sense of belonging that Hoggart deems historically characteristic of the working class, is demonstrably coming apart in this space—a notion that recalls changes underfoot in the way that working-class individuals imagine themselves within their own community. Although Osborne offers no definite solution for these concerns, what *Look Back in Anger* successfully portrays is the lived anxiety of imposed class awareness and the consequences that it produces. Whereas *The Uses of Literacy* provides an ethnographic snapshot that tends to cement preconceptions, a text like *Look Back in Anger* sets ethnography in motion in its ability to portray the repressive forms of social stratification and its effect on those it seeks to stratify. Osborne's representation of social immobility is bleak, but his lack of sentimentality renders the text identifiably authentic and commensurate with the lived experience of many working-class people at that particular moment. Furthermore, it establishes a tone of spatial plight that other texts of the period develop in a way that conveys the potential for change.

Renegotiations of Identity in *Saturday Night and Sunday Morning*

While Osborne's text communicates frustration experienced by many working-class people as the result of social stasis, Sillitoe develops similar themes in his representations of the domestic but introduces the dilemma of choice to explore the possibilities of existing both inside and outside of designated class boundaries. Commonly heralded as one of the best novels of the period, Sillitoe's *Saturday Night and Sunday Morning* unleashed Arthur Seaton onto the world—a culturally revered, binge-drinking, womanizing, weekend-warrior. Sillitoe's intention for Arthur was that of an existential hero, one whose material world had seemingly improved through what Goldthorpe et al. (1967) have referred to as "embourgeoisement"—an increase in perceived affluence through Welfare State reform. According to Sillitoe, Arthur's growth was hamstrung by a lack of spiritual values because "the kind of conditions he lives in do not allow him to have any" (Hanson 1999: 32). Sillitoe casts Arthur, like Osborne's Jimmy, as a figure of identification for people living under comparable conditions—a model of the sort of person inherently oppressed by the contours of their environment. But whereas Osborne's play centers on the consequences of a repressive milieu, Sillitoe's text takes the same problem and frames it as an existential dilemma: rebellion against the "establishment" or resignation to the status quo. Representations of domestic life are central to this dilemma in that to settle down in a newly built home is to submit to a system. Sillitoe's treatment of such representations at least hints at a burgeoning change in conceptions of class from that of passive acquiescence toward a willingness to explore new expressions of class consciousness.

Set in Nottingham, the story opens on a Saturday night in a workingman's club, establishing Arthur as a hard drinker and revealing his affair with the wife of his co-worker and friend, Jack. During the week, Arthur operates a lathe in a factory. He resents his position but also clings to an illusion of autonomy through his entrepreneurial capacity to work hard and make extra money.[24] Like Osborne's Jimmy, he is the embodiment of the disenfranchised younger generation, striving for an existence beyond that of his parents, but discovering that with more opportunities supposedly available to him, pernicious forces hover unseen, imposing limits that will always situate him as working class.[25] Although Arthur's character is, as Sillitoe insisted, "untypical," the environment that he inhabits is exceedingly typical for the time. In fact, much of the suburban surroundings of Nottingham to this day resemble Sillitoe's telling description of "trade-marked houses, two up and two down, with digital chimneys like pigs' tits on the rooftops sending up heat and smoke into the cold trough of the windy sky" (2010: 178). In these environments, factories oversee the space, with rows of housing acting as appendages of industry, resulting in a setting best understood as a toxic dystopia: "backyards burned by the sun with running tar-sores whose antiseptic smell blended with that of dustbins overdue for emptying, drying paint even drier on front doors, rusting knockers and letter-boxes, and withering flowers on windowsills, a summer blue sky up to which smoke from factory-chimneys coiled blackly" (2010: 136). Industry's domination is registered as omnipresent through the constant noise of generators and the smell of cut steel that "permeate[d] the air over the suburb of four-roomed houses built around the factory, streets and terraces hanging onto its belly and flanks like calves sucking the udders of some great mother" (2010: 23). Whereas social forces in *Look Back in Anger* were made manifest through the walls of the flat, here they extend into the community in ways that blur factory life and the sanctuary of domestic space. The text's tension—and, arguably, the tension experienced by many working-class people at this time—is encapsulated in the paradoxical quandary: industry offers new freedoms and an (apparent) elevated status through newfound affluence. But, like Jimmy's attic space, it is an elevated status that remains constricted within structural confines and curbs any real or meaningful social elevation.

The first domestic space introduced in the text belongs to Brenda and her husband Jack, in which Arthur performs the role of surrogate husband and father to Brenda's children while Jack works. The fact that Arthur approaches the home as a territory to be conquered ("He released her and, knowing every corner of the house and acting as if it belonged to him, stripped off his coat and shirt" [1958: 14]) speaks to his own insecurities of not being the head of his own household. In a manner that echoes Doreen's fear of "being left upon the shelf," Arthur's affair with his friend's wife confirms his own domestic plight and the anxiety that cultural narratives of normative domesticity produce, especially in environments characterized by mass housing.[26] The traditional arrangement of the domestic space and the nuclear family is what Arthur initially protests through this vicarious surrogacy, but it also reveals his paradoxical desire to attain such an arrangement for himself as his world dictates that that is what constitutes manhood. Put differently, the choice of rebellion or submission emerges early in the text as the consequence of limitations imposed by the environment and its ideological underpinnings.

Arthur lives at home with his family, and Sillitoe amplifies the constraining role of this space in that Arthur is made to share a bed with his younger brother—an arrangement that both infantilizes and emasculates him.[27] Furthermore, the home can be seen to function as part of the same system that designates social stratification, at times unfairly. Arthur's friendly superior at the factory triggers his anxiety in that, although "basically they were of equal stock," Robboe's world differed due to his ability to buy a "semi-detached in a posh district" (2010: 39). This rests heavily upon Arthur as he shares the lesser housing with his family that includes his father—a man who has dedicated the majority of his life to working at the same factory to which Arthur will, presumably, dedicate his. Arthur's father, like Jack, embodies resignation and merits Arthur's sympathy as the result: "The old man was happy at last anyway, and he deserved to be happy, after all the years before the war on the dole, five kids, and the big miserying that went with no money and no way of getting any" (2010: 22).[28] In fact, the novel's most salient and pressing theme is that of being trapped in a monotonous cycle—a notion most lucidly expressed in the closing scene in which Arthur catches and releases a fish back into a lake, with the narrator's declaration that "As soon as you were born you were captured by fresh air that you screamed against the minute you came out. Then you were roped in by a factory, had a machine slung around your neck, and then you were hooked up the arse with a wife" (2010: 236).[29] The perpetuation of cycles, underscored by the emphasis that Sillitoe places on the drudgery of labor, is the material upon which the narrative is constructed. Arthur's father instills fear in him in that he serves as the projection of Arthur's future; the man's passive haunting of the domestic space outside of work is Arthur's portent of what it means to be "caught."

The Seaton family home is designated as a space of refuge from the week's labor, yet it is also a space where autonomous agency is desired, with family members frequently extolling the virtues of being left home alone for some peace and quiet.[30] The arrangement of this home maps onto Hoggart's description of the way "two-up two-down" housing served multiple, flexible functions, much of which was aimed at integrating the family into the community. The Seaton home, Sillitoe instructs, "function[s] like the neck of an egg-timer: visitors came in through the backyard, and [are] disgorged with gangs of the family by the front door" (2010: 210). Hoggart schematizes northern working-class households, holding that "a good living room must provide three principal things; gregariousness, warmth and plenty of good food" (1971: 33). This is the case in the Seatons's home in that the living room is structured around "A bright fire [that] burned in the modernised grate—the family had clubbed-up thirty quid to have it done—and the room was warm and cheerful, the table set, and the tea mashed" (2010: 20). In this regard, it is a welcoming space and is treated as such by members of the community. But the effect is that the space fails to relieve the occupants from the trials of the workweek as the noise and bustle of the machines are replaced by the noise and bustle of family members and neighbors.[31] In other words, the dividing line between home, community, and factory is eradicated, casting the home as inseparable from the community of labor, inevitably inscribing class status onto its occupants. The upshot is that the characters in the story reach for other ways to escape—for Arthur, it is sex and drinking; but for his father, respite is found through the recent acquisition of a television. So, not only does the domestic space fail as sanctuary against repetitive cycles of labor, it operates as a manacle to that labor in a manner that stresses the servility working-class lives.

Saturday Night and Sunday Morning is a critically astute work through its narrativizing of the way the burden of the daily grind is assuaged by the newfound affluence of the Welfare State and its false promise of social elevation. The relative prosperity of the period following the war is expressed through material and domestic achievement that functions to offset servility. Sillitoe suggests that the stability of labor grants Arthur's father "all the Woodbines he could smoke, money for a pint if he wanted one ... A holiday somewhere, a jaunt on the firm's trip to Blackpool, and a television-set to look into at home" (2010: 22). Intriguingly, Hoggart describes his working-class subjects in almost identical words: "This man is a specially skilled worker and has been doing well for some time, so that he takes his family for a lavish week at Blackpool each summer and bought a television set before anyone else" (1958: 53). This, of course, is one example of many in which fictional representation and Hoggart's ethnographic study cross paths, and it is possible to comprehend the dichotomous nature of Arthur's father's existence: he is either on the clock or spends his free time preparing himself for his next round of being on the clock. The upshot is that "He was either happy and fussy with everybody, or black-browed with a deep melancholy rage that chose its victims at random" (Sillitoe 2010: 21). An environment that provides limited opportunities appears to result in emotional states that reflect these same limits—expressed as the theme of submission that Sillitoe dramatizes throughout. As Arthur's father is the emanation of what Arthur fears he will become, and his friend Jack is heading down the same path of resignation ("You won't knuckle under, Arthur. If you would, you'd enjoy life" [2010: 207]), it can be said that the domestic spaces occupied by both Jack and Arthur's respective fathers serve as models for the protagonist's paradoxical desire to both attain such a space for himself and reject it by undermining cultural norms.

The space that the characters inhabit takes its toll on them in ways similar to Osborne's Jimmy. But where Jimmy's anger is also symptomatic of an amorphous problem rendered material through spatial confines, *Saturday Night and Sunday Morning* speaks to forms of acquiescence and resignation to a world where labor and domesticity are intertwined, fueling Arthur's tension as he vacillates between joining the status quo (taking on a mortgage and essentially signing his life over to the factory) and pushing back against conformity through delinquency. As the result, his own domestic space keeps this existential threat alive, but as a type of space, it confirms that new affluence and conspicuous consumption cannot propel him into the middle class. Although the novel ends with the suggestion that a balance between homogeneity and independence is the ideal, the tone is one of continual class struggle: "And trouble for me it'll be, fighting every day until I die. Why do they make soldiers out of us when we're fighting up to the hilt as it is?" (2010: 238). In his attempt to understand why young people like Arthur continue to take jobs like that of his father, Paul Willis outlines the capitalist apparatus that upholds a servile labor force through a controlled sanctioning of insurgence where "penetrations" (the recognition of inequality or the uncovering of capitalist mechanisms) are met with "limitations" (a manipulation of the cultural field to stem rebellion) (1981: 174). In Willis's model, Arthur's rebellion is stage-managed and therefore futile, but it at least implies revolutionary thinking of something beyond mere acquiescence. In this regard, the consciousness-shaping effect of the domestic environment is explored in a manner that presents submission to class demarcation as the path of least resistance through its capacity to inscribe social status. Yet the text also opens the door to the potentiality of a kind of cerebral insurgence, anticipating the culture shifts that will occur throughout much of the 1960s and concretizing the need for new forms of class identification to match changes underway in the social sphere.

Queering the Domestic in *A Taste of Honey*

Whereas Osborne's play articulates the impact of domestic space on the individual, and Sillitoe's novel shows how domestic anxiety contributed to a burgeoning existential crisis, Shelagh Delaney explores the way oppressive domestic spaces can be reconfigured through shifts in class consciousness. As one of just a handful of women writers affiliated with kitchen sink realism, Delaney was the antithesis of the "Angry Young Man," being neither male nor particularly angry. While still grappling with themes of social alienation and class stratification, Delaney's contribution posed a different approach to understanding one's social position: whereas Osborne and Sillitoe's work illuminated the subtle and not-so-subtle tensions of acquiescence, *A Taste of Honey* unapologetically turns social conformity on its head through its brazen discussion of class, gender, race, and sexual orientation. Given this, Delaney's dynamic reimagining of constrained domestic space is indicative of the unraveling of traditional working-class temporalities in ways that anticipate new articulations of identity.

Originally developing her text as a novel, the nineteen-year-old Delaney took just two weeks to recast *A Taste of Honey* as a play specifically intended to tackle taboo topics and contribute to a revitalization of British theater. Raised within a working-class Irish immigrant family in Salford, and initially failing the eleven-plus exam that would have granted her social ascendency, Delaney imbued her play with a strong autobiographical charge that calls to mind the frustrations and limitations of working-class life but with a notable degree of optimism. In a 1959 interview, the author voiced her desire to represent Salford locals as idiosyncratically unique, proclaiming that "I had strong ideas about what I wanted to see in the theatre … Usually North Country people are shown as gormless, whereas in actual fact, they are very alive and cynical" (Kitchin 1960: 177). The press response to the play was mixed, with the notoriously conservative Daily Mail condemning the Theatre Workshop for even staging the performance, complaining how "Once authors wrote good plays set in drawing-rooms. Now, under the Welfare State, they write bad plays set in garrets" (qtd. in Lichtenstein and Schregenberger 2006: 266). Nevertheless, prominent figures of the time like director Lindsay Anderson and journalist-cum-author Colin MacInnes praised the play's substantiated depictions of northern life and its sparse authenticity.

The play tells the story of seventeen-year-old Jo—a teenager essentially abandoned by her promiscuous mother, Helen. Following a brief relationship with a Black sailor, Jo finds herself pregnant and without resources. In the second act, she rooms with a flamboyant-yet-tormented gay man named Geoffrey, and in a complete inversion of social norms, the pair upend the idea of the traditional household and transform an otherwise uninhabitable space into a new, queer domesticity. But following the dissolution of her shotgun wedding, Helen returns to short-circuit this arrangement, leading the play to its somewhat bleak finale.[32] The text is minimal with terse dialog, resulting in the prominent foregrounding of working-class concerns: the reimagining of a working-class identity based on potential rather than actual conditions.[33]

Set in the author's home town of Salford, the play centers on two flats in the decaying Manchester slums, both of which are deemed inadequate spaces of residence but are cemented as a "type" that had become the norm for young people in northern England. When Helen's fiancé Peter first visits the "ghastly district" containing "tenements, cemetery, slaughterhouse," he exclaims, "Nobody could live in a place like this," to which Jo retorts: "Only about fifty thousand people" (1958: 17). The first residence of the play—a standard-fare "comfortless" room that Jo shares with Helen—is marked as transitory through Helen's aside that "we can always find something else" (1958: 9). Despite its derelict and constraining atmosphere, both Jo and Helen express the working-class trait of "making do" through optimistic spin: "Everything in it's falling apart, it's true, and we've no heating—but there's a lovely view of the gasworks, we share a bathroom with the community and this wallpaper's contemporary" (1958: 9). Similarly, Jo recasts the space as defensible and comforting by dressing up an exposed light bulb with her scarf—a gesture of control that is repeated throughout the play, and one that speaks to Delaney's symbolic stress on illumination as revealing or concealing truth. For Jo, masking reality is compensatory, and her ability to manipulate light sources parallels her capacity to shape her domestic surroundings as needed. For example, when Geoffrey first enters the larger space of the second act, he reaches for the light only to have Jo snap, "No. Don't you dare put that light on" (1958: 46). Moments later, she states that she likes the "romantic half-light of the maisonette," and when she demands that he reveal the nature of his sexuality, she adds "Come on, let's have some truth" while turning on the light (1958: 47). On the one hand, this use of light manipulation as a technical device within the play may be read as a sophomoric metaphor. On the other, it accentuates the play's emphasis on the necessity of adaptation to unsuitable conditions as the result of the housing crisis. In this sense, Jo demonstrates a willingness to reimagine her domestic environs and reinvent herself beyond the accepted demarcations of her designated class through creative, spontaneous gestures.

Thus, what Delaney's text explores—perhaps more saliently in Tony Richardson's popular film adaptation—is the way that less-than-ideal spaces have the capacity to be recast as ideal places. In Richardson's film, there is considerable elaboration in the way the environment is framed in that the two rooms of the play are expanded as part of a more extensive milieu. Yet Richardson is sensitive to the claustrophobic intent of Delaney's text, emphasizing how external space can be just as repressive as that of the domestic. For instance, in the opening scene of the film, Jo is seen in a schoolyard through a moving documentary-style camera that places the viewer into the midst of a yelling crowd of schoolgirls. Later, when Jo and Geoffrey escape the confines of the flat, Richardson depicts them as hemmed in beneath "the arches"—(the actual location of which is a famous viaduct in Stockport, Cheshire) in a scene cropped by a brick frame to simulate the state of entrapment linked to Jo's pregnancy. In this regard, domestic confinement plays as much of a role in *A Taste of Honey* as in *Look Back in Anger*, but whereas Osborne's text focused on dramatizing the psychological harm of constrained domestic space, Delaney's text takes the next step in reinscribing space through the reimagining of social designation and new class consciousness.

Jo's comprehension of domestic space is undeniably optimistic and perhaps naïve. The maisonette is described as dark, enormous, and decidedly unhomely; it is unkempt, as confirmed by Geoffrey's quip that "I can tell it's yours from the state it's in; No wonder you won't put the light on" (1958: 47); the nearby river is "the colour of lead" and filled with "filthy children" (1958: 54); and in Richardson's treatment, the stage set is designed in such a way that it resembles an abandoned factory crossed with a barn. Despite this, the space fits their unorthodox and idiosyncratic needs, with Jo adding, "There's only one of me like there's only one of you" followed by Geoff's remark, "We're bloody marvellous!" (1958: 50–1). No sentimentalizing or romanticizing exists; it is a grim, miserable space. Yet unlike Osborne and Sillitoe's texts, Delaney's play does not linger on notions of poverty; instead, it posits domestic space as a combination of the factual and the conceivable—a way to experience space for what it could be as well as what it is. In his discussion of what he calls heterotopic space, Michel Foucault sketches a similar idea: "a kind of effectively enacted utopia in which real sites, all the other real sites that can be found within the culture, are simultaneously represented, contested, and inverted" (1986: 3).[34] Foucault develops this thought, positing heterotopic space as ideal and beyond hegemony, "As a sort of simultaneously mythic and real contestation of the space in which we live" (1986: 4). For Foucault, such a space can be understood as active and contingent (such as a colony), and *A Taste of Honey*, despite its clear allegiance to kitchen sink aesthetics and class-anxieties, makes no direct reference to class-concerns. The text essentially sidesteps class assignation in lieu of counterhegemonic potentiality, emphasized by Jo's comment that Geoffrey would "make somebody a wonderful wife" (1958: 55). While Delaney keeps working-class anxieties thematically afloat through the topics the play engages, her outlook is markedly different than that of Osborne or Sillitoe, suggesting a new way of conceiving domestic space in order to parry its potential to inscribe class.[35]

But where Jo is represented as most animated is during her time of independence from Helen. Although Helen invades the domestic space of the second act in a manner consonant with the ideological intrusions of *Look Back in Anger*,[36] Delaney takes time to represent the way that domestic structures can be established in nontraditional spaces under nontraditional terms. Similar to the squat of misfits that form new communities in Colin MacInnes's 1959 novel, *Absolute Beginners*, Jo influences space to transcend the kinds of classed-imprisonment prescribed—a gesture that differs from other works of the period through innovative portrayals of class consciousness. In this respect, the text speaks to fractures in class solidarity as hinted at by Helen who puns "Don't worry, you'll soon be an independent working woman and free to go where you please" (1958: 15).[37] Even MacInnes (no stranger to squatting himself) declared "it's the first play I can remember about working-class people that entirely escapes being a 'working-class play': no patronage, no dogma, just the thing as it is, taken straight" (1961: 205).

For Jo, domestic space is not structured upon tradition or allegiance, but upon honesty, symbolically represented by Delaney as light: "I'm not frightened of the darkness outside. It's the darkness inside houses I don't like" (1958: 22). Yet this optimistic reading does not fully cohere to the text as Helen succeeds in dragging Jo back to her world. But what it does suggest is that the narrative conveys a possibility for something beyond what is prescribed—a gesture comparable to the crux outlined by Sillitoe, codified in the closing scene when, for the first time in the stage direction, Helen addresses the audience directly and says "I ask you, what would you do?" (1958: 87). Through this reimagining of the domestic, what Delaney's text reveals—perhaps in a less nuanced but more candid manner than that of Osborne or Sillitoe—is that alongside the cultural changes underfoot in mid-century Britain, the conception of the working class as an oppressed, disenfranchised populace is beginning to unravel in lieu of new, adaptable, contingent subjectivities seeking alternatives to spoon-fed mediocrity.

The grim realism of *A Taste of Honey* was not lost on critics at the time. Lindsay Anderson noted that the play had "all the strength and none of the weaknesses, of a pronounced authentic, local accent" (1958: 42). Alan Brien of the Spectator amended his initial review from "a boozed, exaggerated, late-night anecdote of a play" to "unlike almost any other working-class play in that it is not scholarly anthropology observed from the outside through pince-nez, but the inside story of a savage culture observed by a genuine cannibal" (Laing 1986: 89). Brien's revised observation is telling in that it speaks to many of the kitchen sink texts of the period: although stylized in their own way, they were arguably as sociological and anthropological as they were literary, rendered particularly "real" through their on-the-ground reporting made palpable by the lived experience of their authors. Their avoidance of sentimentality or nostalgia commonly associated with social realism in lieu of celebrating the mundane and the routine is evident. Furthermore, the notion of romantic individualism is also dodged in that characters like Jimmy, Arthur, and Jo are hardly celebrated role models.[38] To return to Hutchings's "Proletarian Byronism," if there were a literary lineage, it would be to the Byronic hero, even though there is nothing extraordinary about these characters. Instead, it is easier to argue that they reproduce a cultural moment with admirable fidelity as commonly recognizable products of their circumstances and domestic environments.

Conclusion

Hoggart's archetypical working-class household from *The Uses of Literacy* reads like a fictional family drafted from a blueprint. The same might be said for Orwell's portrayals in *The Road to Wigan Pier*. That Hoggart's and Orwell's descriptions echo the fictional families represented in kitchen sink realism stresses how documentary-style techniques seen in social realism operate beyond the imaginative; they construct a facsimile of life tacitly endorsed by those represented. Even though the "angry young man" moniker is still applied in a manner that suggests critical oversight, I would argue that the presence of "the kitchen sink" in the "kitchen sink realism" label is similarly overlooked. This underscores the introduction's commentary on the way the labels applied to this body of British postwar writing hold little merit, operating more as a sensational marketing device. However, the mere reference of "kitchen sink" begs for consideration of the way such texts engage space and place in relation to identity. As Osborne, Sillitoe, and Delaney—perhaps the three most defining voices of the movement—demonstrate, domestic space is not simply a backdrop in these works; it is a functional aspect of the narrative and the period. For Osborne, characters struggle to sustain coherent identities in space, with Jimmy's mood vacillations best described as sociopathic. And yet, it is the space itself—what it represents and what it fails to accomplish—that sustains his aggression. For Sillitoe, the domestic is a problem in need of a solution. Arthur wants a home and wants to settle down, but that means subjecting himself to a life that is no longer his own. Viewed in this way, *Saturday Night and Sunday Morning* uses domestic space to stage an existential dilemma that marks a turning point in British working-class culture. The novel does not propose a definitive solution, but it illuminates the problem in such a way that the reader is required to form their own ideas. Delaney's play—perhaps generally read as the most naive and least sophisticated of the three—is the one that maps the clearest path forward. For Jo, her choice is to simply reject the status imposed upon her and to engineer a sense of self that pleases her. This is accomplished through negotiations with domestic space—her ability to transform such spaces in ways that mirror her own transformation as a classed subject. Read in sequence, the three authors identify a problem, illuminate the problem, and then propose a solution. Stylistically, they are distinct; thematically, they are in full alignment in that they portray working-class life in a manner tacitly sanctioned by working-class people while introducing space and spatial metaphors as a canvas against which to construct a new classed identity.

Notes

1   Tynan opens his review by urging critics who hated Kingsley Amis's *Lucky Jim* to "stay well away from John Osborne's *Look Back in Anger*" (1956: 33). He goes on to add how the play "presents post war youth as it really is" (33), highlighting the disconnect between the arts and the vast majority of British people.
2   Even though women gained access to work opportunities, they were still expected to uphold the kinds of unpaid labor associated with the domestic sphere. So, women who did work during this time tended to work part-time in factories designated as sites for "women's work." The texts of the era present a number of male characters who feel emasculated by their displacement in the work force and their usurpation as the sole breadwinner of the home.
3   The 1949 Housing Act also sought to expand the focus of housing needs by allowing local authorities to provide housing for middle-class citizens in addition to the working class. The inclusion of Health Minister Aneurin Bevin's ideas into

the Act certified the socialist principles of postwar urban planning in that Bevin's desire was for a society in which classes were no longer segregated. This was more commonly known as "mixed development" but was never implemented since temporary rehousing took precedence over such endeavors. See Colquhoun (2008) for a more architectural perspective on this topic.

4 It is, of course, worth acknowledging that the appeal of these structures today has far more to do with their location than their working-class history or their apparent links to working-class culture. That said, some remain sought after in that they represent a period of architectural innovation and modern design. Discrepancies in the production of such buildings, once more, illuminate the degree of inconsistency prevalent at the time.

5 This gesture was more evident in later years following the accelerated pace of high-rise development. Because of their scale, such constructs tended to play a more spectacular role as totems of progress whereas low-rise housing's futuristic appeal was communicated as the upshot of innovative construction methods.

6 This reflects observations made by a number of contemporary critics writing about the spatialization of class in Britain. See Ben Gidley and Alison Rooke's "Asdatown: The Intersections of Classed Places and Identities" (2010) for one example. Another would be Beverley Skeggs's *Class, Self, Culture* in which it is argued that "geographical referencing is one of the contemporary shorthand ways of speaking class" (2004: 15).

7 One of the most recognizable examples would be Kensington's brutalist monolith, the Trellick Tower in which a number of former social housing units are now privately owned. Recent sales data suggest that listings range between £400,000 and £800,000.

8 This figure is dated to 2007/2008. See Rosenfield et al. (2011) for more.

9 It should be acknowledged that following the 1980 Housing Act with its emphasis on "the right to buy," there was a distinct shift in such aesthetic uniformity in that ownership of one's home allowed for personalization—which, in turn, acted as a way to communicate social elevation. The emergence of nonstandard window frames and decorative front doors signaled personal ownership in addition to autonomy. This maps onto a long history of social signaling in working-class space, perhaps best understood in the way housewives would compete for the "cleanest" porch stoop in order to signal respectability. Pat Barker's 1982 novel *Union Street* covers this well, and later chapters in this volume will show how rising individualism associated with the Thatcher era exacerbates such atomization and attempts at distinction.

10 It might be argued that timelines played a role in the way prefabs are referenced in literature. For one thing, they came to be around the same time when kitchen sink authors were writing. We might attribute the more common portrayal of

working-class terraced housing as a technical device of verisimilitude—a location perhaps most familiar to the average working-class reader. But we might also consider the fact that it was years after the kitchen sink movement concluded that many of the problems with such housing types arose. Nonetheless, several prescient writers and filmmakers do pinpoint such concerns, with one of the most notable being the depiction of the family home in Tony Richardson's 1962 take on Alan Sillitoe's *The Loneliness of the Long Distance Runner* in which several tropes are combined: the cramped prefab (what appears to be an AIROH house), proximity to the factory, and the dying patriarch. These tropes are discussed in subsequent chapters.

11 It is worth pointing out that many prefabs actively promoted the practice of gardening with a slew of propaganda-style pamphlets preaching a message of community engagement and sustainability. Such pamphlets were part of the Beveridge Social Surveys distributed between 1942 and 1947. Like the emphasis placed on the clean front-door stoop, such pamphlets suggest a burgeoning competition for "most respectable" that, unto itself, prompts consideration of shifts away from notions of solidarity to something more atomized and individualistic.

12 Although the name connotes economic leniency, "No-Fines" refers to the method of construction in which cement was mixed with stone as opposed to using sand. The result was said to produce a more durable wall—which was true—but the design was still prone to problems, largely seen in the pebble-dashed exterior and the joint sections of the walls.

13 This collapse took place in 1968 when a load-bearing wall gave way due to a gas explosion. Ronan Point used Large Panel System building techniques in which prefabricated slabs were assembled on site. The incident, which killed four people and injured seventeen more, was exacerbated by the shoe-string construction methods that failed to support an entire side of the building following the explosion. The Grenfell Tower fire of 2017 is a more recent example of such a tragedy in that the 1974 building was known to be a hazard.

14 The 1956 Housing Subsidies Act put forth by the Conservative government offered better subsidies based on the height of the construction. The result was that high-rise construction was granted even more allure to British citizens.

15 Osborne is somewhat of an outlier in this regard as his upbringing was far closer to middle class with his parents moving to a London suburb for many of the same reasons articulated in this chapter's overview redevelopment. Osborne hated the suburbs, thinking of them as culturally vacuous. Such an attitude, of course, is seen in the character of Jimmy who gravitates to working-class characters such as Cliff Lewis and Hugh Tanner, assisting the latter in creative acts of class warfare. Jimmy's class antagonism is rarely compared to Osborne's own desire to antagonize London's theater-goers. But that is, after all, what the play aimed to accomplish.

16 It can be noted that Sillitoe was well traveled, living in Malaya, France, Spain, and Mallorca. An argument could be made that, as with many expatriates, distance from home increases the fascination with home and its strange allure.

17 As Stanley Chapman claims, the emergence of industry in the Midlands is "very poorly documented largely because the industry had contracted to smaller proportions before the age of the Victorian chroniclers and commentators" (1965: 526).

18 The "Manchester School" centers on figures such as Harold Brighouse, Stanley Houghton, and Allan Monkhouse, all writing in the 1910s. In an article for *Observer*, Heilpern states: "For me, they created a rosy, sentimentalized image–just the sort of cozy picture of the North that goes down well in patronizing London" (2002).

19 Most of Delaney's head shots—professional or otherwise—use particularly dreary backdrops. The 1959 image referenced here is far less staged than others.

20 In "Function as the Basis of Psychiatric Ward Design" (1957), Osmond sought to build connections between the needs of mentally ill people and the architects who design the spaces that they inhabit.

21 It is relevant to consider the link between domestic innovation that exposes the inner workings of the domestic space and the concerns that British people expressed in terms of new appliances. The persistent permeability of domestic space—especially in the postwar period—seems central to such neuroses.

22 This, of course, sums up the cultural moment perfectly in that the rise of the Welfare State promised new opportunities that failed to flourish, primarily because the class system remained so inflexible that mobility was near impossible for many.

23 Colonel Redfern (Alison's father) and Helena—one of the play's symbolic manifestations of the elevated class—function within the text as misplaced conduits for a complex and fluid set of social anxieties that *Look Back in Anger* skillfully exploits.

24 This, of course, is disposable income that Arthur mostly spends on expensive suits and beer.

25 Arthur's plight is well articulated by Kenneth Tynan's characterization of the archetypical Angry Young Man: "a new sort of hero—a lower-class intellectual with a ribald sense of humour, a robust taste for beer and sex, and an attitude of villainous irreverence toward the established order" (1961: 190–1).

26 Doreen Gratton: A young woman Arthur dates while Brenda is pregnant. She works at a neighboring factory and is bullied by her co-workers to find a husband and settle down.

27 This forced emasculation can also be read as a contributor to Arthur's desire to cuckold Jack, driving the narrative to Brenda's inevitable pregnancy and her

subsequent attempts to abort the baby. It is also worth recalling Sillitoe's own experience, mentioned earlier, in which he describes growing up in a house with "an attic at the top where we children slept on one bed" (Sillitoe 1995: 19).

28 As an aside, the submissive father is an unmistakable trope across many of these texts. In several (*The Loneliness of the Long Distance Runner* and *Absolute Beginners*, for instance) the father dies (after suffering, we are to believe) at a relatively young age, supposedly as a consequence of his labor, emphasizing the existential threat of complacency and resignation.

29 At several points in the text, the narrative voice changes from third person to second person, rendering it unclear as to whether the narrator has assumed Arthur's character who is now thinking out loud, or whether the narrator is providing a narrative overlay of commentary and addressing the reader directly in a didactic manner.

30 This is an option that, it is worth recalling, was also unavailable in the Porter's flat of *Look Back in Anger*.

31 Incidentally, noise plays a significant role in this text. The factory is metonymically reduced to a series of deafening sounds, the pubs are rarely presented as anything but a sea of noise, and the domestic space is equally as rambunctious. Karel Reisz's 1960 adaptation emphasizes this point as well, with a constant stream of non-diegetic rumbles and groans of machinery. At several points in the narrative, Arthur craves chaotic noise, implying that he cannot function without it. Sillitoe's intention here is clearly to demonstrate how the environment has written itself into Arthur's DNA in that the factory and working-class community will always be a part of him.

32 I would argue that the pessimistic ending that counters Jo's otherwise optimistic worldview is one of aesthetic allegiance. Delaney was clearly as in touch with the political dimensions of her play as her audience would have been. A "happy ever after" ending would have detracted from the play's goals, but such pessimism also calls to mind the paradox faced by Arthur—a gesture toward resistance that still acknowledges social inevitabilities.

33 Whereas Osborne's play can be read as a stand-alone work, the framework of *A Taste of Honey* is gaunt and appears more fleshed out in Richardson's 1961 adaptation of which Delaney wrote the screenplay.

34 Needless to say, a more developed and nuanced discussion of this concept will be taken up in Chapter 3 where spaces of resistance are discussed.

35 Perhaps the best way to think of this is not as an attempt to simply overlook class, but rather as a state of disinterestedness—the emanation of a set of subcultural ideals akin the notion of the outsider.

36 It is possible to think of Helen as a recurrent reminder of the restrictions of class designation, a foil for Jo's attempts to subvert such designations. This

echoes the way cultural frustrations that make their way into the Porter's flat send Jimmy off the deep end.
37 Arthur Marwick acknowledges a kind of fragmenting of familial solidarity in a similar manner but cites, specifically, the rise of the Welfare State as the reason. He argues that with the availability of better public resources, there was less reason to "call in a grandmother or raise a loan from a more fortunate uncle" (2003: 41).
38 Although I would argue that all three have admirable qualities.

2

"Off Down the Local"—Institutional Borders in Working-Class Communities

In 1961, the Warwickshire County Council became the first regional commission to recommend a country-wide ban on an internationally acclaimed film: Karel Reisz's 1960 adaptation of Alan Sillitoe's *Saturday Night and Sunday Morning*. The council's chair remarked that the film was not only "shocking" and bore "no redeeming features," but that "it should be banned as harmful to public morals" (*The Birmingham Post* 1961). Although the film contains violence, as well as language colorful enough to warrant an x-rating, the decision seems more aligned with the committee's subsequent claim that "it presents a most unsavoury picture of factory morals" with the council's chairman adding that "I have had a lot to do with factory workers, and I think a great deal better of them than the film-makers apparently do" (*The Birmingham Post* 1961). Sillitoe, a one-time factory worker himself, noted how the British Board of Film Censors influenced the screenplay he developed alongside Reisz, resulting in what he considered to be "a much watered down version of the book" (1995: 259). Even though Sillitoe would later confess his pleasure in antagonizing authorities, Reisz served as a mediator between the cranky author and the relatively progressive and permissive censor.[1] But, what the committee's contentions show is the social and political sway of the kitchen sink movement and its legacy. Contention centered not on the film's violence, the dialog, or even its controversial abortion sequence; the issue was that the film confronts the monotony of working-class life, staging factory-floor insurrection and antiestablishment sentiments as a way to counter the drudgery and repetition conveyed in the title. The Council's anxiety was shared by J. K. Cordeaux, a conservative MP from Nottingham, who claimed that insubordinate workers like that of Arthur were an anomaly: "These young offenders form a very small faction of our young people as a whole, most of whom are doing a good job of work to the best of their ability from Monday morning to Saturday noon, and spend their weekends in natural and healthy recreation and social contacts" (*Nottingham Evening Post* 1961). At a moment in which efforts to reignite the postwar economy through labor were prevalent, it is revealing how novels, plays, and films exploring the impact of working-class space on the individual were viewed as plausible threats to the status quo by those who most benefit from its preservation.

This chapter builds on the last by broadening the scope of analysis from representations of domestic space to representations of the community, exploring how portrayals of constraint and frustration are represented through shared space and attendant symbols of community. Turning explicitly to spaces and institutions central to working-class life (although not exclusive to them), this chapter traces the social history of community space in working-class culture, its role in the crystallization of class identity, and their representation in kitchen sink texts. Consequently, it considers how spaces of presumed social and cultural sustenance not only fail to provide adequate substitutes to domestic sanctuary but also adopt a disciplinary stance by reinscribing class boundaries and reinforcing social limits. Considering Émile Durkheim's notion of collective consciousness, this chapter explores how classed environments sustain collective working-class ideals in ways that maintain passivity and acquiescence to one's "lot in life" otherwise understood as "knowing one's place." The texts of the kitchen sink era confront such sites through representational strategies. In doing so, they raise questions about such sites' value as components of community given their tendency to produce states of resignation. Instead, the texts under scrutiny here can be seen to counter the relative dreariness of working-class environs by highlighting social insurgency and subversion through new modes of class articulation. Expanding on the previous discussion of Sillitoe's *Saturday Night and Sunday Morning* and introducing studies of David Storey's *This Sporting Life* and Nell Dunn's *Up the Junction*, the chapter explores links between domestic and communal space. It shows how spatial motifs prominent in kitchen sink texts reveal the way working-class life is institutionally contoured and policed in a manner that maintains existing conditions. It can be said, then, that kitchen sink texts question the idea of a working-class monolith through their insistence on "outsider" ontologies of resistance in which the individual is simultaneously within and without the community.

Shared Space and Working-Class Institutions

If postwar domestic space was considered a sanctuary, then what is it a sanctuary from? This chapter seeks to consider such a question, specifically looking at the way working-class environs inscribe and reiterate identity similar to that of the working-class home. Rob Imrie, drawing on research by David Binns and Gerald Mars, shows how domestic sanctuary is compromised when "the home environment becomes the product of withdrawal from wider social networks" (2004: 100). What Imrie suggests is that when the home is seen as a reprieve from a repressive environment, it operates as an annex of the same environment through its necessity. As stated in the previous chapter, texts such as *Look Back in Anger* depict the domestic as a failed defense in that, not only do ideological aspects of the outside world infiltrate, but the cramped, cluttered space itself serves as reminder of the protagonists' distance from the comfort they desire while also standing in for repressive power dynamics that limit movement. That said, identity is still renegotiated and concretized through communal and shared spaces, and kitchen sink texts' emphasis on the working-class milieu serves as an indicator of such operations.

As outlined in the previous chapter, ineffectual attempts at slum-clearance and rehousing projects exacerbated anxieties about working-class space. Whereas physical reminders of the Blitz littered communities with rubble and waste, identities based on shared struggle were impacted by the breakup of long-standing social networks and their dispersal to the urban periphery. John Braine's 1957 novel, *Room at the Top*, is just one example of a text that deploys images of war-torn space meant to act as a counterpoint to the middle-class life championed by social mobility and aspiration. The depiction is polyvalent in that it illuminates a symbolic marker of class difference but also functions as a memento mori, linking working-class life to concerns about health and well-being: "On my way to the Siege Gun that evening I went past my old home ... I paused by the gap where our house had stood; I had no desire to receive old memories but instantly, unbidden, the events of that morning in 1941—the Bad Morning, the Death Morning—unreeled themselves like a film" (1980: 98). Braine's story is powered by the protagonist's trauma: a childhood home destroyed by a WWII bomb that also claimed the lives of his parents. Images of poverty and destruction of the old community and community life are pitted against middle-class spaces characterized by plenitude and wealth. The text both idealizes and romanticizes working-class space, even in a state of dereliction infused with trauma. When contrasted against the vacuity of the middle-class world the protagonist accesses, it is the ruined home that conveys a greater sense of sanctuary. In this sense, the landscape reiterates the notion of the working-class home as a failed defense while illuminating the communal principles tied to working-class life.

In addition to shifts in the built environment, as well as changing gender dynamics in society, the decline of Empire and new waves of immigration from former colonies also contributed to a generalized anxiety. Yet, the previous chapter's discussion of multigenerational households divided along ideological lines is germane in that attitudes toward race and race relations chronicled a split between traditional and progressive values. Immaterial anxieties existing beyond the realm of the domestic also break through the boundary in the form of ideology and social upheaval. What the texts of the kitchen sink era reveal is that the home is an illusory sanctuary at best—one that provides little protection from social forces and developments underway in British culture. Therefore, this chapter will survey salient aspects of working-class environs in order to gauge their function relative to the domestic, outlining the way spaces such as these establish and enforce comprehensions of class and, in turn, prompt new modalities of class consciousness in response.

It would be incorrect to suggest that all working-class communities in Britain are built from the same blueprint, but striking similarities and parallels do exist regarding urban planning and social institutions. The result is that portrayals in cultural production can offer a coherent summation of lived experience through consensus, consonant with Williams's "knowable communities" noted in the introduction as well as in the previous chapter. For instance, Keith Waterhouse's 1959 novel *Billy Liar* goes to lengths to portray the fictional Yorkshire town of Stradhoughton as an archetypical representation of a great number of northern working-class communities. Larger towns like Nottingham or Manchester tend to be represented more by way of their suburban offshoots or peripheral districts, with areas like Delaney's Salford or Sillitoe's Nottingham enclaves representing a cross-section of traditional working-class life; with few exceptions, kitchen sink narratives anonymize their setting to position them as representations of "everytown"—an extension of the humdrum "everyman" character prominent in fiction and meant as a reflective representation of the reader. The use of anonymous yet ubiquitous "everytowns" functions similarly by simulating the lived experience and social circumstances of a text's designated audience.

But even in texts in which the portrayed region is part of a larger, more populous area—such as Dunn's *Up the Junction* or MacInnes's *Absolute*

Beginners—kitchen sink spatial motifs suggest boundaries and limits that sequester the community from the larger metropolis in a manner that recalls traditionally insular manifestations of working-class space. What emerges from these texts is that, despite geographical and regional distinctions, working-class communities tend to operate through recognizable structures with institutions, rarely distinguishable in terms of urban design or municipal entities. That is to say, they draw on ciphers of working-class life structured through spatially driven forms. Aside from the domestic spaces outlined in the previous chapter, the most commonly inhabited sites of working-class life are epitomized by known institutions: the factory, the school, and the pub. While such institutions by no means characterize the totality of working-class communities, such spaces are frequently centered in kitchen sink texts as sites in which identities are renegotiated.

The Pub

Aside from the factory, the space perhaps most synonymous with British working-class culture is the pub—a space whose historic development acts as a mirror to social change and altered class delineations in telling ways. In his comprehensive history of the topic, Paul Jennings offers an overview of British drinking culture, focusing on the way social change dictates shifts in the pub's communal function. For example, in a chapter devoted to decor and traditional design, Jennings situates the pub's evolution in relation to social and economic transformations. Beginning with a survey of "the 'golden age' of the inn," Jennings shows how the pub's primary purpose was to house travelers such as merchants and judicial servants while doubling as hubs of social activity (2016: 72–3). During this period, the clientele of the pub expanded from one "dominated by the male poor to one in which the middling and upper ranks of society and women made greater use of its spaces" (2016: 75). However, the institution's capacity to delineate class is made clear in that, during the Victorian era, pubs were divided by the drinks served. "Beerhouses" were generally considered the province of the working-class and, therefore, off-limits for more "respectable characters" (2016: 78). It was not just the drinks served that divided the patrons; the buildings themselves reflected social stratification which, by extension, made pubs a rich index of class consciousness.

Jennings discusses the way interiors of Victorian pubs often resembled nearby homes, distinguishable by their signage, their seating, and their penchant for carved wood and terracotta tiles. Despite being subtle in their distinction, such elaborations helped grant respite from the working world through a degree of aesthetic flare designed to replicate the familiarity of the domestic. In the postwar years, when the utilitarian architectural styles of prefab construction dominated, pub development upheld a veneer of Victoriana or, as Jennings notes, many were built in "a neo-Tudor or neo-Georgian style, which attempted to recreate a version of the traditional inn" (2016: 86). This practice reflects to the prevalence of engineered nostalgia in British culture, to the modicum of comfort such symbols offered disrupted communities, and to the function of escapist fantasies grounded in a loosely defined sense of tradition. This is especially telling with regard to a younger generation who, as noted previously, questioned the symbolic markers favored by the previous generation's proclivity for Victoriana. The younger generation would inevitably turn away from "the local" by seeking out more modern and adventurous clubs that offered livelier nightlife. In addition, Jennings comments on how Victorian-era pubs saw internal segregation that mimicked social microcosms with pubs tending to have a "best room" reserved for middle-class patrons. Twentieth-century pubs followed a similar plan, but interwar renovations introduced a mixed "lounge" that Jennings lists as "a gender-neutral space which appealed to some working-class and, in some places, middle-class couples and women drinkers" (2016: 86). Even in pubs without such obvious segregation, Jennings remarks that social microcosms still formed: "There was the 'public space' of the middle-aged regulars at the bar; the 'negotiable space' of the non-seating areas by various groups of customers; and the 'closed' social space where couples sat alone" (2016: 87). The famous opening sequence of Sillitoe's *Saturday Night and Sunday Morning* is attuned to such nuance, painting a picture of a mixed social space in which people who might not ordinarily commune are forced together with questionable results—a point made known when Arthur vomits on a couple noticeably marked as representations of the previous generation.

Whereas Victorian-styled pubs provided a sense of escape by simulating imperial heritage, new pubs of the postwar era minimized aesthetic fanfare in lieu of functional practicalities. With the aesthetics stripped away, such pubs promoted escapism not through heritage decor but through alcohol consumption. In these cases, the impression of unanimity was less driven by symbols of Britishness and more by insular notions of locality characterized by drowning shared sorrows. One example is the working men's club—a space whose name alone is suggestive of the way social position is upheld through institutions. Working-men's clubs began in Australia as private social clubs with both recreation and education in mind. They spread to the industrial areas of the midlands and northern England in the nineteenth century, accompanying the rise in industry with the intent to operate as nonprofit organizations. Their incentive differed from that of a traditional pub in that they formed as a more institutional, functional space aimed at serving rather than entertaining patrons. As Katie Engelhart (2014) has it, working men's clubs acted as a mechanism to placate revolutionary potential by "subduing and socializing the wily menfolk of industrial England"—an objective that ran counter to their origins. Kathleen Woodroofe claims that, in 1862, social reformer Reverend Henry Solly hoped to create environments that would "persuade young working men to give up drinking at public houses, to carry on education by means of evening classes, and to develop 'a deep vital interest in religious truth'" (1975: 20). She adds that Solly's plan was also to build bridges between social classes—not necessarily to permit social elevation, but to improve inter-class relations as a gesture of goodwill (1975: 20). The primary intent of Solly's clubs was threefold: to help working-class men become fully self-sufficient, to engage with local worker's unions, and to maintain an apolitical stance while furthering its own cause (1975: 21). At first, such clubs were designed to be free of alcohol, providing instead a space for "social intercourse, amusement, and 'rational recreation'" (Beaven 2005: 21). But, by the 1870s, the ban on alcohol was lifted, increasing membership and moving the institution away from the founders' reformist intent (Beaven 2005: 28). Working men's clubs reached their apex in the 1970s, gaining notoriety as classed spaces marked by excessive drinking—a sanctioned working-class alternative to the traditional pub. As Ruth Cherrington points out, such clubs were seen as "safe spaces" in the community and were, by design, flexible enough to accommodate an array of community events (2012: xiii). In order to retain such flexibility, the clubs eschewed decorative flare, opting instead for utilitarian buildings and spaces—oftentimes open rooms with minimal decor, furnished with the most basic seating available along with a makeshift bar. As with other institutional spaces like sports clubs and youth clubs, working men's clubs offered little in the way of characteristic flare, relying instead on the social capacity of the guests to furnish the space.

The distinction between pubs that prioritize symbolic heritage and pubs focused primarily on alcohol consumption renders clear the ways urban planning inscribed and reiterated social class. Pubs and clubs serving a specified community tended to feel more like an annex of the home, and postwar rehousing programs were generally designed in ways that incorporated such sites as part of their overall design. In a number of cases, pubs were built into postwar housing estates—which, in terms of alcohol consumption, reinforced the idea of drinking as an escape from day-to-day drudgery. This speaks to a point made in the previous chapter pertaining to John B. Calhoun's concept of behavioral sink—how destructive behavior can be understood as both a symptom of, and a response to, environments that cannot adequately support the needs of their inhabitants. Given how readily kitchen sink texts foreground working-class space, it is not surprising that pubs and clubs make frequent appearances. But it should be acknowledged that such texts also make full use of the wide range of pubs in British culture to accentuate class distinction. This is registered in the way that patrons align themselves with a particular type of pub's social position or by performing subversion—imposing a working-class status onto a pub aimed at a higher social register. The latter is a move perhaps captured most pointedly in one of *This Sporting Life*'s set pieces discussed later in this chapter.

Lewis MacLeod's (2012) discussion of drinking in Alan Sillitoe's *Saturday Night and Sunday Morning* provides an effective precis of the role of pubs within the narrative, arguing that alcohol serves as both escape and a means to challenge class confines. MacLeod's reading is compelling, aligning with the growth of British drinking culture in the postwar years. But, in a text where drinking informs so much of the plot, it is also advantageous to consider the conditions from which a text such as this might emerge. As MacLeod argues, Sillitoe was attuned to the role of alcohol in society and its social function, but I would suggest that *Saturday Night and Sunday Morning* also helps clarify the way classed identities are renegotiated through social institutions linked to alcohol consumption. The region of Nottingham where Sillitoe spent his youth was filled with pubs, and the nearby city center has a rich history of drinking culture. Yet Sillitoe opts to focus on "the local," showing how pubs act as part of a close-knit working-class community. As mentioned, Sillitoe's ability to capture working-class space and people so precisely is due, in part, to his own voluntary exile in that his relative distance awarded him a degree of clarity by which to consider drinking spaces and their effect on communities. This chapter's subsequent analysis of Sillitoe and Storey's work, in addition to Dunn's more subversive consideration of pubs, highlights the significance of drinking culture in portrayals of working-class space as well as the way such spaces inform and reiterate classed identities.

During the 1950s and the 1960s, the rising popularity of underground clubs and niche social spaces impacted the popularity of traditional pubs. As Jennings denotes, the interwar and immediate postwar years marked a time when the traditional pub was known as "a legitimate, even respectable place of leisure" that was "good for morale" (2011: 86).² He continues to note how a postwar decline can be attributed, in part, to the "erosion of [the] male working-class base" and the weakening of industry that would span the remainder of the century (2011: 86). Clearly, pubs and drinking culture responded to social changes underway in the postwar era, and Jennings's observations suggest an increased atomization of British subjecthood. New residential areas stemming from postwar regeneration policies regularly included their own dedicated pub or similar communal space as part of their design, producing a more isolated and less integrated social experience (2011: 87). This helps reveal how such shifts increase notions of social stratification and regimented boundaries, appearing not just as a convenience in their proximity to the home, but as sites of amalgamated resignation based on shared struggle.

Despite their preference for modern clubs, young people did frequent "the locals," but their drinking patterns differed. Jennings registers an increase in "pub crawls" among younger people that situates the idea of "the local" as part of an older, more rigid classed identity: "In place of the old community local, where customers stayed most of the night, drinking places were now, it was argued, 'fashion items'—places for the staging of self-emancipation from the older generation and distancing from its values" (2011: 87). Whereas the younger generation retained aspects of traditional working-class identities, they were more inclined to reject spatial manifestations of class as understood by regular attendance at "the local." This phenomenon is most evident in the 1970s and 1980s according to Jennings, but I would suggest that generational divides and young people's increasing interest in more expansive articulations of classed identity laid the groundwork at least two decades prior. Once more, the texts of the kitchen sink era can be seen to document subtle social changes in a recursive and culturally responsive manner.

Whereas representations of drinking culture in literature run the gamut from communal spaces of joy to dens of iniquity that connote the socially condemned, kitchen sink texts tend to present pubs in a matter-of-fact way, emphasizing the everyday importance of the institution for those who frequent them. In this sense, postwar class-conscious writing demonstrates a unique paradox; it presents drinking culture as a pharmakon, offering a solution to social limitations (drinking to escape) while also reproducing the problem itself (perpetuating the cycle). James Gindin writes:

> The contemporary writer turns to the traditional values of the working class not to find a proletarian utopia, not to endorse some vague notions about improving conditions or the equality of all men. Primarily, the writer values the working

class for its traditional responses within a society it cannot control, for learning to live within a limited compass. The problems of the working class have, in one sense, become those of many of the thoughtful men in the whole society: how to assert and defend oneself in the midst of chaos and indifference.

(1962: 105)

As this book contends, kitchen sink writers seem exceptionally invested in the potential of literature to accomplish such goals, especially literature's ability to provide a sharper understanding of the vicissitudes of working-class life. The texts analyzed in this chapter tend to nuanced turns in class consciousness by amplifying the way working-class space determines class articulation. Pubs and clubs in texts such as *Saturday Night and Sunday Morning*, *This Sporting Life*, and *Up the Junction* depict the social environment as it was—at times chaotic and boisterous, and at other times mundane and glum. But most important is the fact that these texts consider the dynamics of character in relation to spaces such as these, inviting interpretations of social behavior that signify new forms of classed identity.

Schools and Education

Shifts in the British postwar education system are complex, but educational institutions play important roles in kitchen sink texts, oftentimes due to their absence in the narrative. Connections can be made between class and educational opportunities that parallel the design and function of educational spaces themselves. One of the major shifts in education in twentieth-century Britain followed the 1942 Beveridge Report, generally heralded as the origin of the modern Welfare State. The report, led by economist William Beveridge, earmarked a range of social ills and proposed solutions designed to combat issues like squalor, disease, and "ignorance." "Ignorance" was the first issue addressed through the 1944 Education Act which initiated a comprehensive primary and secondary educational program and offered government subsidies to fund post-secondary education and training. The proposal sought to close class divides by increasing access to educational pathways. While secondary schools had previously charged for attendance, the Education Act removed fees, allowing working-class children to attend institutions otherwise only accessible to middle- and upper-class children with viable resources. However, the system funneled students down one of three channels, reiterating and reinforcing traditional class distinctions: the grammar school for those figured as academically astute; the secondary comprehensive school for a general, practical education; the technical school for more mechanical and labor-based training. One's path was determined by one's performance on the "eleven-plus"—a standardized test meant to assess academic potential. As with all standardized gatekeeping practices, class bias dominated in that the system could be gamed, principally through for-profit coaching—an option unavailable to many working-class children. Furthermore, access to grammar schools became increasingly competitive because there were not enough technical schools available to accommodate the demographics the exam produced. Criticism of the process was swift, and regional results were telling: children in the southern part of the country scored considerably higher than those raised in northern industrial towns. Subsequent studies found that a disproportionate number of middle- and upper-class children scored well relative to working-class children. Thus, attempts to thwart class bias only served to reinforce bias and privilege even more, and this was reiterated in the way educational spaces operated as well.

The prewar years saw the construction of new school buildings but mostly in large urban hubs such as London. In heavily populated areas, emphasis centered on multistory construction whereas new schools in suburban areas prioritized single-level builds with a greater focus on light and ventilation (Harwood 2010: 51). In an effort to minimize problems like the spread of illness through shared spaces, school development before the twentieth century favored expansion of existing buildings, some from as far back as the seventeenth century. Eighteenth- and nineteenth-century schools still remaining bore markings of charitable schools—institutions given the dubious name of "ragged schools," generally affiliated with industrial areas and the working poor. Revivalist designs of nineteenth-century buildings—what became known as The Queen Anne style—were also popular, spreading to midlands communities like Sheffield and Leeds (Harwood 2010: 42). By the turn of the century, local authorities moved away from the decorative revivalist style and toward a more utilitarian appearance (Harwood 2010: 52). Designs focused less on making grandiose statements, leaning instead toward spaces that met the needs of the community more squarely. Although the interwar years saw innovation in school design and building development, a poor economy hampered implementation and construction. By 1925, the focus turned to the production of cheaper, more makeshift schools that cut back on interior space by reducing ceiling height and, therefore, abandoning the prior emphasis on good light and ventilation (Harwood 2010: 64). This led to what were known as open-air schools—spaces that, while somewhat repressive indoors, promoted outside learning to assuage the experience of confinement.

In the wake of the Education Act, the new secondary system called for a vernacular architecture of its own. Continuing the push to build new schools in a timely and cost-effective manner, the Ministry of Education, in 1943, turned toward prefabricated materials. By 1949, the use of low-budget construction and ultra-rationalist designs was state-mandated (Harwood 2010: 73). Grammar schools favored existing, established buildings from the past whereas technical schools embraced the more modernist, prefabricated formats (Harwood 2010: 70). Secondary comprehensive schools lacked a singular design of their own, and for many northern areas, the cost of constructing or developing all three formats was not feasible. So, local authorities turned toward the possibility of building "bilateral" schools—schools in which two of the three educational tracks were combined (Harwood 2010: 77). Unsurprisingly, bilateral schools tended to combine the secondary comprehensive model with technical schools, insulating grammar-school students from the "chaff." In certain ways, this period of educational reform paralleled mass-housing in that the more problematic developments were modeled on better quality plans and designs. As was true of much mass housing, canonical architectural case studies exist, like Alison and Peter Smithson's Hunstanton School in Norfolk (1949). However, such designs are anomalies in that much postwar rebuilding borrowed general design principles but tended to cut corners where they mattered most. Such high-minded aesthetic projects were notably uncommon in communities where budgets were tight. Open plan, flexible spaces were standardized with a shift from innovative design to a more doctrinaire approach led by educational authorities seeking utilitarian and economic construction. By the late 1950s, the British educational landscape resigned itself to its existing stock of buildings. What new construction did emerge was limited by budget restrictions. Similar to the way utilitarian pubs became part of housing estate designs, educational spaces also encoded classed identities. Grammar schools acted as signifiers of history, tradition, lineage, and architectural grandstanding whereas secondary comprehensive and technical schools, by comparison, bore little architectural interest. The inadvertent reinscription of tripartite class hierarchies, in accordance with the class-based gatekeeping of the eleven-plus exam, is linked to the physical make-up of school buildings, ensuring space informs certain kinds of social identities.

In a touching letter to Joan Littlewood, Shelagh Delaney declared "I want to write for theatre but I know so very little about it. I know nothing, have nothing—except a willingness to learn—and intelligence" (Littlewood 2016: 515).

Littlewood would become a supporter of Delaney's writing, though later conceding that her work required considerable editing. Delaney's statement is apt in that access to a formal education—or a lack thereof—is commensurate with the lived experience of a number of the kitchen sink writers and, inevitably, their work. In a 1982 essay on his career as a writer, Alan Sillitoe noted that after failing the eleven-plus twice, it was clear to him "once and for all that [he] was not cut out for education" (1982: 8). Delaney failed the exam multiple times, as did Arnold Wesker, Keith Waterhouse, and others. Stan Barstow began grammar school prior to 1944's Education Act leading him to a career as a draftsman in the engineering industry, and David Storey passed the exam and attended a grammar school before studying fine art in London. John Osborne funded his education through an inheritance from his father's family, yet it is perhaps his work that critiques Welfare State education plans most pointedly. While the key figures of the movement registered a general desire for higher learning in working-class communities, access remained limited. Those who did attend higher-ranked schools clung to their working-class roots rather than embracing (in their work, at least) social elevation and the supposed elevation tied to the grammar school. It can be said that those kept from furthering their education tended to incorporate motifs of alienation and rejection into their narratives. Even as Sillitoe proclaimed that he was not cut out for education, there is a sense of cynicism in his claim—as if limited access to education cannot diminish intellectual curiosity or an appreciation for the arts, marking a distinction between assumptions of class and access to cultural capital.

Kitchen sink texts' engagement with academic opportunities is hardly a "them and us" affair, though; the texts complicate the relationship between working-class intellectualism and cultural capital in ways that echo the lives of the authors themselves. For instance, John Osborne's inheritance may have given him access to educational opportunities, but *Look Back in Anger* shows that even when opportunities are available, the same class hierarchies persist. Jimmy's anger is, in part, the result of a perceived failure of Welfare State policies. Despite the character's access to education, his chances to succeed are still hamstrung by his social position—a point made known through a judicious spatial metaphor that situates him as elevated yet restricted. Despite failing the eleven-plus multiple times, Shelagh Delaney's persistence eventually enabled her to transfer from Broughton Secondary to Pendleton High School—then considered a grammar school as part of the tripartite system.[3] During the Blitz, Pendleton functioned as a refuge for displaced families and the school went through a number of structural changes to incorporate several other local schools into its campus.

At the time of Delaney's attendance, it reflected the postwar utilitarian format of economic paucity. As such, it is possible to consider how Delaney's eventual acceptance into a grammar school may have proven disappointing. The school itself failed to live up to idea of the grammar school as academic utopia, perhaps because her arrival there was so delayed by gatekeeping in the form of the eleven-plus. Jo, in *A Taste of Honey*, appears accustomed to disappointment, mining resiliency from adversity—a characteristic that seems aligned with Delaney's own resolve. In contrast, Sillitoe lacked Delaney's persistence. After failing the eleven-plus twice, he dropped out of school to work in the local Raleigh bicycle factory—an event that shaped *Saturday Night and Sunday Morning*'s narrative. Nottingham is home to the prestigious Nottingham High School—a traditional school known for its Gothic revival style. In Sillitoe's time, the school was exclusively for the privileged with few educational alternatives in the surrounding area. This helps frame the central narrative of a text like *The Loneliness of the Long Distance Runner* in which the protagonist's only viable opportunity for education comes from the punitive borstal system. Sillitoe attended schools close to his home: Radford Boulevard School and Forster Street School, the former still standing but long since abandoned; and the latter, an elementary school, since demolished and replaced with council housing. In other words, in contrast to the postwar utilitarianism of Delaney's Pendleton School, the buildings where Sillitoe received his brief education would have likely resembled the same ramshackle Victorian housing of the children they served.

Grammar schools, known for using architecture as a link to the past, communicated social elevation through their traditional design. Although raised in a working-class environment, David Storey attended Queen Elizabeth Grammar School in Wakefield—a school founded in 1591 and housed today in an 1854 building designed by Richard Lane. The school's motto—Turpe Nescire, or "It is a disgrace to be ignorant"—emphasizes the ramifications of class division in Britain. As John Sutherland has noted, the ability to attend a grammar school represents "The primal scene in Storey's fiction" in that the characters' ability to transcend their surroundings is largely hinged on their ability to pass the eleven-plus (2011: 698). For working-class young people who managed to be "saved" (Sutherland's telling term for passing the exam), attending a grammar school would regularly lead to a kind of identity crisis. Sutherland cites Storey's own commentary on his 1963 novel *Radcliffe* in which he refers to the central character, declaring that "Grammar school broke him in two" (2011: 698). Certainly, Storey's early domestic life as the son of a coal miner would bear little resemblance to his life as a young academic. In this regard, it can be understood that, even if social impediments were eradicated through the Welfare State's Education Act, other concerns would still remain.

The spectrum of educational experience seen in the writers of the kitchen sink movement proves interesting in that it raises questions about the oft-cited assertion that the realist mode is little more than a byproduct of institutionalized art theory. That several of these writers were denied access to traditional avenues of study suggests that lived experience and determination took precedence over technical comprehension and formal technique. As this book has already claimed, one of the most significant tropes of kitchen sink realism is its unwavering commitment to fidelity. Writers such as Delaney and Storey—despite disparities in their educational experiences—produced texts that capture their environments and their ramifications in a similarly realistic and honest manner, suggesting that writing in the realist mode stems from a range of lived experiences rather than merely adherence to aesthetic principles. In the case of Sillitoe, whose formal education was brief, his training as a novelist can be best understood through his voracious consumption of literature. That so much of the work produced during this time appears as incidental and culturally responsive suggests a window in which artistic gatekeeping was momentarily curtailed. This, in turn, allowed writers who may have otherwise struggled to gain access to the arts, to participate. As Ian Watt submits in *Realism and the Novel* (1952), traditional forms of literary realism relied on institutional forms of knowledge of the arts, but the kitchen sink movement suggests that formal education can only go so far, and that lived experience matters just as much. Hoggart is interested in this dynamic in *The Uses of Literacy*. In his discussion of the way working-class voices became a commodity in the eyes of publishers, he points toward "the 'earnest minority'"—a group that, despite lacking the education usually required to access the arts, offers a new perspective worthy of consideration (Hoggart 1971: 260). This particular discussion will be taken up further in Chapter 4 where I suggest that kitchen sink texts augment traditional forms of the realist mode through democratic gestures of access that run counter to the kinds of gatekeeping prevalent in twentieth-century British culture.

The Factory

As E.P. Thompson holds in *The Making of the English Working Class*, social class is less of a tangible formation and more of a set of cultural experiences shaped by "traditions, value systems, ideas, and institutional forms" (1963: 10). Therefore, the site most synonymous with the working class is the workplace itself, and representations of factories and work environments are omnipresent in the kind of kitchen sink texts under consideration. The factory space is rarely considered a site of architectural fascination but, like much postwar rebuilding, factories are built with function in mind. That said, designs are nuanced and have the capacity to document changes in society as well as changes in labor practices. Early factories in Britain—specifically those associated with the silk industry—relied on local resources such as rivers and streams by which to power machinery. So, bucolic settings played a role in their operation. Furthermore, early factories—specifically those designed and created up until WWII—connoted permanence through the use of brick construction. While such designs were hardly strong enough to withstand the Blitz, the symbolic fixity of the space conveyed a form of stability. In fact, it was the internal organization of factories that saw the most culturally responsive shifts in that architects and planners considered how the building could operate as a machine, the workers acting as cogs and parts.

As Gillian Darley proclaims, factory design varies, from simple, utilitarian sheds to grandiose municipal statements, the latter regularly acting as "an apt metaphor for progress and change" (2003: 8). Darley adds that turn-of-the-century structures signaled technological determinism as "potent architectural icons" designed to respond to an early twentieth-century "fascination with the machine and all its works" (2003: 8). Furthermore, Gössel and Leuthäuser have shown links between factory design and the products made. In such cases, the building sought to promote the industry it housed as part of a process of "nobilization" (2001: 94). Such practices function as a gesture of chauvinism and national pride tied to forms of promotion intended to "impress the workers" and instill pride in labor (2001: 94). The authors also note tension between form and function in the development of industrial buildings with "architecture" responsible for symbolic totems of productivity, and "design" responsible for maximized efficiency (2001: 95). Walter Gropius, defending the role of the architect in the process of factory development, suggested that workers and owners alike benefit from grandiose architectural statements, asserting that "They will work more happily towards the creation of great common values in workplaces which are designed by artists to satisfy the sense of beauty with which we all are born and which enliven the monotony of mechanical work" (qtd. in Gössel and Leuthäuser 2001: 95). Although some factories in northern England adopted designs analogous to the gothic revivalism of grammar schools, most replicated their uninspired surroundings, acting, as it were, as an extension of the domestic. For many working-class British people, the factory was well within reach of the home, and, in some cases, harnessed to it. This served purposes of convenience for factory owners, but it also designated and sustained a servile class in that an individual born and raised within housing that serviced a central factory almost certainly guaranteed them a future in the same factory.

In kitchen sink texts, the image of the dying patriarch is a frequent trope. The sick or dying father calls to mind health concerns based on proximity to the factory, acting as a metaphor of the laborer's death under capitalism and as a perennial harbinger for the younger generation. As discussed in the previous chapter, regeneration and renewal programs such as slum clearance and gentrification sought to address matters of public health, aiming to distance the worker from the workplace and minimize the impact of pollution. An example of this exists in the New Towns movement that thrived between the 1940s and the 1970s, setting the standard for new forms of urban development. But as Anthony Alexander comments, many of the New Towns were "derided for having unspectacular architecture or dismissed as a failed social experiment" with "reputations [that] have been tarnished by pockets of extreme deprivation and a vicious spiral of decline, and in some cases, chronic problems of maintenance, widespread abandonment and ultimately demolition" (2009: 4). Since postwar planning tended to prioritize expedience through corner-cutting, such plans resulted in an array of new issues. Despite an emphasis on "design" as a way to maximize productivity, factories themselves ran into similar issues in that they were plagued with worker health problems, requiring continual adjustment via regulation. The fabric industry, for example, required humid conditions and the air contained a great deal of dust. Even though the introduction of masks assisted with breathing, problems like eye inflammation, ear infection, and "mule-spinners" cancer were common diagnoses. These work conditions, combined with long hours, also led to accidents, from loss of limbs to machine-related fatalities—an occurrence documented in David Storey's *This Sporting Life*.

After failing the eleven-plus that would secure him a seat in the world of higher learning, fourteen-year-old Alan Sillitoe joined the labor force becoming a lathe operator at the Raleigh bicycle factory. Sillitoe described the factory as a "marvelous brick hall with its high dark windows, and gangwayed forest of intricate and awe-inspiring machines" (Hanson 1999: 5), adding how the space left an indelible mark and informed his writing. Sillitoe explains the effect that the space had on his sense of independence, commenting that work in the factory was "neither arduous nor unpleasant" although pointing out that it took time for him to adjust to the noise (1995: 58). He characterizes the noise as "rhythmic"—an effect that, when combined with the mechanical repetition of the task, would inevitably produce a state primed for contemplation. The factory in question—a since-demolished industry landmark in Nottingham—is kept alive in memory through websites such as "I Worked at Raleigh," with images and documentary clips portraying the factory space as a Fordist dream, with individual work stations allotted to each employee. Sillitoe recounts the pride that stemmed from manning equipment of his own, suggesting how entrepreneurial spirit flourishes in spaces where productivity is tied to stage-managed autonomy. Despite this, Sillitoe felt frustrated by a fluctuating pay scale based on performance, especially when the production line's speed was manipulated by the foreman—a practice all-too-common in the pre-WWII factory years but gradually phased out due to increased union protection and progressive Factory Acts. However, this did not prevent Sillitoe from protesting when his wages dropped below previous pay scales and eventually seeking work elsewhere. At the time, the process of leaving a position was complicated due to 1941's Essential Work Order which sought to prevent employers bidding against each other for labor in order to help sustain worker attrition. Yet, striking workers forced the foreman to submit release documents to the Ministry of Labour allowing Sillitoe (and others like him) to access alternatives. Soon after, he started work at A.B. Toone and Company, a factory that he described as similar in structure (1995: 60). This space, a "five-storey red-bricked mill which stood between two streets of small houses, manufacturing plywood for Mosquito bombers and invasion barges" (1995: 60), produced the same repetition and rhythmic noise as the Raleigh factory only with more sawdust in the air that led to "an occasional gob of orange spit flashed into the gutter" on the way home from work (1995: 60). Sillitoe mentions that while he shared commonalities with his colleagues and found them cordial, few of his fellow workers showed interest in the arts or events beyond the realm of their immediate community. Given this, Sillitoe's experience in the factory space can be seen to anticipate the dilemma faced by his protagonist: to resign oneself to the monotony and repetition of the production line, or to try and imagine new possibilities. Although Arthur likely settled for a life tethered to the factory, Sillitoe himself chose a different path, claiming that "School was the basic condition of life, home a place to stay while going there, and the prospect of labour in a factory something that could not be allowed to spoil my enjoyment of the present" (1995:54). In this sense, factories produced more than salable goods; they also manufactured the opportunity for simulated autonomy as well as subversive, strategic class insurrection articulated and modeled through forms of mid-century writing.

While Sillitoe depicts factory labor as an inevitability of working-class communities, David Storey's *This Sporting Life* offers a depiction of machine work in a different form. Frank Machin—a character whose surname is unmistakably similar to "machine"—is drafted into a professional rugby team, promising an escape from his prophesied future as a coal miner. The novel is highly autobiographical in that Storey was also drafted to play rugby for Leeds Rugby League Football Club (RLFC), granting him a path to continue his education and eventually complete a degree in fine arts from the London Slade School. The novel depicts the sudden rise to stardom of a young working-class man, emphasizing the sense of displacement that comes from leaving one's roots and illuminating the challenges of social mobility. Like Keith Waterhouse's *Billy Liar*, *This Sporting Life* constructs a fictional northern town as its setting, but does so in a manner that would make it identifiable to northern working-class people. As Edward White has stated, Storey's depiction of the town tells of "a stern, unforgiving place in which outbursts of gruesome violence on the rugby pitch are mirrored in the industrial accidents and domestic abuse that punctuate everyday life" adding that "the casual matter-of-factness with which Storey relates those incidents shocked readers of the time" (2016). Storey merges the field with the factory throughout the novel and his first-person narrator frequently comments on the foreground and background in unison: "I had my eyes fixed on the twin buds of the power station's cooling towers and watched a cloud of white steam escape across the valley and come over the pitch" (2000: 40). Throughout, the natural world and the factory are linked by their narrative proximity, with Frank's gaze often vacillating between both: "I looked to the life that wasn't absorbed in the futility of the game—to the tall chimney and the two flowering cylinders of the power station, half hidden by cloud" (2000: 251).

Although Nell Dunn's 1963 novel *Up the Junction* arrived late relative to other kitchen sink narratives, with Ken Loach's TV adaptation and Peter Collinson's feature-film adaptation arriving in 1965 and 1968 respectively, the text is significant in its analysis of the way the factory impacts class expression. Unique to the movement, Dunn was born into an elevated social position in that her mother was the daughter of an earl and her father was a knighted farm owner. In 1959, Dunn, along with her then husband and child, moved to the relatively impoverished area of Battersea and began assembly-line work in a sweet factory.[4] Prior to this, the couple lived in Chelsea on a street that Dunn disliked as "it wasn't a talking street" (Ironside 2003).[5] In Battersea, Dunn found an area in which community thrived—one where people lived in close quarters, forging a sense of shared culture. Her interest in working-class communities was driven by the discovery of something unavailable beyond the spaces designated for working-class life: the sense of solidarity that stems from less-than-ideal conditions.[6] Similar to David Storey, Dunn's own lived experience structures the narrative as *Up the Junction* tells of a privileged woman who joins a working-class community and develops close bonds with her female coworkers from the local sweet factory. It is the factory that unifies the members of the community and brings them together each day with a singleness of purpose. In this regard, it is possible to grasp the appeal of working-class life as a motif of kitchen sink realism, particularly in the way that such texts celebrate rather than simply depict working-class communities. Explored further in the following chapter, *Up the Junction* offers a unique portrayal of social environs from the viewpoint of a relative outsider—a text whose ability to represent the boisterous spaces of the factory and the pub is based on commemoration rather than exploitation.

During WWII, propaganda was deployed to promote factory work as a gesture of national support in that production transitioned to military supplies and arms. It was suggested that those at home played as vital a role as those fighting overseas with notices proclaiming that "The attack begins in the factory" and "Back them up!"—a widely circulated poster featuring a British battleship crushing a comparatively smaller German war vessel. In the 1950s, however, propaganda veered toward anti-communist rhetoric, and the promotion of factory labor was tied to the nuclear family—most notably the promotion of household appliances and commodities that promised to differentiate the home from the workplace. Thus, the "era of affluence" that followed postwar austerity was defined by consumerism and better living as an antidote to alienated labor. Literary depictions of factories become more nuanced when considered alongside cultural narratives powered by government propaganda. The period's texts certainly reflect the nationalist attitudes affiliated with postwar reconstruction, with characters influenced and shaped by consumerist choices. Yet they undermine the efficacy of propaganda by reminding the reader of the monotony required for conspicuous consumption. Viewed in this light, the texts of the era provide a crucial insight into society in that they illuminate how consumerist rewards tied to rehousing and redevelopment obfuscate the way labor sustains social stratification. In other words, where culture at the time shifted its focus from labor as a gesture of nationalism to that of material acquisition, imaginative writing re-centers implications of labor in light of rising commodity culture.

Collective Consciousness and Shared Experience

The consequence of institutional space in working-class environs is that they assist in the formation and sustenance of shared experience and collective consciousness. In turn, the principle of collective consciousness is beneficial in clarifying the ways frequently visited sites define and frame working-class identities. The term can be traced back to Émile Durkheim's 1893 text, *The Division of Labour in Society*, with the central idea further developed by Lukács and others. For Durkheim, the idea of collective consciousness speaks to instincts and persistence, especially the idea that a social group's steadfastness is predicated on the upkeep of shared beliefs and values. Beliefs and values that define a group act as behavioral guidelines but also as a mechanism that holds a group in stasis. Put differently, collective consciousness is based more on the capacity of a group to regulate an ideological social body that acts as the sum of its parts. Durkheim viewed this as a positive factor pertaining to a group's tenacity, indicating that what he termed as "mechanical solidarity" (1984: 31) responds to like-minded thoughts and actions naturalized over time.[7] That is to say that the durability of a group is determined by its capacity to retain its ideological form, even if the form itself is based upon immiserated states. From this perspective, it can be understood that a working-class identity is sustained and reiterated through participation in shared spaces and institutions, but is not necessarily produced by the spaces themselves. Instead, the upkeep of classed identity stems from the navigation of such spaces—the kinds of actions and performances that spaces such as these promote. As this chapter has suggested, specific sites have the capacity to boost ideological messages about one's social rank and, in the absence of a definable source, they can appear as the source.

It might be said, then, that the built environment acts as a mirror of classed identity in that buildings and institutions tend to reflect the people they house. But when urban planning is involved, architecture emerges as a prescriptive apparatus designed to impart class consciousness as part of an ideological process. This is most perceptible in terms of postwar rehousing, and is perhaps most aggressively recognizable in the form of high-rise construction. In this sense, parsing the built environment is further complicated by the notion of collective consciousness and a desire to sustain identity through social turmoil. Following Durkheim's logic, a working-class space characterized by shared struggle might promote behaviors and responses that serve to sustain the struggle itself. To a degree, this invites consideration of Lefebvre's spatial triad—specifically the category of perceived space in which subjectivity informs the nature of perception. Kitchen sink writing speaks to this principle in that it portrays interactions with classed space in detail. For instance, a character may challenge a site they deem repressive by insisting that the space performs in a different manner entirely. Put differently, the texts of the period celebrate traditional beliefs and values tied to working-class life while mapping out alternate articulations of identity. As I suggest in Chapters 3 and 4, this is one of the major contributions of the movement in that the realist mode is revised as a critical rather than an aesthetic modality.

Given this, it can be understood that classed environs—specifically shared social spaces—are dialectical and contingent, as much a construction of the status quo as a construction by and for the people they house. Such sites demonstrate the curious capacity for agency and personal articulation of classed experience. It might be said that the urban environment acts as a two-way screen in that hegemonic forces impose identity from one side while subjects respond through spatial concessions. Classed environs are therefore rich sites for inquiry, and, as this chapter shows, kitchen sink realism is instructive in that it stresses setting through detailed, visceral devices by which to stage new modalities of class articulation and, by extension, class consciousness. In a way, such tropes call for a revolution of thought and identity, inferring that the working-class individual should claim ownership of space rather than relying on the collective to determine class awareness. However, they are also texts that honor and venerate the idea of community and shared struggle, calling for forms of reciprocal engagement between self and other. The principle of collective consciousness, it can be said, is informed by geographic limits that, while perhaps difficult to transgress with regard to social mobility, can be breached through the imaginative potential of the individual, remapping space in ways that subvert or permit radical conceptions of one's social position.

While the third chapter tends more to the way spaces can be remapped as sites of resistance, it is important to note how texts linked to the movement intensify environments marked by hegemony and the way space necessitates certain practices and behaviors. By foregrounding the setting of working-class space in such a manner, these texts perform multiple functions: they elevate the lived experience of a social group historically sidelined in the arts; they confront a bourgeois readership predisposed to more comfortable modes of class tourism; they advance their own aesthetic agenda with spatial metaphors acting as a genre-specific trope; and last, they offer a series of potential examples of the way working-class people might renegotiate their social standing through space. I suggest that the presence of the factory, the school, and the pub in texts of the movement surpass mere representation; instead, these texts respond to the pressures of conformity prescribed by Durkheim's notion of the collective through the elevation of the "outsider"—a character who thrives both within and without the community. Such characters simultaneously venerate and reject their social position through dynamic disputes and the articulation of new possibilities of autonomy and agency.

What follows is a consideration of the way documentary-style portrayals of working-class environs reveal their role in the enlargement of working-class identities. Furthermore, this analysis shows how working-class space itself operates as a motivator for change through portrayals of restricted autonomy. By delineating social limits and narrativizing breaking points, such texts help eke out ways of parsing identity through interactions with classed sites and environs. Alan Sillitoe's *Saturday Night and Sunday Morning*, David Storey's *This Sporting Life*, and Nell Dunn's *Up the Junction* are exemplary in their representations of working-class cultural institutions, providing an implicit critique of the way such spaces aim to maintain social order. When paired with the previous chapter's analysis of domestic space, it becomes increasingly obvious how everyday environments affiliated with working-class communities impact class consciousness and prescribe identity. In doing so, the following analysis aims to highlight how kitchen sink texts articulate spatial limits, how such limits impact the individual, and how these texts advance new ways of being without abandoning one's connection to traditional working-class sensibilities.

Shared Space and Identity Formation in
Saturday Night and Sunday Morning

Sillitoe compiled *Saturday Night and Sunday Morning* from a sequence of loosely connected stories about his hometown of Nottingham. Although published in 1958, he began work on the text in 1954 at the recommendation of the poet Robert Graves. In a 1962 article in *Shenandoah*, he describes his time in Majorca where, in 1953, he met with Graves after sending him some poems of his own. Upon learning that Sillitoe hailed from Nottingham, Graves suggested he focus on the city exclusively: "Nottingham: I hadn't seen it for some time, and the word came like a shock, bringing a sudden clear vision of packed streets and factory chimneys, of tar melting between cobblestones in summer, of riotous public houses on Saturday night" (Sillitoe 1962: 49). By this point, Sillitoe had penned several novels on themes quite removed from the themes central to the kitchen sink era.[8] Following Graves's advice, he wrote "Once in the Weekend"—a short story that would become the opening chapter of *Saturday Night and Sunday Morning*. This shift in thematic focus is matched in his writing practice. Preliminary drafts of *Saturday Night and Sunday Morning* and *The Loneliness of the Long Distance Runner* were handwritten over the typescript of an abandoned novel called *The Deserters* in a large and elaborately bound manuscript he had produced to impress potential publishers. By writing his new work over the top of the old, he essentially abandoned what came prior in exchange for class-centered themes and motifs that would inevitably grant him literary success.

In contrast to his unpublished novels, *Saturday Night and Sunday Morning* is structured around slice-of-life vignettes that paint a vivid image of a working-class milieu. Sillitoe organized the vignettes under the heading "Short Stories on the Same Theme," assigning some to "LDR" (*The Loneliness of the Long Distance Runner*) and others to "SNASM" (*Saturday Night and Sunday Morning*).[9] Parallels between the two texts are no accident as both texts originated from the same grouping. Vignettes emphasizing specific regions and locales like "Canning Circus" and "Once in the Weekend" were incorporated into a larger suite of writing, threaded together by a series of new stories for a more coherent narrative. The result is a stylistic shift in which attention to the details of space and spatial interactions is foregrounded; the nature of the short story mandates repeat references to space and setting which, when compiled into a novel structure, offers a kind of rhythmic regularity of spatial detail. While both *Saturday Night and Sunday Morning* and *The Loneliness of the Long Distance Runner* offer coherent narratives, the use of impressionistic snapshots underscores dedication to spatial and geographic awareness as well as the mimetic reproduction of working-class culture.

Sillitoe's capacity to present working-class environs with authenticity stems from his experience living and working in such spaces. The working-class sites he frequented as a young man are commensurate to those of Arthur, and perhaps it might be said that his clarity in defining the world of Colin Smith from *The Loneliness of the Long Distance Runner* can be read through his own experience with the British education system. Yet, during his self-imposed exile from Britain, Sillitoe also read widely on the topic of imprisonment. In 1956, hoping to review books on criminology, he received a shipment of texts that covered "prisons, borstals and their recidivist inmates" with "some analysing and commenting on the penalties handed out to anti-social elements of the British population, books written from every point of view except that of the criminal"

(1995: 226). Since his own experience in Nottingham did not include prison time, such texts surely helped flesh out discrepancies in coverage. Of note is his claim that many of the authors he read on the topic "looked on the lawbreaker as little more than a statistic, giving only cursory attention to individual psychology and social conditions" (1995: 226).

Saturday Night and Sunday Morning offers scenes that, while split between the pub, the factory, and the home, integrate working-class institutions as a gestalt milieu in a manner that recalls the social unity associated with class allegiance and Durkheim's collective consciousness. Sillitoe's fascination with environments is made apparent in his discussion of D.H. Lawrence, with his observation that "Place is everything—soil in the throat, under the feet, in the hands, the nostrils clouded with soot and pollen, the first smells and sounds of life still immediate" (qtd. in Gindin 1987: 37). Sillitoe's fascination with cartography, stemming from his time in the military, also contributes to his dedication to locale and vicinity. For Sillitoe, a childhood obsession with maps prompted a fondness for travel but it also signified the importance of understanding the specifics of space and environment:

> The stronger the sense of place, and mine couldn't have been more rooted, the more I wanted to know the rest of the world. One part of me was bound for ever to where I was growing up, but the other told me I had to know the whole world if my head was not at times to burst from sheer misery. Such a project could not be embarked on until the territory over which it was possible to walk from the front door of the house had been thoroughly mapped and understood.
>
> (1995: 18)

In this regard, Sillitoe's novels replicate his investment in mastering locale—not simply through mimetic replications of place (as that was the province of cartography), but through the manifold resonances of space and identity that replicate aspects of culture itself.

Saturday Night and Sunday Morning opens with one of the more memorable scenes of postwar working-class fiction: a Saturday evening in the White Horse Club—the "best and biggest glad-time of the week" (2010: 4)—where a "rowdy gang of singers" observe an inebriated Arthur tumble down a flight of stairs. The pub, ordinarily subdivided by class and gender, has adopted a more egalitarian community spirit for the night, "spread[ing] a riot through its rooms and between its four walls" so that "Floors shook and windows rattled, and leaves of aspidistras wilted in the fumes of beer and smoke" (2010: 3). The cause for celebration is a Notts County football team win, and the subsequent party reflects the way stratified spaces adapt when community interest beckons. Arthur, ordinarily excluded from such socially elevated affairs, is granted access by accompanying Brenda in place of her middle-management husband.

This opening scene is significant because it introduces the kind of loosening of class structures that periodically occur in spaces otherwise meant to reiterate social hierarchies. It also helps to situate Arthur as an intermediary, liminal figure. His class designation is conveyed through a series of behavioral signifiers—acts of delinquency he reserves for "one of the fifty-two holidays in the slow-turning Big Wheel of the year" in which "the effect of a week's monotonous graft in the factory was swilled out" (2010: 4). His momentary social elevation that comes from gaining access to the supporter's club floor is undermined by an older patron who dismisses him as "Dragged-up, I should think, getting drunk like this. Looks like one of them Teddy boys, allus making trouble" (2010: 11). Of course, the trouble in reference is Arthur vomiting on a middle-aged couple—the scene's climactic moment, and the narrative action central to Sillitoe's initial vignette. In its early short-story form, the scene served as an example of raucous drinking in a working-class space. When framed in the context of a novel, one that situates the protagonist in a liminal position marked by generational divides, the vomiting on representatives of his own social group is a telling gesture of generational revolt.[10] Sillitoe paints the victim as similarly class-conscious through his own actions and clothing ("Look at what the young bogger's gone and done ... My best suit ... Only pressed and cleaned today ... It cost me fifteen bob. As if money grows on trees" [1958: 10]). The scene is rich, representing the complexity of relational power structures. But, most significantly, it is a scene that establishes Arthur's precarious position as a postwar subject by revealing his inner conflicts about his role in a community in that "bliss and guilt joined forces" causing a stubborn dismissal of his delinquency and moral disregard: "Couldn't care less, couldn't care less, couldn't care less" (2010: 12). For Sillitoe's purposes, the opening scene in the White Horse allows him to introduce his protagonist who, while very much a part of that world, is both alienated and self-alienating.

While *Saturday Night and Sunday Morning* is not a text that focuses on the role of education in society, education is present within the text. Robboe, Arthur's factory superior, is educated. This grants him social elevation, both in his role in the factory as the administrative gaffer and in his ability to own his home, which is ultimately Arthur's goal. Sillitoe's depiction of Robboe is one of tenacity, but also resignation: "a bloke of about forty who had been with the firm since he was fourteen, having signed on as an apprentice and put in a lot of time at night-school" (2010: 37). Arthur considers this a mistake as he believes that Robboe, despite his elevation, is more enslaved to the factory than anyone else in that "he was a human being afflicted with the heavy lead-weight of authority when a rebellion always seemed on the point of breaking out" (2010: 38). His allegiance to his work undermines his elevated status in that Arthur views him with resentment and envy. As with Sillitoe's own experience after failing the eleven-plus, Arthur treats educational institutions with skepticism and cynicism in that he knows his bravado will only take him so far. Once more, the choice between acquiescence to a prescribed life and the potential thrill of insubordination is worked out through space and interactions.

Arthur, while working at his lathe, ponders the theme of repetition conveyed by the novel's title, recalling "dim memories of the dole and schooldays behind, and a dimmer feeling of death in front, a present life punctuated by meetings with Brenda on certain beautiful evenings when the streets were warm and noisy and the clouds did a moonlight-fly over the rooftops" (2010: 136). Arthur clearly seeks to live in the moment, and the novel's position on educational institutions seems to be one of dismissal, characterized by Sillitoe's description of Arthur's "lack of spiritual values" that are less of a personal choice, and more the result of postwar culture. In the "Canning Circus" scene in which Arthur and Fred witness a young man attempting to steal a vase for his mother's grave, the nearby church and school are described as "standing deserted like unwanted corpses" (1956: 119). Although seemingly innocuous as a passing reference, the line confirms that an environment which fails to provide its inhabitants with basic, necessary moral training will be subjected to criminal and delinquent behavior. Arthur's own alienation from cultural institutions beyond that of the factory links him to the young man's delinquency in that, when the shop's window is smashed in the attempted robbery, Arthur is "stirred by the sound of breaking glass: it synthesized all the anarchism within him, was the most perfect suitable noise to accompany the end of the world and himself" (2010: 114).

Sillitoe further develops the relationship—or lack thereof—between the school and delinquency in *The Loneliness of the Long Distance Runner*. Although published a year later than *Saturday Night and Sunday Morning*, the text contains a number of parallels with the main difference being that the protagonist's heightened frustration pushes him toward committing crimes rather than the kind of antisocial acts associated with Arthur. Told in a sequence of flashbacks at a borstal school, the narrative conflates educational institutions with the prison system as part of its class-based social critique. The tacit insinuation is that for postwar working-class young men, prison grants greater opportunities than either the factory or the schoolhouse. It is the borstal that, like Arthur's lathe, grants Colin access to autonomy. But whereas Arthur resigns himself to a weekly cycle of labor, the borstal offers an illicit space of rebellion that permits irresponsibility and recklessness rewarded by subversive forms of knowledge. Sillitoe's own contentious feelings about education are apparent in both texts, but his resentments are tempered. By challenging its efficacy in both narratives, Sillitoe reproduces prevalent anxieties in a moment when, in spite of the Welfare State's promise of equal access, education was neither as accessible as promised nor did it "save" working-class young people from a life like that of their parents.

That said, the factory is the most prominently featured space in the text and, as such, it replaces the school as a site of education while also incorporating aspects of the home. The presence of the factory in the story is akin to factories in many northern industrial areas: omnipresent. In an early scene in which Arthur and his father leave the house to head to work, its presence is registered instantly:

> Once out of the doors they were more aware of the factory rumbling a hundred yards away over the high wall. Generators whined all night, and during the day giant milling-machines working away on cranks and pedals in the turnery gave to the terrace a sensation of living within breathing distance of some monstrous being that suffered from a disease of the stomach.
>
> (2010: 22)

The novel presents the factory in full sensory detail with sound described as "infernal" and making "the brain reel and ache" (2010: 26)—an effect replicated in Karel Reisz's film adaptation through a regular and rhythmic use of non-diegetic industrial noise. Yet, the factory building—despite its prominence in the community—disappears early only to become a larger metaphor for perpetual labor and imprisonment: "And so it was possible to forget the factory, whether inside it sweating and straining your muscles by a machine, or whether swilling ale in a pub or loving Brenda in her big soft bed at the weekend. The factory did not matter" (2010: 42). Consequently, its omnipresence is naturalized as an inevitability; inside and outside blur together in that to exist in the community is to exist as part of the factory. The effect is that work is abstract and duration loses meaning: "Living in a town and working in a factory, only a calendar gave any real indication of passing time, for it was difficult to follow the changing seasons" (2010: 137).

Inside the factory, individual work stations promote a sense of entrepreneurial independence as well as the atomization that inhibits solidarity. The way Sillitoe depicts the environment is that labor is primarily a relationship between the laborer and his machine, and any violation of that relationship is met with worry. For example, when Arthur wanders over to Jack's workbench and tells him to "Udge-up" so he can sit next to him, Jack's concern is more that Arthur will disturb the work arrangement he has of "a clamped-on vice and a carborundum wheel" next to "a mug of the firm's tea" (2010: 30). Jack's issue is that Arthur's violation of space will lead him to knock over his tea, thus disrupting his efficiency. While such a scene might ordinarily seem inconsequential, it is wise to recall that, unbeknownst to Jack, Arthur has already violated and disturbed his world by engaging in an affair with his wife, playing a surrogate father role to his children, and making himself at home in Jack's bed while Jack is at work. Both Jack and Arthur's livelihood rely on their ability to defend their personal space; only Robboe exists beyond such limitations in that his social and economic superiority grants him a wider berth of movement and literal mobility, "walking from bench to bench, machine to machine" (2010: 59). The factory building, then, functions as a totem of class but is subordinate to labor practices and the relationship maintained between the worker and his machine. Accordingly, the mechanics of Sillitoe's aesthetic choices are laid bare, and the text encompasses much of what the kitchen sink movement aimed to achieve: a portrayal of the way spaces and identities are renegotiated rather than simply how the spaces themselves appear. Despite Sillitoe's text painting an authentic picture of working-class life in Nottingham, his emphasis on local environs also serves to depict the way working-class spaces can be comprehended as the sum of their parts. Sillitoe presents a familiar world to working-class readers and offers a protagonist who questions his place within it.

Class Migration and Social Stasis in *This Sporting Life*

David Storey's *This Sporting Life* introduces fame (rather than notoriety) to the kitchen sink narrative archetype in order to explore social mobility within working-class space. Similar to Sillitoe's writing, Storey's novel was semi-autobiographical with details of Frank Machin's life matching his own. Also similar, Storey was responsible for developing the screenplay, with Lindsay Anderson directing the widely acclaimed 1963 film adaptation. The novel was equally popular, winning the 1960 Macmillan Fiction Award, its success perhaps due to a growing interest in kitchen sink aesthetics following Osborne, Sillitoe, and Delaney's earlier efforts. The novel tells the story of a traditional Angry

Young Man-type figure whose penchant for pub brawls gains him the attention of rugby league recruiters hoping to profit from his aggression. The subsequent narrative documents the broadening divide between his social ascendency as a professional athlete and his subjugated social position as working class. A romantic subplot is introduced when the protagonist initiates a troubled and abusive relationship with his widowed landlady (Margaret). The romance ends in tragedy with Margaret's death, denying either of them the chance to make amends. Much of the subplot serves to counter the aggressive machismo of the main narrative, placing Frank and his love interest on somewhat equal grounds with Margaret acting as a threat to Frank's masculinity through her advanced age and life experience that positions him as a naive child by contrast. In a manner consonant with the way the recruiters exploit Frank for their own personal gain, Margaret does the same, using Frank to assuage the guilt she bears from her failed marriage and her ex-husband's subsequent suicide. The romantic subplot corresponds to the main story's focus on exploiting others for personal gain and the compound effects that such practices can have.

Storey wrote *This Sporting Life* when he was just twenty-one years old, and, as William Hutchings has observed, its complexity and nuance are surprising for such a young writer—a point that Hutchings attributes to Storey's having already produced several novels prior to its release that remain unpublished (1988: 8). While a 2016 article in Rugby Today celebrates Storey's narrative as one of the best depictions of the sport, the novel was not always so highly considered—especially by the Rugby League fans who felt that it played into stereotypes (White 2016). Rugby, in British culture, has long been tied to working-class industrial regions with players supposedly lacking the social graces required to play more "respectable" or "gentlemanly" sports. Furthermore, historic attempts to elevate the social status of the sport have failed.[11] Still, Storey's personal experience with rugby was insufficient to offset criticism from those who felt he contributed to negative stereotypes. This raises questions of verisimilitude: does Storey's work promote a false narrative or reinforce existing stereotypes? As Steven Lacey has argued, Storey was very much engaged with the idea of moving authenticity forward in that "what emerged at this time is not simply a particular kind of realism but a new cultural 'moment', in which representations of class would assume an importance not only for the theatre, but also for the way that the myths of affluence and consensus were contested in a range of cultural and artistic forms" (2002: 71). The depictions of rugby in the novel were likely discomforting not because they reiterated cultural stereotypes, but because they portrayed a world that had, up until this point, never been shown with such honesty. Although *This Sporting Life* certainly depicts a brutish, exploited class, the text is much more of a mirror to the reality of the time than a caricature or exaggeration.

Similar to Sillitoe's text, Storey places the site of labor at the narrative center, flanked by other social institutions associated with working-class space. Set in the fictional town of Primstone, the narrative casts the rugby club as an institutional archetype, blurring the line between the fictional and the tangible. The novel engages the dilemma of class acquiescence in a manner that recalls Sillitoe's Arthur. Storey reports that the name of the text stemmed from a phrase he heard on the radio while traveling from art school to play rugby in Leeds: "This sporting life is going to be the death of me: I'm going to settle down" (qtd. in Redhead 2007: 100). The domestic aspects of the narrative involve a series of terraces ("Little black hutches nailed together by those pegs of chimneys" [1960: 32/2000: 37]), with homes that are clearly insufficient to protect their inhabitants from social and psychological onslaughts ("I banged the door on the way out. The house trembled. I could imagine how she felt when all her house trembled" [1960: 41/2000: 46]). However, the novel's emphasis on the working-class milieu reveals links between shared communal space and identity. The rugby field itself acts as a symbolic stand-in for the factory floor, and the novel's engagement with pubs—specifically Storey's attention to the distinction between "the local" and the more high-brow pubs on the edges of town—highlights the novel's larger concerns about social mobility.

This Sporting Life frequently stresses the rugby field's connection to violence. It also connects the field to the harms of labor by first situating Frank as a lathe worker in a local factory. Whereas Storey himself would spend his days as a student and his nights and weekends as a rugby player, Frank vacillates between a laborer in a factory and a laborer on the field. Since he practices after work during sunset, the field is cast more as a space of mystery than that of a space of monotony: "When I ran on to the field it was almost dark. A heavy mist hung over the valley and enclosed the ground in a tight grey wall of drizzle … Everything outside of the dark wreath of the crowd and the wooden pinnacles of the stadium was hidden. We were isolated" (2000: 20). It is also a space that works on Frank in a hypnotic way: "The field had grown, its limits disappeared into that suffocating mist. The ground continually surged up to absorb me. I listened to the thud of my vanished feet as they pushed up automatically against the earth" (2000: 22). The mechanical nature of Frank's actions recalls the trancelike state Arthur experiences while working on his lathe. Accordingly, the novel stresses the atavistic and primitive characteristics that Frank's employers seek to exploit. Although the field incorporates the kinds of violence that leads Frank to lose his teeth, the factory's violence is registered as threatening when Frank reminds Weaver, the Rugby Club chairman, of the funeral of one of his fellow workers: "How'd he get killed?" Weaver asks with Frank responding "On a lathe in 'D' shop. Quite nasty" (2000: 61). Through this, Storey links rugby to labor but insinuates that the violence of the sport is less violent than what working-class people experience in the factory.

As Hutchings declares, individuals in kitchen sink texts are routinely figured as automatons in their world echoing Marx's observation that "[factory work] confiscates every atom of freedom, both in bodily and intellectual activity" (1987: 35). Hutchings pinpoints the role of leisure time as a momentary escape from the monotony of labor, but rightly argues that sport is a form of leisure susceptible to labor exploitation. This is not merely an economic endeavor, even though financial gain is a chief motivator for both player and manager in the narrative. Hutchings concludes that "the expropriation of athletes" as seen in texts like *This Sporting Life* and Sillitoe's *The Loneliness of the Long Distance Runner* is more a reflection of social dynamics in that such a practice has "its origins in the power of one person or group to 'have the whip-hand over' others, demanding allegiance to an institution, class, city, or state" (1987: 46). Whereas the state-driven exploitation of Colin in *The Loneliness of the Long Distance Runner* is considerably more palpable in that he is not only "owned" but held captive by his owners, Frank is one who mimics the fantasies of many aspiring athletes. Yet, the narrative explores the more nuanced and less perceptible ways that a figure like Frank is still owned, not only through contract, but in his role as a local celebrity obligated to perform and, ultimately, entertain the people of his town. The rugby field itself, distinct from the punitive constraints of the borstal or the time-clock-based constraints of the factory, is open space, metaphorically marked by possibility and potential. In the end, it is Storey's depiction of the space as isolated and distanced from the rest of the community that situates Frank as a figure to be ogled and provoked for pay.

Storey makes it clear to his reader that traditional tripartite class assignations remained prominent in the postwar era despite attempts to curb such divides. One of the novel's most instructive examples can be seen when Frank convinces Margaret to join him on a trip to Howton Hall—"an old country house converted into an hotel and an eating place for the sort of client who can afford to drive out there for an evening, or a week-end" (2000: 84). The scene is noteworthy in that it recounts the way pubs operated in Britain by distinguishing between "locals" that served the immediate community and pubs distanced from "the local" in ways that reiterate class separation. Storey notes that Howton Hall is "an equal distance from three large industrial towns, and approachable from two more—the distance acting as a kind of social sieve. But with the bigger hand-out of cars and other crap propaganda since the war it's stepped down a peg or two" (2000: 84–5).

Storey initially suggests that the rise of commodity culture has reshaped the experience of class, but the scene certifies that status is still sanctioned by social institutions. The novel recounts how the building divided its clientele by segregating the upwardly mobile from more traditionally affluent groups, essentially splitting the building in two: "On one side, overlooking a deep wooded valley and a lake, is the residential sector and the restaurant, and on the other is a car park, a bicycle rack and a café" (2000: 85). This sense of social division is valorized in the text through Margaret's working-class discomfort of entering the upper-class restaurant ("I tried to get Mrs. Hammond to go in the cocktail bar, but one look at the plush interior and the Riding cloth merchants, and she wouldn't budge past the door" [2000: 85]). Her anxiety is compounded by the way they are treated by the staff: "I did all the talking with the waiter, who made no attempt to hide his feeling we'd strayed over to the wrong side of the hotel. He coughed a lot, and pointed out the big prices to emphasize the dearness of everything" (2000: 85). But despite Frank's demonstration of his new fortune and elevation, he cannot mask his class status or the source of his finances in that he is forced to wear his rugby boots after soaking his shoes in a lake. The scene, albeit contrived in relation to the rest of the novel, confirms the persistence of class bias—perhaps more so in the era of affluence when those most invested in sustaining social hierarchies struggled to discern the dividing line between "them and us." From this, it is clear that Howton Hall offers a decisive glimpse at the way postwar British society fought to preserve class demarcation in relation to changes pledged by the Welfare State.

The social exclusion that Frank experiences—from both inside and outside his own community—is one that he has little recourse to fix. Storey casts Frank as an oversized brute, one whose emotional capacity is that of an undersized adolescent. His attempts to navigate emotions are suitably brutish yet they serve to counter the emotional barrenness of Margaret whose world, we are given to understand, has led to her frail psychic state. What *This Sporting Life* indicates, therefore, is in alignment with other novels of the time: that the environment inhabited by working-class people serves to maintain subjugated states of being. But whereas other texts of the period raise awareness about classed confines or put forth alternative modes of being, Storey's text provides little in the way of redemption. Although Margaret's fate is sealed early on, Frank's fate unfolds as the novel progresses as it becomes clear that athletic success extends few substantive advantages with the promise of fame masking the limits of social mobility. Malcolm Pittock has argued that Frank's obliviousness to the effects of his environment suggests that Storey did not want his characters to appear "as determined by their environment" (1990: 104), but it seems plausible that Frank's chief characteristic, aside from his brutishness, is his naïveté. Furthermore, Jane Mansfield has suggested that Frank's aggression is consistent with representations of aggressive masculinity seen in other texts of the time reflecting the "period of national insecurity" (2010: 34). But Storey's emphasis on space as a locus of alienation cannot be overlooked in light of the way the field is presented as a heterotopic site distinct from the town. Similarly, Howton Hall is separated but embedded within a national framework of class assignation. Frank's obliviousness as to the effects of such spaces on his behavior is commensurate with his emotional immaturity present throughout the text.

Andy Harvey has suggested that, despite Frank's failed attempt at class migration, the attempt alone is enough to prove that alternative modes of existence can be imagined within oppressive conditions. Frank's failure, he claims, is the result of him being "too inarticulate to succeed" and that his "anxious but unspoken attempt at a different kind of masculinity thus fails to materialize" (2010: 12). Whereas Harvey is focused on Frank's approach to gender relations, it helps to keep in mind the effect of class confines on one's capacity to transform behavior. In a space of systematic oppression, the ability to engage radical transformations of being is hamstrung without the imaginative capacity to do so. It is wise to recall that Storey, in naming his character "Frank Machin," undoubtedly intended his protagonist to be likened to a machine. And, as a cog in a mechanism, Frank has limited capacity to effect significant change.[12] In this regard, Storey's text is a bleak example of the way that working-class environs can be mobilized to place limits on social elevation. Yet, it is also a text that furthers the notion of accumulation and status as simulations of class transgression.

Even with substantial income and a degree of local notoriety, Frank is still held in place by social forces. The novel closes with Frank driving toward a game, passing by the factory while registering the way it pollutes the surrounding environment, reminding himself of "the assurance my place of work provide[s]" (2000: 239). However, the pollution he describes—"the brown industrial water [that] foamed in great arcs over the weir and swirled in slow volutes past the stone embankment of the factory wall" (2000: 239)—differs little from the subsequent description of the game in which "the dampness went through to the bone, numbing. Black unknown faces, streaked with skin or blood, slow black limbs. Moved continually past, interlocking, swaying, beating, followed by steam, seeping from the skin, polluted by the mud, vaporizing in the cold air" (2000: 249). By the end of the novel, little has changed about the way Frank comprehends his labor; he thinks of it as elevated, yet Storey stresses how such elevation is stage-managed and ultimately illusory. Frank's inability to fully understand the nature of the environment he inhabits situates him closer to Osborne's Jimmy with the significant difference being that Jimmy's education helps him to understand the way his environment works against him. Frank lacks Jimmy's intellectual ability, and the novel closes with Frank tending to his injuries in the locker room baths: "The water rose to my shoulders. It pressed on my chest and I fought for breath, coughing in the steam. Its heat brought my bruises to life" (2000: 253). Frank is doomed to repeat the same cycles of violence and reward, and the reader is given no guarantee that his career will sustain him. While Storey's novel tells a story of stasis and limitation, the novel itself provides the working-class reader with insights into how such stasis is established and maintained through spatial means. In other words, this is a novel that illuminates a problem in the hope that the reader will come to conclusions about their own position relative to working-class space.

Contours of Class and Mobility in *Up the Junction*

Nell Dunn published *Up the Junction* in 1963, relatively late in the kitchen sink realism cycle. With Ken Loach's 1965 TV play and Peter Collinson's 1968 film adaptation in tow, the novel played a significant role in transforming access to abortion services in Britain. In an interview with Margaret Drabble and Jenni Murray, Dunn claims that she did not plan the text to have such a high degree of social impact, swearing that "it would not occur to me that any politician would have read anything that I'd wrote" (Dunn 2013b). Regarding concerns about class tourism and exploitation, she adds that "I didn't know what exploitation meant at the time" (Dunn 2013b). This is in response to the fact that Dunn herself used documentary-style realist techniques as well as dialog lifted from women in the working-class region of Battersea. Rather than appear exploitative, the text reports with eagerness and care. Dunn, herself, was invested in representing the lives of working-class people with sensitivity, focusing specifically on the distinct voices of working-class women as a retort to the mostly male-dominated voices of the "Angry Young Man" label. Scraps of overheard conversations and gossip fragment the text to simulate the jump-cut edits of documentary film. The novel tells a story of three young working-class women from the slums of Battersea. All three work in the McCrindle's sweet factory during the week and, on the weekend, they head "up the junction"—an area of Clapham known for its bars and nightlife. Focusing less on an engaged plot and more on slice-of-life vignettes, Dunn's text provides a glimpse into women's work at a time when gender politics were under revision. The narrative closes with a harrowing depiction of an illicit abortion, and it is this scene that is often attributed to helping change abortion laws in Britain. Her link to the kitchen sink movement is clarified by Merseybeat figurehead, Adrian Henri, who reminds us of the term's origins in David Sylvester's comments on figures like John Bratby. Henri points out that one of Bratby's early canvases is of Dunn and her then-husband, Jeremy Sandford, stating that "the gritty, down-to-earth concerns of the so-called 'kitchen sink school' of painters precisely parallels Nell Dunn's search for beauty in the unpromising environs of working-class Battersea" (Dunn 1988: XII).

Although *Up the Junction* is propelled by dialog, the text still details working-class locales in depth, offering a new perspective from that of the more male-dominated texts. For instance, the text opens with a chapter entitled "Out With The Girls" which introduces the reader to the pubs of Clapham Junction where the three central characters make clear their goals: to drink and have sex with an array of men.[13] The scene is followed by boisterous skinny dipping "up the common" in a local coke quarry—an area off-limits due to the characters' need to "clamber over a high wall" (1988: 4). The bulk of the text is split between scenes in the factory and various domestic spaces—many of which depict pre-regulation slums listed for demolition. Similar to the rugby field in *This Sporting Life*, Dunn punctuates her settings with images of industrial production and pollution. That said, McCrindle's sweet factory is deemed less of a repressive space and more as one that functions as a site of communal gathering. Dunn tells of her own experience working in a Battersea sweet factory, particularly how women in her role worked a handful of hours per day and were allowed to eat as many of the chocolate liqueurs as they liked. This, apparently, led to occasional intoxication, and it paints a different picture than that of Arthur at his lathe of Frank in his scrum.

The most dominant characteristic of the novel is the use of vernacular—colorfully expressive and tonally authentic in its depiction of South London. However, as a text so driven by its dialog, depictions of space are generally colored by flourishes of speech that reframe them in new ways. For example, in the chapter entitled "Prison Visit," incarceration is figured as a viable alternative to working-class institutional spaces in a manner similar to that of *The Loneliness of the Long Distance Runner* with one character commenting "They say Borstal's all right—sort of university for them what can't afford Oxford" (1988: 104). Much of the text engages the notion of repurposing space for both individual and collective gain, and this will be taken up more forcefully in the following chapter. For now, though, Dunn's text puts forth a clear-eyed perspective on some of the more prosaic working-class institutions pertinent to this chapter: the factory, the pub, and the school. Of note is the way that Dunn—like Delaney—uses such sites to model renegotiations of identity as the upshot of shared conditions.

The novel distinguishes between different forms of industry indicative of postwar "women's work"—a reflection of the rise of women in the workplace under conditions inherently gendered. For one thing, the text's spaces all exist under the shadow of the power station—a famous Battersea landmark—that "blows violet smoke" into the surrounding area (1988: 49). In contrast, the factory where the women work is presented less of a space of imposing industry and more as a feature of the community developed for purposes of socialization. In contrast to the individual work stations of Sillitoe's Raleigh bicycle factory where Arthur plays out his entrepreneurial fantasies, the workspace occupied by the characters of *Up the Junction* is designed with conversation in mind: "We laugh, twenty-five women hunched over three long tables, packing cheap sweets for Christmas" (1988: 19). During WWI, women were employed in specifically gendered roles, performing what was frequently deemed "delicate work"—tasks characterized by intricate production such as assembling fuses as the result of physiognomic qualities considered more appropriate for such tasks (Hammond 1919: 157). This continued in WWII when women joined factories to replace the men fighting overseas. Dunn seemingly pushes back against such gendered and essentialist assumptions by describing the factory workers as having "Thick red fingers, swollen with the cold" (Dunn 1988: 19). Despite its capacity for social engagement, the factory space is still restrictive—small, with just two rooms, the narrator claiming that "My eyes begin to ache in the cold electric light. There are no windows in the room where we have been sitting since eight in the morning earning our two-and-fivepence an hour—tenpence an hour for the under eighteens" (1988: 21). Furthermore, the space is damp, causing an older employee to "spit into a rag" claiming "Got the guitar, get it every winter" and adding how the factory "Used to be a laundry you know—that's why it's so damp" (1988: 20–1). There is no on-site cafeteria or breakroom; workers take breaks in a cloakroom, sitting on a cold cement floor (1988: 22). A sign by the lavatory patronizingly instructs workers to "WASH YOUR HANDS AFTER USING THE TOILETS. THIS IS A FOOD FACTORY" (1988: 22, emphasis original) while an older employee instructs the protagonist not to bother as "it'll take them five minutes to thaw out" adding that "what the eye don't see the heart don't grieve" (1988: 23). In other words, the space is one that pushes workers together into close proximity in a manner that lends itself to conversation and shared experience in contrast to the relative autonomy of Sillitoe's lathe workers.

Dunn describes her own work in the factory as more pleasurable, telling of how the space produced female-centric discourse. In an interview with Philip Fisher, she comments on her aptitude for recreating authentic voices, professing that "If somebody I got to know in the street, and I then wanted to put them into a situation where they got murdered or something, I would sort of be able to pick up how they spoke" (Dunn 2016b). In this sense, the setting of the factory is secondary to the kinds of dialog the work environment produces—coarse, graphic, and often very funny. But the factory space itself is responsible, both through the physical proximity created by the workspaces themselves and through the shared experience of working in a role that is social yet laborious. Given how close confines unite characters in ways that extend beyond work hours, Dunn offers a markedly different representation from the masculinized portrayals of factory life perceptible in *Saturday Night and Sunday Morning* and *This Sporting Life*—spaces that produce isolation and competition rather than new articulations of shared struggle.

During the same interview, Dunn discusses the process of transforming *Up the Junction* into a Wednesday Play with Ken Loach.[14] She tells of how Loach was already an established figure at the BBC, and how the pair spent considerable time walking the streets of South London to discuss the kind of spaces that the broadcast should reference. In contrast to a text like *This Sporting Life* or *Saturday Night and Sunday Morning*, *Up the Junction* centers on the urban-industrial landscape—an area that saw heavy gentrification in the immediate postwar years. Furthermore, the region is significantly less provincial than northern towns. The result is a landscape that provides a variety of spaces for interaction as opposed to just a handful of pubs or a single school serving the proximate community. In addition, the fragmented structure of Dunn's novel allows for a greater sense of movement throughout what is ultimately a sprawling space. Clapham Junction is named after the railway station serving the Wandsworth borough of London, granting links to Clapham Common and Battersea's town center. Accordingly, *Up the Junction* is a composite of interconnected regions (South London), but the regions themselves are distinct. The Wandsworth region in particular was a high-profile target for German bombers during the war due to the prevalence of industry in addition to the iconic power station. Like Colin MacInnes in his London trilogy, Dunn suggests that postwar rehousing policies are as much a cause of destruction and damage, saliently recounted through Adrian Henri's commentary: "Battersea, like Brick Lane, like Islington and The Isle of Dogs, has succumbed to the new disease of 'gentrification': affluence at a lower level, of cheap mail-order clothes, rented video sets, hire-purchase furniture, has eclipsed the sort of street culture celebrated in Richard Hoggart's *The Uses of Literacy*" (1988: XIV).

Like Sillitoe's Nottingham, the range of institutions represented form a cohesive whole—classed environs in which like-minded individuals congregate, their shared status made clear through Cockney slang that stands in contrast to the narrator's Chelsea "sloane-speak." Given the novel's dedication to dialect, and Dunn's commitment to replicating vernacular, *Up the Junction*'s spatial demarcations are also cemented through the use of speech patterns. Early in the text, the narrator goes shopping with another character from the area, and subsequent scenes demonstrate the effect of consumer culture on the individual in that the narrator—hailing from upper-class Chelsea—registers every aspect of war damage while her shopping partner's attention is split between the latest fashions displayed in shop windows and local gossip. For example, the posher narrator's articulation of space—"Past some torn down prefabs and we walk over the erupted foundations looking for the drains" (1988: 13)—is strikingly different to her companion's understanding of the same space—"There's a gorgeous bloke what works in the breadshop. Shall we go in?" (1988: 13). Such contrasts permeate the text, offering clues to the way poor working-class people sought to offset impoverished circumstances by focusing on conspicuous consumption and the pursuit of pleasure as a way to counter working life. Many of these spaces are rendered anonymous as institutional archetypes akin to other kitchen sink texts, yet their significance denotes class in colorful ways: "We are at a party in a block of LCC flats: plates of ham sandwiches, crates of brown ale and Babysham, the radiogram in the lounge, pop-song oblivion with the volume knob turned to full" (1988: 27). On several occasions, what appears to be a club or a pub is little more than a vacant lot to be inhabited temporarily: "We go through the bricklayers' yard and down some filthy stone steps. The club is an old cellar poshed up with hardboard and flashy paper … Outside in the yard the toilet is aswim with piss" (1988: 29). Like MacInnes's representations of London discussed in the next chapter, the effect is one of a destabilized, perpetually shifting community, with clubs opening and closing with regularity. Dunn's characters navigate these spaces with ease when in each other's company, and the novel creates the sense that they have a grasp over the territory that they inhabit, despite its precarious state.

Aside from the urban nature of the space, its effect on the characters can be aligned to other texts of the period—specifically the way that space reiterates class position while also producing the need to seek alternatives. As a later text, albeit one developed prior to its publishing date, *Up the Junction* responds to shifts underway in British culture that signal the move from austerity to affluence. Stephen Brooke has approached Dunn's novel as an example of "class slumming." He posits that the text presents "class consciousness and identity [as] positional and relational, particularly with regard to consumption, geography and the perception of other classes, rather than only rooted in economic structure" (2012: 431). I would argue that Dunn's text acknowledges a wider turn toward commodity culture as a way to pacify aspects of social neglect. I would also argue that *Up the Junction* is a text more about spatial reclamation—the impulse to make a space one's own and develop new communities based less on spatially driven class assignations and more spatial interaction. As new doors opened for women in the late 1950s and early 1960s, the ability to conceive of one's social position beyond the kind of limits imposed is linked to such opportunities, demonstrating how certain spatial freedoms can lead to entirely new structures of cognition.

Up the Junction, as Henri's introduction clarifies, is "a distillation of experience" (Dunn 1988: XII), one fueled by a search for authenticity that Dunn found through a "symbolic crossing of the River Thames" (1988: XIV) into areas radically different from her own. Although the transformative qualities of Dunn's text are usually associated with the impact of Loach's TV adaptation and the subsequent debate over the 1967 Abortion Act, what is also apparent is how the spaces depicted require their inhabitants to seek out alternative ways of existing. While the text portrays the local color and native vernacular relevant to the area, it also grants a deeper understanding of how inadequate spaces were rethought in a manner that propagates new forms of community to help replace those destroyed by the process of gentrification. Whereas Brooke suggests that the text sidesteps politics and acknowledges class solidarity, any solidarity that exists within the text is contingent and fragmented. Close female bonds are formed in response to spatial limitations in the factory. But such bonds do not produce traditional forms of class solidarity; instead, they lead to a kind of solidarity that exists within loose contours of class. The relationship between Rube, Lily, and Sylvie is structured less on a historical sense of social stratification, and more on the way groups of people carve out new kinds of identities in relation to the physical environments they inhabit and share. The following chapter will explore this idea further, arguing that *Up the Junction* serves as a prime example of the way kitchen sink texts test the limits of geographic confines and, in turn, offer models of class articulation based on negotiations of spatial limits.

Conclusion

What this chapter has sought to illuminate is how the "kitchen sink" of kitchen sink realism signals not just the domestic space in which much of the action takes place, but the surrounding environment that acts as an extension of the home. As noted, working-class communities were designed to situate the worker in close proximity to the factory, generally at the expense of their well-being. From this angle, the institutions affiliated with working-class communities can be seen as performing a similar function as working-class homes, inscribing identity through ideological and programmatic processes. Yet, following Lefebvre's model of spatial production, the working-class subject is granted a degree of agency in their ability to renegotiate identity in space. On the one hand, this can be a process of acquiescence in which the working-class subject resigns themselves to limited opportunities presented in the space. On the other, the novels of the movement reveal how spaces tied to working-class life promote new modes of class consciousness coupled with a sense of autonomy that stands in contrast to the prescriptive nature of spaces such as these. This calls to mind Durkheim's notion of "mechanical solidarity" as well as Pierre Bourdieu's concept of habitus, but it also underscores how the elaboration of a working-class identity is dialectical and contingent rather than as the result of a top-down, imposed process. In the case of *Saturday Night and Sunday Morning* and *Up the Junction*, the fragmented, vignette structure denotes the need for frequent, repetitious descriptions of setting. Yet, the same is true for texts like *This Sporting Life* that follows a more traditional narrative structure while tending to space in detail as well. The upshot is that the kitchen sink era elevates the role of setting not only to reinforce the text's realism but also to introduce the possibility of spatial negotiations. Although the following chapter will explore further the way new forms of identity are made possible through such means, this chapter demonstrates the degree to which the movement's texts position space and place as a crucial component of their aesthetic and ethical agenda.

In doing so, working-class representation is elevated from prior portrayals, especially pertaining to portrayals of class in realist texts of the late nineteenth and early twentieth centuries.

Notes

1. I take up this debate extensively in a forthcoming article on Karel Reisz's film adaptation of *Saturday Night and Sunday Morning*—specifically the role Reisz played in mediating between Sillitoe and the British Board of Film Censorship. The back and forth between the parties involved is as engaging as any of the kitchen sink narratives.
2. Jennings comments that such thinking ran counter to the decimated state of the social psyche following WWI and that the benefit provided was mainly intoxication. "Good for morale," in this sense, can perhaps be read more as "pacifying."
3. By the time Delaney's transfer was approved, she was already fifteen years old—almost at the end of her designated high school years.
4. There is little in the way of biographical writing on Dunn, possibly because, at the time of this book's publication, she is still living. There seems to be no record of the factory where Dunn worked, but the factory scenes of the film (that Dunn helped develop) appear to be The Charterhouse Works in Petergate—now, perhaps unsurprisingly, condos. Similarly, the Battersea Power Station—a statuesque and iconic art deco factory—now houses a "mixed-use neighborhood," or multi-million-pound condos and high-end retail. As of 2022, the Battersea website refers to the power station as "a legendary landmark that's a symbol of hope and positivity" while insisting that prospective residents "Join an incredible line-up of tenants and don't miss out on being part of London's most exciting new destination" ("Battersea Power Station"). In fairness to the current tenants, the building stood vacant and in disrepair when one half was decommissioned in 1975, the other in 1983. While its current state as a "destination" is hardly encouraging, at least the building still stands. Developers have wrapped the building with expensive glass condos—a sort of cladding of the social elite.
5. Cheyne Walk—the same street where George Eliot lived.
6. Dunn commented on the destruction of this aspect of working-class life at the hands of developers who "pulled down all those lovely Battersea cottages, where people had chickens, and dogs, and rabbits and pigeons and gardens, and put up these badly made estates" (Ironside 2003).
7. Of course, the machinic nature of the working-class as part of the means of production is an unmistakable irony.

8   Sillitoe's early, unpublished novels are voluminous, including *By What Road* (1950), *The Man without a Home* (1952–1953), *The Deserters* (1950–1953), *Mr. Allen's Island* (1954), and *The Palisade* (1957). Aside from *By What Road*, the rest were written while abroad with themes of exile and island living threaded throughout. While all show signs of promise, none has the vitality of *Saturday Night and Sunday Morning*, highlighting the impact that Graves's had on Sillitoe's work.

9   This plan—along with much of the first draft of both novels—was written on a reverse page of the typescript for *The Deserters*. This specific page can be found in Mss. II, box 3, folder 15, tab 3 in the Sillitoe Mss. at the Lilly Library, Indiana University, Bloomington, Indiana.

10 The fact that the scene is literally "revolting" is most likely an unintended pun.

11 For more on this, see Tony Collins's 2009 text of the development of rugby in *England: A Social History of English Rugby Union*.

12 It is worth commenting (as the third chapter will argue) that *The Loneliness of the Long Distance Runner*'s protagonist as the kind of cog that breaks the machine.

13 It is wise to note here that *Up the Junction* is a text widely praised for its unambiguous embrace of female sexuality and as one of few texts at the time that depicted women with sexual agency of their own.

14 *The Wednesday Play* series ran on BBC1 from 1964 to 1970 offering weekly television dramas culled from sources such as novels and plays. The series was known for bringing social issues to light through narratives in which taboo topics were highlighted. According the British Film Institute, the series was surprisingly successful in swaying public opinion on topics, and the televised version of *Up the Junction* represents the series at its most controversial, prompting "accusations that it [the series] was deliberately contravening the BBC's pledge of impartiality" (Wake). Parallels can be found between *The Wednesday Plays* and similar productions like *Armchair Theatre*, and a larger discussion of this topic will take place in the fourth chapter as part of my overview of Channel 4 programming.

3

Spatial Transgression and the Working-Class Imaginary

In an interview with Selina Robertson, Nell Dunn discussed her 1959 move from Chelsea to Battersea, commenting that the gritty working-class environments just two miles south felt more "more real" than the relatively privileged neighborhood she shared with her screenwriter husband, Jeremy Sandford. Dunn downplays the politics of the move in response to Robertson's question of whether *Up the Junction* hinges on the practice of class tourism: "It [the move] was no big experimental business, you know ... it didn't have that charge, I liked it and I moved in" (Dunn 2016a). For Sandford, the move was more strategic: "Nell and I had become intrigued by North Battersea, just the other side of the river, at the time one of the poorest parts of London" (2006).[1] Despite Dunn's dismissal of motivating details, Sandford suggests that a drastic shift in living conditions and community was part of the appeal: "It was she who had found us a terraced slum house in Lavender Road that, she decided, would suit us better than the Georgian mansion we occupied on the embankment in Chelsea" (2006). In fact, Sandford claims that the move was deliberate, adding that "Both of us were firmly inhibited by the politically correct socialist ideals of the time and both trying to get away, as we say it, from our privileged backgrounds ... And if there was ever to be a proletarian revolution, North Battersea would be a safer place than Chelsea" (2006). Despite the social, political, and professional advantageousness of the move—a move that *The Daily Express*, Sandford adds, denounced as an affront to the couple's elevated class status—Dunn clearly sensed the community spirit present in the area. Sandford would describe Battersea as poverty-stricken but "also [with] an unexpected feeling of security," akin to a culturally gated community as though "entering an enclosed society where everyone, it seemed, had been to school together and everyone knew each other" (2006). While Sandford concedes that the move was tainted by romantic idealism bordering on class fetishism, the work that the pair produced both before and after the move does indeed reveal how communities and environments marked by neglect can register as sites of vigor and plenitude through a reconceived class consciousness.[2]

This chapter seeks to extend the analysis of spatial metaphors in kitchen sink realism by illustrating how new articulations of classed identity emerge as a consequence of spatial limits. By staging such deliberations, the texts of the period suggest that disaffecting sites can also be experienced as sites of abundance and possibility. Returning to texts discussed previously, this chapter clarifies kitchen sink realism's investment in augmenting aspects of class expression through spatial awareness. Drawing on key theories and concepts associated with "the spatial turn"—specifically, Michel Foucault's heterotopic space and Henri Lefebvre's socially produced space, as well as subsequent evolutions of both concepts advanced by figures such as David Harvey and Edward Soja—the chapter maps the subversive potential of modified social relations through a nuanced comprehension of the way classed spaces are established and upheld. As Lefebvre submits, spaces are produced through an amalgamation of the tangible, the conceptual, and the experiential—the latter introducing subjectivity and relative agency into an otherwise objective framework. By prioritizing the subjective, class-conscious postwar writers show how marginalized spaces can be reimagined as a stage upon which new forms of class insurrection can arise; bomb sites become centers of community, prisons become spaces of independence, and factories become hubs of subcultural provenance. The chapter examines the way texts like Colin MacInnes's *City of Spades*, Alan Sillitoe's *The Loneliness of the Long Distance Runner*, and, once again, Nell Dunn's *Up the Junction* use spatial metaphors to reveal undercurrents of power central to social stratification. It suggests that kitchen sink texts offer ways in which such dynamics can be undermined or, in some cases, reversed. This form of subversive class autonomy—a practice of challenging spatial limits by redefining classed subjecthood—is what I refer to as a "working-class imaginary." The phrase signals a new state of being, demonstrated through spatial motifs and spatial interactions in a number of kitchen sink texts. That said, a "working-class imaginary" should not be read as an attempt to eradicate social class or to simply deny existing models of social stratification; instead, portrayals of subversive spatial negotiations chart new ways of parrying top-down, programmatic class assignation in a manner that responds to the kinds of existential crisis faced by characters such as Sillitoe's Arthur. The texts promote a paradoxical working-class subjectivity which entails existing both within and without the community—a move that anticipates Foucault's heterotopic space as well as Soja's thirdspace. While relatively utopian, the "working-class imaginary" can be read as the upshot of kitchen sink writers' desire to recalibrate the ethical and the aesthetic objectives of realism, underscoring the texts' didactic response to the Welfare State's inability to address social inequality in an adequate manner. By cementing this concept as a central motif of postwar class-conscious writing, this chapter allows for a greater consideration of kitchen sink realism's subsequent impact in the arts and in society itself.

Theorizing Spatial Transgression: From the Production of Space to the Non-Place

The shift toward space and place as a viable approach to literary analysis is regularly understood through Soja's discussion of the "spatial turn" which represents an interdisciplinary attempt to think beyond chronology as an arranging principle in the arts and social sciences. As Leo Mellor writes, "Conceptualising any aesthetic in terms of locale can be useful, since it gives texture to particularity, specificity and the happenstance juxtapositions of geography that could remain obscured" (2011: 3). The use of language like "texture" and "particularity" is common in writing linked to the spatial turn, suggesting how analysis of spatial details has the capacity to reveal certain constructs previously taken for granted or at face value. Mellor continues, "There has recently been the growth of synoptic area studies, and these trace the relationship between literature and the urban experience: with the city as character or at least shaper of a particular consciousness and the possibility of knowledge" (2011: 3). The kind of knowledge produced through spatial awareness is multivalent. But, for the purposes of this study, such knowledge can be understood in terms of negotiating identity as a consequence of space.

As Bertrand Westphal's geocritical methods suggest, fictive representations of place are useful when piecing together an overall perspective of a locale and its occupants' conception of spatial relations. As noted in the introduction, Westphal's approach to analysis stipulates a mode of reading that "seems to be more sensitive to those qualities of spatial and geographical formations that are most difficult to detect from within the established, formalized explanatory frameworks of the physical and social sciences" (2011: 14). Westphal's method proposes that when representations of space in fictional texts are merged with empirical data, the grain and patina of place are clarified. In Westphal's words, this textured depiction is rendered most complete through a composite of the real with the fictional in that the fictional "actualizes new virtualities that had remained unformulated, and then go on to interact with the real according to the hypertextual logic of interfaces ... fiction detects possibilities buried in the folds of the real, knowing that these folds have not been temporalized" (2011: 20).[3] Viewed in this way, what kitchen sink texts offer is something akin to a consensus of lived experience related to working-class life, sanctioned by responses to the movement's representational strategies.

Yet, whereas Westphal excluded spaces that lack a pre-existing body of cultural work, or spaces that cannot be recognized as a registered locale, Eric Prieto amends Westphal's model by showing how *types* of space can work within this framework. Referencing Paul Ricoeur, Prieto writes that "the indirect referentiality of metaphor and fiction, enables them to act as a kind of midwife, drawing nebulous and spatial intuitions out of their conceptual purgatory and making them available for other, nonliterary uses" (2011: 14). So, Westphal argues that sites like domestic space are beyond his purview (what he defines as "non-geographical places" [2011: 119]) while Prieto suggests that *types* of place convey a universal charge comparable to the geographic locations Westphal favors. For Prieto, such an example of *types* might be squatter cities or shanty towns. It is not a stretch, then, to see how spaces like council estates or working-class environs might also produce similar results without having to fully align to Westphal's insistence on an existing body of literature. In this regard, the "knowable communities" discussed in previous chapters act as paralogical discourse that validates comprehensions of working-class life.

In the wake of the spatial turn, scholars across disciplines have increased their dedication to site-specific analysis as a way to consider new modalities of lived experience. Gieseking et al. refer to this as the "geographical imaginary," adding that "As we move through our everyday routines, it is possible to imagine and enact alternative ways of living" through a process that "involves new understandings and representations of our place in the world" (2014: 357). As the authors note, comprehension of spatial production permits certain forms of transgression. This sentiment was explored by both C Wright Mills in the 1960s and David Harvey in the 1970s, particularly through analysis of the ways space is experienced by individuals rather than as a populace. For Gieseking, such an approach acts as "a tool for reaching greater understanding of self and other, while making plans to change the injustices of everyday life" (2014: 357). Gieseking, et al.'s analyses map identity across global continents, but the methods used are structured on concepts formulated by figures who laid the groundwork for the spatial turn.

Henri Lefebvre's pioneering *The Production of Space* centers on the idea of the local environment as socially constructed, a phenomenon understood through tension between three categories. "Perceived space," or "Spatial practice" encompasses the social construction of space—the commonly held understanding of the way a specified space exists in society. In the most reductive sense, perceived space is the physical or material plane of reality. "Conceived space" or "Representations of space," however, exist as imagined space, or the space conceptualized by architects or planners prior to development. "Lived space" or "Representational space" not only registers one's experience of space, but also suggests the kinds of space adaptable for an individual's own needs. Lefebvre contends that such categories should not be considered discretely; instead, they operate dialectically, and attempts to analyze a space should account for all three. The challenge, according to Lefebvre, is that "lived space" is not readily perceptible whereas perceived and conceived space register with ease (1991: 38). What makes comprehension of "lived space" so challenging is the fact that space is experienced passively. A shopping center, for instance, may be understood as a building designed to facilitate consumerism, but the ways in which the space was planned and designed to encourage and increase consumerism are less perceptible to the individual passing through. On the one hand, Lefebvre's conception of what is referred to as a socio-spatial triad posits that there is far more to a space than meets the eye; on the other, it implies that space can be remapped through awareness of spatial production.

As discussed previously, working-class space communicates diminished social status and, in doing so, prescribes behavior and identity. Yet, following Lefebvre's line of thinking, such messaging can be short-circuited and rewired for alternative experiences. Lefebvre refers to this as the recognition of "differential space"—a sort of oppositional negative space that "carries within itself the seeds of a new kind of space" that is inherently productive "inasmuch as abstract space tends toward homogeneity, toward the elimination of existing differences or peculiarities, a new space cannot be born (produced) unless it accentuates differences" (1991: 52). Such "new" spaces are based upon a transformation of social relations in that identification of differential space "will also restore unity to what abstract space breaks up—to the functions, elements and moments of social practice. It will put an end to those localizations which shatter the integrity of the individual body, the social body, the corpus of human needs, and the corpus of knowledge" (1991: 52). Put differently, the identification of differential space can be read as the contestation of social narratives that prescribe behavior.

Lefebvre deems this to be a form of resistance, following the line of thought developed by the Situationists:

> We know what counter-projects consist or what counter-space consists in—because practice demonstrates it. When a community fights the construction of urban motorways or housing-developments, when it demands "amenities" or empty spaces for play and encounter, we can see how a counter-space can insert itself into spatial reality: against the Eye and the Gaze, against quantity and homogeneity, against power and the arrogance of power, against the endless expansion of the "private" and of industrial profitability.
>
> (1991: 381–2)

According to Lefebvre, "counter-spaces" must exist in opposition to, rather than in tandem with, spaces of power. Lefebvre argues that seemingly emancipated spaces are illusionary, often simulating counteraction but with little lasting impact:

> The situation has consequences that seem paradoxical at first. Certain deviant or diverted spaces, though initially subordinate, show distinct evidence of a true productive capacity. Among these are spaces devoted to leisure activity. Such spaces appear on first inspection to have escaped the control of the established order, and thus, inasmuch as they are spaces of play, to constitute a vast "counter-space". This is a complete illusion. The case against leisure is quite simply closed—and the verdict is irreversible: leisure is as alienated and alienating as labour; as much an agent of co-optation as it is itself co-opted; and both an assimilative and an assimilated part of the "system" (mode of production).
>
> (1991: 383)

Such thinking aligns with Paul Willis's work on resignation in *Learning to Labour*, but also adds clarity to the function of the rugby field in Storey's *This Sporting Life* discussed in the previous chapter. Thus, Lefebvre's model of accessing and understanding spatial production constitutes an active and engaged strategy of oppositional behavior rather than simply an attempt to make space palatable. For Lefebvre, what is required is a radical reexamination of the way that spaces are used as well as the interactions that occur within them. Viewed in this way, the objective limitations encoded within space bear the potential to be altered through subjective, subversive intent.

David Harvey considers how space acts as an analog for discussions of capital. He builds on Lefebvre, and his 2012 text *Rebel Cities: From the Right to the City to the Urban Revolution* explores links between urbanism and capitalism in order to uncover differential spaces of contention. He adds that subversive transformations of space must function as a collective endeavor rather than as a practice engaged by discrete individuals (2012: 25). Whereas Lefebvre posits a dialectical triad, Harvey, in a 2006 lecture on the topic, includes three more categories to merge with the original concepts of perceived, conceived, and representational space. In doing so, Harvey allows for a more tangible way of grasping Lefebvre's elusive "representational" category—the immaterial component of space structured upon social interactions.[4]

Harvey's additional categories consist of absolute, relative, and relational space, emphasizing the role of subjectivity as part of the process of spatial production. Absolute space is simply Euclidian space—fixed, rigid, and grid-like. But what distinguishes it from Lefebvre's perceived space is that it combines objectivity with subjective renegotiations. Relative space can be understood as an overlay of absolute space, comprehended as positionality or worldview. Relational space is parsed through consideration of the impact of time on a space. Although Harvey notes that his relational thinking is as slippery and elusive as Lefebvre's, he offers tangible examples of how such analysis might work. In discussing the site of the 2001 World Trade Center attacks, for instance, Harvey shows how the space was transformed physically as well as symbolically in people's minds based on a particular moment in time. By doing so, he confirms that spaces are susceptible to alteration and renegotiation as a consequence of temporal events. This implies that their social meaning or representation can change in ways that are not restricted to the material form alone; a type of space, for example, might be seen in a different light following an incident of a magnitude sufficient enough to register in the cultural imaginary. While Harvey's elaboration of Lefebvre's triad increases complexity, its function is similar. He recommends that such a matrix should not be approached as a tool for the categorization of space but as a way to identify productive tensions as a framework for analysis. This is what Harvey denotes as "aesthetic spaces of transit" (2006a: 9), borrowing the term from the artist, Judith Barry. As Lefebvre's triad alerts us to the hidden complexity of space, it is Harvey's matrix that allows for a way to understand the nature of such complexity with more precision—particularly the more subjective nature of lived experience felt by a community.

Although Michel Foucault's work on space sidesteps concerns of socioeconomic inequality, his methods center on understanding disseminated power. For Foucault, chronological time has always subjugated space in terms of parsing reality, the main reason being that space is experienced as a concrete fact and is therefore accepted at face value. His essay "Of Other Spaces" transpired from a series of lectures given in 1967 outlining how conceptions of space have shifted over time. Here, he discusses the way space was initially understood through a structuralist lens: a church is a church because it is not a store. Spatial awareness grew, he claims, alongside fifteenth-century painting's devotion to depth of field, suggesting proximity as an aspect of space unto itself. He maintains, though, that it was during the Enlightenment era that chronology supplanted space as a dominant metric of analysis. "Of Other Spaces" is invested in a pre-Enlightenment consideration of spatial proximity, specifically focusing on the significance of space between two points as a way to unify binaries and conceive of them as a single, reciprocal phenomenon. To make this claim, he focuses on spaces that hold strange, dualistic relations to one another with the example being that of a mirror. A mirror, he argues, provides a virtual replica of the real yet it exists within the real, and the combined real/virtual abstraction is what he refers to as "heterotopic space"—spaces that act as a counter to their original intention through reversal or neutralization. Contrasting Lefebvre's "perceived" or Harvey's "absolute" space, heterotopic space is theorized as a manifestation of space that somehow rebels against the space considered most tangible. In this light, heterotopic space acts as potentiality—a space that operates within the confines of tangible space but offers a kind of alternative that unsettles and disturbs standard perception. Heterotopias, when fully realized and consciously accessed, can act as gestures of reclamation and resistance to dominant norms and ideology made manifest through the built environment.

Soja's concept of thirdspace realigns Foucault's heterotopia with socioeconomic concerns. Introduced in the 1996 book of the same name, the notion of thirdspace is grounded in contingency, following Lefebvre's representational space and amplifying the complexity of its potential. Thirdspace is understood through its relation to first and secondspace, with firstspace most closely aligned to Lefebvre's perceived space or Harvey's absolute space. Firstspace represents tangible, objective comprehensions of space. Secondspace is similar to Lefebvre's conceived space in that it registers an awareness of a space distinct from the tangible (the experience we may gain of a place by reading travel brochures, for example). Thirdspace posits an active combination of first and secondspace. Soja's concept is, like much of the spatial turn, an attempt to undermine dominant epistemologies of spatial experience through the insertion of critical, speculative potentiality into more rational, naturalized comprehensions of working-class environs. Distinct from the dialectical tensions of Lefebvre's triad or Harvey's matrix, Soja's thirdspace seeks to integrate the perceptual with the conceptual to construct a third entity. One example is the Orientalist notion of the way the west produced the east.

By manipulating perceptual representations of the east as a conceptualized, exocitized other, the west not only transforms the east into a thirdspace but transforms itself in the process. If the process of Othering the east is done in the service of delineating the west as superior, then the same process of combining the perceptual with the conceptual is identified. In "thirding" the east, the west colonizes itself as a geographic reality that is reliant upon its own imagination and image-making.

Soja's thirdspace resembles Foucault's desire to reconcile spaces "strangely" related which, in turn, recalls an impulse in kitchen sink realism to reinscribe sites of class identification. While Foucault's conception of the heterotopia conveys the potential for political subversion, it is first and foremost a space that acts on the individual by defamiliarizing the environment as a means to disarticulate the self. In the case of the mirror, the author finds himself erased: "In the mirror, I see myself there where I am not, in an unreal, virtual space that opens up behind the surface; I am over there, there where I am not, a sort of shadow that gives my own visibility to myself, that enables me to see myself there where I am absent" (1986: 4). Although destabilizing, the upshot of heterotopic space is that it separates the subject from normative temporal and spatial orders, thus revealing new potentialities. For Soja, thirdspace is more of an event than an effect. As such, it corroborates Lefebvre and Harvey's claims that for a spatial revolution to occur, counter spaces must be established and understood collectively rather than experienced individually. And this is perhaps the fundamental distinction between the two: that thirdspace is a tool by which to comprehend geographic makeup whereas heterotopic space represents a later turn in Foucault's work centered on "technologies of the self," or autonomous self-care. If kitchen sink texts' emphasis on spatial interactivity offers insight into new forms of class articulation, then it is evident why such conceptions of spatial rethinking help delineate this salient thematic of the movement.

Building on similar principles of heterotopic space is Marc Augé's conception of "non-places" outlined in *Non-Places: An Introduction to the Anthropology of Supermodernity*. Here, Augé discusses sites of transience that produce dissociative effects. If a space can be comprehended as a physical location and a place understood as space with an attached social narrative, then Augé's conception of a non-place rests on the idea that certain spaces fail as places because they repel the kind of interactions that grant them meaning (2009: 77–8). The kind of spaces that Augé deems "non-place" are defined as liminal, transitional sites like airports, freeways, and corridors—spaces of movement required to transition from one identity-forming destination to another. In this sense, Augé's work builds on Foucault's interest in the exploration of proximal, in-between spaces, but his argument centers on globalization and a networked society. For Augé, a place (as opposed to a non-place) is one produced by history, social relations, and identity; the non-places that connect them, by contrast, are figured as alienating. However, as Augé adds, non-places are also sites that strip the individual of character, deeming all who enter as anonymous and relatively equalized. Despite the purportedly equalizing nature of spaces like those outlined by Augé pointing toward something like a classless society, it is important to keep in mind that such sites are non-places—places that exist outside of the realm of sites that hold meaning. While Augé would most likely view a site like a council estate as a destination in which identities are formed and maintained, their precarious nature situates them more with the transitory protocols of the non-place. Augé's project centers on material representations of capitalism and its effect on the individual, but the kind of environments considered a non-place certainly resemble a number of postwar spaces developed in Britain like council estates and makeshift housing. When Augé describes such spaces as spaces designed to be "passed through" (2009: 104), it is wise to recall that much of the housing developed in the postwar era was meant to be temporary. Given the inherent promise of social elevation implicit in the rise of the Welfare State, council housing can perhaps be read as transitory—a *non-place* that one momentarily inhabits while on the path to a more substantial destination.

Such theorizing of space as adaptable and transgressive is worthwhile in terms of understanding the impact of spatial representation in postwar texts—especially texts engaged with social identity. For Lefebvre and Harvey, spaces are not simply the result of their physical components; they are produced by social interactions and power relations. The growth of mass housing was a necessity of the immediate postwar years to meet the needs of the housing crisis. But, comprehending such processes as an example of "spatial production" raises concerns about the magnanimity of such projects. Foucault, Soja, and Augé add texture to such ideas by presenting frameworks to understand the more abstract manifestations of social space. What is perhaps most vital in this discussion is the idea that space can be contested and challenged without necessarily changing the physical environment. By understanding how environments are produced, and potentially undermining said production through subversive, alternative conceptions of a given space, and individual can potentially short-circuit a site's programmatic intent. Arguably, the texts of the kitchen sink era allow for such consideration, principally because of the way they construct working-class spaces with precision and cast their characters as models of spatial transformation. What follows are studies of a number of sites endemic to working-class communities that, in some manner, possess the potential for subversive thought.

Transgressive Space and Postwar Potentiality

The kind of sites conspicuous in postwar working-class communities exceeds the kind of dominant institutional spaces explored in the second chapter. Yet, the sites discussed here represent environments that align with the ideas central to the spatial turn—sites rife with transformative potential. Whereas the pub, the factory, and the school generally denote sites associated with powerful ideological forces, ruins, underground clubs, public facilities, and leisure space tend to denote a greater degree of flexibility in terms of use, function, and transgressive potential. The texts of the era, I suggest, offer examples of sites that are reclaimed as zones of arbitration in a gesture that indicates ways in which postwar working-class identities might confront and challenge the more prescriptive, ideological messages circulated through the built environment.

For instance, one recurring space of note is that of the bomb site—a residual reminder not just of the Blitz but also of the dearth of resources available to rehouse and repair impoverished communities in inner-city areas. From 1940 to 1941, air raids conducted by the German Luftwaffe targeted a number of British cities with the capital seeing the greatest concentrated damage—specifically the attacks that began on September 7 in which the city was bombed for seventy-six consecutive nights with just one day of respite (Bullock 2002: 4). In London alone, the bombing resulted in more than 20,000 deaths and, by October of that same year, the Blitz had left 25,000 citizens homeless and in need of shelter (Bullock 2002: 4). The initial damage was especially felt in the east side of the capital, but by September, the attacks had moved west, spreading out into the more suburban areas and culminating in the most expansive attack on October 15. Northern industrial regions were prominent targets with Birmingham, Sheffield, and Manchester—cities known for their industry and economic vigor—subjected to a series of raids. While the main targets were factories and transportation hubs such as ports, by the end of the attacks, two million homes were destroyed. In areas like Manchester, historic landmarks were also ruined, and well-established working-class communities were similarly devastated with regions like Salford losing more than 8,000 homes.

Although bombed-out buildings might ordinarily lead to abandonment, a general acquaintance with dereliction as a classed inevitability (perhaps stemming from ineffectual slum-clearance projects) rendered such sites as part and parcel of the postwar landscape. Rather than avoid the bomb sites' implicit dangers, city dwellers incorporated bombsites into the new landscape and eventually recast them as spaces of aesthetic interest and productive engagement. Commenting on a shifting public opinion about bombsites, Leo Mellor notes how

> For while every bombsite could be a useful metaphor and also a unique ruin, en masse they were to become an unavoidable fact on the ground, and a manifestation of how modern warfare literalised the phrase "Home Front" with violence. As time passed they could be aestheticised into picturesque ruins or politicised through surrealism, observed through the templates of archeology or natural history or the phantasmagoric—or merely played on by children.
>
> (2011: 2)

Whereas Mellor's extended argument points toward modernism's reliance on themes of decay, he also registers the temporal shock achieved through radical shifts in the environment in that:

> bombsites contain absolute doubleness. They are inherently both a frozen moment of destruction made permanent; as much as they capture the absolute singular moment, the repeated cliché of the stopped clock exposed, battered blast but still affixed to a wall in a bombsite: yet they also act as a way of understanding a great swathe of linear time previously hidden or buried, offering history exposed to the air.
>
> (2011: 6)

Destruction and social decay would have been naturalized as part of the postwar urban landscape by the time the kitchen sink texts took hold, making bomb sites rather ordinary, therefore positioning them well as sites of narrative class renegotiation.

Mentioned prior, John Braine's *Room at the Top* depicts bombing and its impact as a metaphorical reminder of social and familial dereliction. Joe Lampton is an orphan, his parents killed when their home is destroyed by "Dufton's one and only bomb" (1980: 82). For Joe, the bombsite is uncanny and heterotopic, "a gap where our house had stood" (1980: 98), calling to mind Harvey's discussion of the way spaces change meaning following certain destructive events. Joe recollects the moment as though it played out like a film, granting it the title of "the Bad

Morning, the Death Morning," describing the now-transformed structure as an abject deformity: "The pavement had been roped off that morning: among the debris was the bathroom mirror, which somehow had survived the explosion and seemed to wink derisively in the August sun, as if it had survived at my parents' expense" (1980: 98). Furthermore, the space demarcates class distinctions. As Joe contrasts the destruction of Dufton ("Dirty Dufton, Dreary Dufton, Despicable Dufton" [1980: 104]) with his new, socially elevated life in Worley ("Worley had shown me a new way of living; for the first time I'd lived in a place without memories. And for the first time *lived* in a place" [1980: 104, emphasis original]), it is certain that Braine employs the bombsite as a metaphor for working-class communities long since abandoned yet still inhabited. In Jack Clayton's 1959 film adaptation, when Joe returns to Dufton, it is characterized by clichéd social markers: children playing on piles of rubble, covered in filth, entertaining each other with remnants from bombed-out buildings. In this sense, Mellor's commentary of the way bomb sites became part and parcel of the postwar landscape recalls the way poverty itself was naturalized and accepted. By foregrounding such spaces, texts like *Room at the Top* illuminate the classed dimensions of space, particularly the way such sites operate as reminders of neglect. Yet, in the process of doing so, the texts of the movement reveal the heterotopic potential of such sites, suggesting how they might function as a stage upon which to perform new articulations of self.

Analogous to the repurposing of derelict space, underground and illicit clubs serve a similar function and appear in a number of the period's texts. While the history of underground clubs in twentieth-century Britain is expansive, the 1950s and 1960s mark a time in which their popularity and subversive value coalesce. Although pubs dominate the texts under analysis due to their conspicuous place in British culture, clubs featured in work by figures such as Colin MacInnes offer new ways of comprehending social relations and spatial production.

The preposition "underground" is instructive in that it implies a subjugated space but also one cast into the margins. Dave Haslam claims that the blueprint for the British club can be located within the genre of the music hall with the earliest nightclub dating back to the mid-1840s (2015: 1). But it was the rise of the jazz club in the 1920s that provides the earliest manifestation of what is understood as a nightclub today. Referencing the Hambone—a club founded in 1922 in Soho's Ham Yard, Haslam points out how one attendee, Trevor Allen, incorporated the club into a novel called *We Loved in Bohemia* (1953), prompting a reviewer to recount the space as a "shrine of anti-convention and the home of talented rebels" (2015: 2). According to Maurice Bottomley, the Hambone was just one of several clubs occupying the space at 41 Great Windmill Street with as many as ten separate clubs operating there through the 1920s and 1930s (2012). Bottomley adds that the Hambone was the most notorious, drawing an exclusively bohemian crowd from the arts including the painter Augustus John and the poet Radclyffe Hall. Although the Hambone's legacy endured, and the Ham Yard went on to house one of London's most famous clubs of the 1960s (The Scene), multifunctional and dynamic sites like the Ham Yard reflect the transitory and ephemeral form of underground clubs more broadly.

WWII led to a general decline in club activity, and a number of the nightclubs of the 1920s and 1930s saw damage from bombing. Yet, in the successive postwar years, clubs like the 100 Club on Oxford Street emerged and, by the mid-1960s, club life was in full swing once more. Colin MacInnes's London trilogy—*City of Spades* from 1957, *Absolute Beginners* from 1959, and *Mr Love and Justice* from 1960—document of the role of underground clubs in the postwar capital, with *City of Spades*, in particular, focusing on the way illicit clubs and patterns of immigration intersect.[5] This sequence of texts provides a tour of London's most diverse and energized areas, emphasizing the value of the underground as a sanctuary. In addition, the texts stress the need for clubs to remain ephemeral and makeshift as a response to police harassment. MacInnes was familiar with the intricacies of Black underground clubs like the Hambone, devoting a chapter in *City of Spades* to a fictional club called The Moonbeam in an obscure location: "Soon we reached the outskirts of Soho; and being already, as I imagined, one of the freemasonry of the street coloured underground, I did not hesitate to ask the way to the Moonbeam club from any dark face I saw" (2005: 73). The space's illicit and enigmatic nature is reiterated by the narrator, Montgomery Pew's remark that, "But never had I thought that the bombed site across the way contained, by night, in its entrails, the Moonbeam club" (2005: 74). Montgomery continues to note how the war-torn space was repurposed as a space of cultural vitality, claiming that "the horrid little restaurant was dark and shuttered, and the bombed site alive with awnings, naked lights, and throngs of coloured men" (2005: 74). The club itself—an empty basement, marked only by "past coloured photographs of American Negro singers and white starlets" (2005: 75)—sells no alcohol, only sodas, teas, and coffees, affirming its underground status through its inability to receive a license. As the novel progresses, rumors are heard of clubs raided and shut down, only to open once more in other underground spaces. In this regard, MacInnes's text depicts the way that, despite the popularity and prevalence of nightclubs at the time, an underground movement served the marginalized through the use of spaces considered outside the norm.

Despite their illicit and makeshift nature, London underground clubs dominated night life in England throughout much of the 1950s and 1960s. In northern England, though, new kinds of clubs formed in response as the cosmopolitan nature of the capital maligned London clubs as elitist and exclusive. Such attitudes are linked to the rise of the Northern Soul movement in industrial towns in which spaces ordinarily designated for more parochial events (bingo nights for the elderly, for instance) were recast as sites where youth subculture could flourish. Spaces affiliated with Northern Soul like the Wigan Casino or the Blackpool Mecca were less makeshift than their London counterparts, generally recognized as shared-community buildings housing a range of local and community-based events. Other venues were composed of repurposed buildings tied to industry, like the Wolverhampton Catacombs—a space that, despite the name connoting the capital's underground clubs, occurred on the second floor of an old lead smelting plant in the area where the furnaces once stood. Of import to this discussion is that the clubs accompanying the rise of subcultures exist less as defined spaces that hold events and more as defined events taking shape in existing spaces. In other words, the meaning and purpose of an existing space are transformed. In turn, this highlights the potential of marginalized groups to form social connections through the appropriation and reclamation of sites designed to serve other functions. It also highlights the need to create spaces of sociality and belonging beyond spaces designated for such activities. That texts like MacInnes's trilogy outline such interactions reaffirms the era's emphasis on spatial formations and means by which to renegotiate social positions.

Anne Power has shown how young people—most notably those in disadvantaged communities lacking resources—use public facilities as a means to establish identity. This, Power adds, can lead to generational conflict in that spaces such as these are shared by a range of community members (2007: 85). Public spaces and facilities designed for momentary assembly like bus stops, phone boxes, street corners, parks, and benches—as well as spaces less frequented, like abandoned buildings, warehouses, or railroad tracks—are claimed by such groups for social activity, especially in areas that lack dedicated opportunities for sociality by other means. Power remarks that such sites are habitually marked by graffiti or damage as a gesture of territoriality, creating the impression of youthful disobedience and reinforcing class stereotypes of delinquency. While antisocial behavior is hardly commensurate with a particular generation or a regional demographic, claiming space through marking can be understood as an extension of the behavioral sink concept discussed in the first chapter: regions that fail to cater to burgeoning identities lead individuals to seek out nontraditional spaces of identity formation instead. As Brad Beaven has commented, the practice of socializing in transitory space is frequently tied to the nineteenth-century term, "hooligan"—a term limited not just to youthful loitering but characterized instead by "the culmination of twenty or thirty years of city life, a symbol of the growing lawlessness that seemed endemic to urban living" (2005: 115). Yet the term's usage considers antisocial behavior as innate rather than symptomatic of spatial and class-based abandonment, part and parcel of a younger generation's apparent disregard for traditional values. Kitchen sink texts tend to juxtapose young people against the previous generation, one frequently resigned to their homes, their work place, or their local pub. Although such practices are generally aligned with young people, it is also possible to consider the way that working-class people more broadly, whose environments lack similar resources for socialization, carve out spaces designated for other activities on their own terms.

British psychologist Tony Gibson has argued that delinquency—specifically in young, working-class men—is understood as part of the process of developing a moral compass. He suggests that "To ask what is the cause of juvenile delinquency is to pose the wrong question" adding instead how "one might ask why such behavior is refrained from so often by so many people" (1993: 105). Gibson is interested in the production of a socially conscripted conscience, arguing how a young person develops a sense of right and wrong not through scolding but through the threat of losing the approval of an authority figure: "If the child grows up in a condition of affectionate emotional dependence on his parents [sic] withdrawal of parental approval is a very strong sanction" (1993: 106). Therefore, if the child is deprived of affectionate emotional connections, then the consequences or penalties that might stem from acts of delinquency carry less weight. Gibson adds that a "Society gets the delinquency rate it deserves" (1993: 107), suggesting how behavioral problems are as much a consequence of space as that of supposed parental neglect. Logic would dictate that the moral abandon stemming from a lack of parental affection would apply to an environment that demonstrates a similar lack of concern. That is to say, if the environment fails to convey an interest in an adolescent's wellbeing through resources or sites of productive socialization, then, following Gibson's thinking, not only would there be little allegiance to the environment, but possibly even disdain for it. Public spaces like bus stops, street corners, lamp posts—spaces that can operate as hubs of sociality for young working-class people deprived of resources and dedicated social space—are frequently defaced or destroyed through delinquency. Hence, it is possible to understand how such acts might be comprehended as a response to a perceived form of abandonment caused by the environment itself. Desecration of public space reflects a combination of a classed responses: the marking of territory as an effort to claim it for one's own social purpose; the lack of consequences Gibson alludes to above from emotionally engaged authority figures; and the transference of animosity to a municipal signifier as a gesture of contempt for an environment that fails to support their needs. Perhaps one of the most well-recognized icons of British culture and traditional heritage is the red telephone box. It should be no surprise that such icons were vandalized with regularity. So, while spaces designated for public use are repurposed in ways that counter their original function, the reasons for doing so suggest attempts to adopt a space as one's own in addition to other complex reasons tied to a perceived sense of class-based abandonment.

As Willis notes in *Learning to Labour*, sites of recreation and leisure not only offer a momentary respite from work but also tend to assuage challenges to the status quo. For Willis, the upkeep of the labor force is structured upon the upkeep of a reward system in which the worker is momentarily pacified through commodity culture and leisure activities. Peter Borsay describes how, following the shift from austerity to the era of affluence, an increase in leisure activity corresponds to heightened income and the general perception of improved economic conditions (2006: 88). Furthermore, Borsay identifies connections between leisure activities and the sustenance of the local community in that "Investing in the community was a practical way of safeguarding against the risk of falling seriously into poverty, providing a support network that could be called upon when times proved difficult" (2006: 87). In the texts of the kitchen sink era, such developments are registered but critiqued in that a number of the characters participate in the practices outlined by Willis while aligning themselves with communities in a manner similar to Borsay's claim. Sillitoe's *Saturday Night and Sunday Morning* is a good example in that the protagonist thrives on conspicuous consumption and heavy drinking as though these practices were a leisure activity. Borsay registers such incidents, certifying how

> Heavy drinking and rowdiness have also been frequently associated with the lower orders, and although the accusations of drunkenness and violence were regularly deployed as a tool to stigmatize the common people, there is little reason to doubt that generous corporate and public consumption of alcohol and high levels of inter-personal and inter-communal violence were woven closely into the fabric of (at least male) popular leisure.
>
> (2006: 87–8)

In this regard, the kind of affordances offered as a means by which to offset insubordinate desire is replicated through leisurely practices and leisure space.

Activities and pastimes affiliated with working-class culture of the 1950s and the 1960s generally revolved around the affordances permitted to pacify revolutionary potential. Designated spaces might include sites carved out for gambling or outdoor areas marked for community sports such as cricket and fishing. Churches and working-men's clubs would also serve to house weekly entertainment events like bingo night and dances. Yet, such forms of leisure activity are marked by rigid geographic limits that often position them within a general working-class vicinity. Given that such activities grant little in the way of cultural tutelage or, perhaps, an introduction to the arts, the repetition of relatively mindless leisure activities underscores the imperative behind Willis's claim: that working leisure activities worked to placate under the guise of reward. Borsay emphasizes this effect, claiming that

> Working-class pastimes might be seen as the surviving vestiges of a pre-rational, pre-Enlightenment culture, characterized not only by roughness, but also by a deep conservatism, an emphasis upon oral and visual modes of communication rather than literacy, and a naive dependence upon luck, fate, and magical forms of explanation.
>
> (2006: 88)

In Borsay's view, working-class leisure spaces and activities emerge as a shared experience akin to an atavistic celebration of a community albeit one marked by immobility (2006: 174). Yet, kitchen sink texts articulate how such sites and practices still carry the potential for transcendent thinking, at least with regard to the way class consciousness was experienced. In essence, the era's texts document such moves and ear-mark them for critical inquiry.

According to Brad Beaven, the British government's interest in developing leisure activities increased following WWI. This interest, Beaven observes, corresponded to reports of the failure of borstals to successfully rehabilitate young working-class people. From this, the state's interest in leisure activities and the availability of sites designated for sociality can be comprehended as a hypothetical mechanism of behavior modification (2005: 163). The kind of state-sponsored leisure spaces built during this time included sports facilities constructed in proximity to new communities, multi-purpose community centers, and open expanses of space designed to function as hubs of sociality. As Beaven registers, the emphasis on building leisure sites devoted to physical development—at least during the interwar years—is linked to eugenics and nationalism, aligning physical health and well-being with the symbolic health of the body politic. Furthermore, David Downes has suggested that the kind of spaces designated for outdoor activities historically favored more prosperous regions with resources in poorer areas paling by comparison. In other words, leisure space developed as part of a state-sponsored mandate to improve the general health of British citizens implies a biopolitical function in that such spaces became "classed." According to Downes, the classed nature of state-sponsored recreational space required working-class people to adopt pastimes more aligned with the principle of "do-it-yourself"—a form of self-sufficient entertainment and recreation beyond spaces assigned for such activities. While access to recreational facilities illuminates aspects of social inequality, Downes points out how participation in sports acted as a way to establish class equilibrium (2013: 134). This is perhaps most clear in Sillitoe's *The Loneliness of the Long Distance Runner* in that the cross country race Colin and his borstal participate in is not against a neighboring borstal or a working-class community, but against a prestigious public school that serves to highlight class distinction. It is a text that recognizes the implications of state-sponsored leisure and proposes a model that seeks to undermine such efforts. The kind of leisure spaces represented in kitchen sink texts, then, can be interpreted as potentially transgressive and valuable in terms of framing the challenges seen in a text like Storey's *This Sporting Life* in which a socially elevated character such as Frank Machin struggles to adapt to an economically elevated position. Given this, Lefebvre's comments on leisure space bear repeating: "leisure is as alienated and alienating as labour; as much an agent of co-optation as it is itself co-opted; and both an assimilative and an assimilated part of the 'system' (mode of production)" (1991: 383).

Perhaps the most common municipal site of recreation is the public park, the full history of which extends beyond the purview of this chapter. That being said, given their periodic representation in the texts of the kitchen sink movement, parks are worth brief consideration in terms of their subversive and transgressive potential. In ways, public parks resemble other spaces discussed so far in that they act as symbolic representations of a community's health and its connection to the nation as a whole. While Ebenezer Howard's Garden City movement—an example of urban planning prioritizing natural, recreational space—is linked to early reformist utopianism, the intention was to counter the overcrowding and pollution of urban industrial centers. Originally formulated in the late nineteenth century, Howard's proposal failed to receive government support, leaving him to purchase land and develop the concept alone. The Garden City movement never took hold, but it laid the groundwork for the postwar New Towns movement also designed to address concerns of overcrowding and congestion. Headed by Frederic J. Osborn, the New Towns movement incorporated much of Howard's emphasis on intentional zoning. In the same way designated recreational spaces formed a major component of Garden City plans, the New Towns stressed the social function of communal space through the incorporation of public parks, playgrounds, and shopping centers. Even though Howard's utopian ideals hoped to mix social groups, the New Towns movement would mirror British society as it stood in the moment, rendering new developments as predominantly classed and segregated, tied to slum-clearance and postwar rehousing (Aldridge 1979: 106). Wealthier suburban areas were guaranteed parks and verdant recreational space, but less-wealthy sites focused more on maximizing residential units in order to address the housing crisis. As such, council estates, for example, saw less emphasis on open social spaces and considerably less maintenance in ensuing years. The expansion of more economically conservative urban plans designed to house the working-poor was more likely to skimp on elements aimed at heightening social interaction.

As the first chapter argues, new developments aimed at rehousing those displaced by slum clearance and WWII damage tended to prioritize occupancy over resources. Less-prosperous projects would see shopping centers reduced to one or two basic stores (usually a liquor store or a betting shop). Similarly, spaces meant for communal activities were scaled back, resources for children such as playgrounds were minimized and prone to neglect, and central parks were replaced by unfinished cement zones since they required no municipal upkeep. Somewhat ironically, any patches of green or natural space tended to be accidental—little more than space that escaped planning or development. The result is that the recreational space made available for working-class people in the communities they inhabited could be read as an index of their social position—a material signifier of their worth in relation to the rest of the country's postwar urban design.

However, parks and public spaces in the texts of the kitchen sink movement challenge such limitations by depicting recreational space as sites of transgressive potentiality. For instance, Stan Barstow's 1960 novel *A Kind of Loving* describes the town's central park as a space split between generations. In the novel, daytime activity is generally attributed to an older generation who use the park for its intended purposes. At night, the space is inhabited by a younger generation who use it as backdrop against which to carve out postwar identities. Yet, much of the text centers on protagonist Vic Brown's fantasy of moving into the new estates on the edges of the town, largely due to their modern appeal and their promise of private outdoor space: "I look up at this little modern semi standing up above the road with the garden tumbling down to the fence. Two thousand five-hundred at today's prices, I reckon" (2010: 61). Throughout the novel, the park is presented as a space of illicit interaction, be it intimate meetings with Ingrid Rothwell ("This is the worst time of year for open-air courting and Ingrid and I mostly go to the pictures on our night out. But now and again, we just have to go into the park, even if it's only a shelter" [2010: 233]), or as a site of negotiation where plans for their subsequent pregnancy can be determined. In this regard, the park operates as a multivalent site of social interaction based on privacy, granting a move away from the more communal aspects of the local environment.

Yet, the idea of community formed and sustained through shared space also shifts in the postwar period with new developments and a lack of social resources reflecting a turn toward more private, insular lives that speak to a hypothetical breakdown of shared working-class identity. This can be seen in *A Kind of Loving* in that new estates act as a mark of social elevation. It is further defined by increased autonomy and atomization registered through the appeal of personal, private green space, the aforementioned "garden tumbling down to the fence" (2010: 61). Early parts of the text pinpoint confinement and restriction, expressed through Vic and Ingrid's sharing a home with her parents after the news of her pregnancy. This overcrowding produces a desire for freedom that, in Vic's mind, is something that must be achieved on the outskirts of the community—essentially a home with a small, private park that only he and Ingrid can inhabit. In this sense, the novel's emphasis on recreational space as a site of intimacy and arbitration suggests how spaces such as these can be mobilized to conceive of new articulations of self; in the case of Vic and Ingrid, as a family who "makes do" with their current predicament. So, the park's intended use as shared, community space is transformed in a manner that echoes modifications underway in terms of the way working-class life was understood and experienced.

Changes in the postwar landscape that assisted in transforming shared, communal working-class space into something akin to fragmented, atomized sites underscore the necessity of new articulations of self. Arguably, this is one of kitchen sink realism's most dominant thematics: the way new conceptions of classed identity transpire relative to transformations in the built environment. Yet, whereas such plans for postwar redevelopment imply a prescriptive set of class delineations, the texts of the period suggest ways of existing that push back against plans and designs that might otherwise inform identity. In this light, the way space and spatial production are discussed by writers like Lefebvre, Harvey, Soja, Foucault, and Augé allows for a reconceptualization of the way kitchen sink writers of the time grasped the significance of environment in terms of shifting class consciousness. For example, the need for underground clubs to remain fluid—conceptual rather than fully realized and fixed—folds multiple transgressive practices into a single space. Furthermore, Foucault's notion of heterotopic space is perceptible in that underground clubs exist within a culture that would ordinarily denounce such cultural insurgency and subversion. Depictions of space in kitchen sink texts reveal how negotiations of space act as a counter to heterodox environments—a spatial form of emancipation stemming from the inequities of social division and class. What follows is analysis of three prominent texts of the time to demonstrate how writers understood working-class identities as active and pliable rather than as fixed and prescriptive. By viewing the texts in this manner, it becomes increasingly clear that the kitchen sink realism movement surpassed mimetic portrayals associated with the realist mode; rather, it modeled and proposed new ways of articulating one's class position through creative and innovative engagements with space.

Spatial Transgression and the Working-Class Imaginary in *Up the Junction*

As mentioned in the previous chapter, Dunn's *Up the Junction* preexisted its 1963 publication date as a series of vignettes, several of which were published in The New Statesman. The text was inspired by the British documentary filmmaker Dennis Mitchell, who instructed the author to "keep very close to [her] material" and to "be absolutely true in [her] observation" (Dunn 2013a). Mitchell's own credo was to use vernacular to "give voice to the voiceless"—a motif clearly aligned with Dunn's aesthetic. While the text underlines cultural changes afoot in such a way that it reflects other publications of the time, *Up the Junction* offers a glimpse into new forms of women's labor and the female bonds consolidating around assembly line work. Whereas other texts emphasize alienation and stasis related to male-dominated working-class communities, Dunn's text presents a world that is less confined and limiting due, in part, to its willingness to explore transgressive modes of being in working-class space.

Much of *Up the Junction* is set in and around a small working-class community, yet the characters leave their local milieu often to travel into neighboring areas. In doing so, Dunn contours territory and marks difference between "home" and "away." Stephen Brooke has commented on this demarcation, arguing that Dunn's text "represents 1960s London as a city whose internal borders continue to be based on a strong sense of class difference" (2012: 431). Geographic boundaries are not merely the result of arbitrary divisions, though; where industry is present, a working-class neighborhood will likely exist. In northern industrial communities, demarcations are less definitive in that entire towns appear structured with labor in mind. In urban sprawls, boundaries were often drawn territorially as part of the community. As an area known for landmark power station as well as its copious railroads, Battersea was destined to be a working-class community. As Brooke suggests, geographic and physical boundaries are bolstered by ideological delineations which validate the idea of class as a spatial phenomenon: "Within that boundary, Dunn presents a recognizable, resilient and autonomous working class shaped by both the past and the present" (2012: 431). Viewed in this way, the region the novel centers on can be read as emblematic of Lefebvre's claim of space as a social product in that the area was conceived of as a site of labor, it exists as one in reality, but it is also a site in which working-class sensibilities coalesce to form an implied boundary of their own based on shared experience. Given this, it might be said that the text's engagement with space is one of the more salient examples of Lefebvre's lived experience—space made manifest through collective action and shared beliefs.

However, it should be understood that the community that Dunn's protagonist, Lily, experiences is hardly monolithic; the space connotes a subcategory of class, or a new conception of working-class identities marked by creative emancipatory impulses. The space is classed, but it is also a subversive, heterotopic space in that the women of the novel reject the class and gender-based expectations prescribed. Through their actions, the characters of *Up the Junction* transform the working-class environment into a working-class utopia that meets their own needs at any given moment. Despite this, tension still exists between the imagined environment and its class-based limits. The text mobilizes new articulations of lived experience in response while also drawing attention to municipal lack in a manner that enacts tangible change.

Dunn's text was celebrated for its thematic content, building on the kitchen sink movement's drive to feature topical concerns as part of its realist motif. *Up the Junction* saw an extraordinary backlash from morality groups with the noted fundamentalist critic Mary Whitehouse demonizing Ken Loach's 1965 adaptation, arguing that the abortion scene should serve as moral warning to young women that "clean living could cut out a great deal of this problem at the root" (1967: 168). The issue that Whitehouse and other conservative voices took was that the narrative celebrated women's autonomy and agency. But as was the case with other texts of the period, the outrage was a front for more deep-seated discomfort with the elevation of working-class life. While the abortion scene is usually what the text is remembered for, it broke new ground in terms of depicting women as free agents whose labor grants them access to the world the novel portrays. In an interview, Dunn cited the influence of Betty Freidan's *The Feminine Mystique* (1963) and Germaine Greer's *The Female Eunuch* (1970) (Dunn 2016a). Yet, *Up the Junction* predates such works, suggesting that liberatory ideals were already well underway as part of a cultural zeitgeist. As outlined in the previous chapter, shifts in the postwar workforce resulted in higher employment for women in factories and a subsequent alteration of domestic norms. And this is what *Up the Junction* captures so saliently, and part of the reason why critics such as Whitehouse took issue.

Aside from the abortion scene, the novel addresses women's rights in society by staging a cast of characters who reject traditional domestic roles and take ownership of their lives. As Nicola Wilson has written, "the flip side of the home in Dunn's fiction entails entrapment for married women" (2015: 161), and much of the novel's action and the general freedom that the characters express through the use of coarse language are carried out in non-domestic, or at least nontraditional forms of domestic space. The text promotes an alternative to the mid-century British woman as passive housewife, emphasizing instead a rejection of traditional domestic roles and reiterating Delaney's transgressive themes from *A Taste of Honey* in the process. Furthermore, the use of vernacular not only upsets established literary norms; it grants ascendancy to local color in a manner that defies historically stereotypical representations of regional accents by making them dominant within the text. In this sense, dialect contours space more than prescribed social roles and positions. The themes and topics in *Up the Junction* galvanize ideas put forth in other texts tied to the era while challenging the limited function of the "Angry Young Man" moniker. It accomplishes this by showing how kitchen sink texts can convey female voices that, while youthful and exuberant, are perhaps less motivated by aggression.

The narrative of Dunn's text takes place around the general Battersea area, with specific emphasis on the factory where the main characters work and the local hot spots where they congregate. The novel opens in a pub—one of several featured in the text—in which Sylvie, Rube, and Lily stand rather than sit "up against the saloon door, brown ales clutched in our hands" (1988: 1). Traditional power structures are inverted in that the three men who flirt with them remain seated, suggesting dominance on the part of the women. Both the scene and the dynamics shift immediately, with the women all mounting a motorbike "each behind a boy" and taking off to swim in an abandoned coke mine (1988: 2). Such swift movement through space is a characteristic of Dunn's text, representing the way that the main characters' sexual freedom is reiterated by their relative mobility through space. Whereas kitchen sink texts prior often presented female characters as relatively static—the most famous characterized by Alison Porter's inert stance behind *Look Back in Anger*'s ironing board—Dunn's women demonstrate agency, expressed by their mutable states. Furthermore, much of the domestic action—the space historically offered as the realm of female characters—is set aside, with domestic space in the text figured as transitory, spaces in which to regroup after a night out "up the junction." Instead, the factory (a space that produces both confections and female agency), the general vicinity (spaces in which female agency can be staged), and the pubs and underground clubs (spaces in which gender norms can be overturned) replace the dreary existence of the housewife, situating *Up the Junction* as a text that challenges the initial framework of kitchen sink realism by essentially abandoning both the sink and its attendant kitchen. Chapters such as "The Deserted House"—a vignette set in an abandoned block of LCC flats—further stresses the rejection of the home as a space of female sanctuary.

Throughout the text, a range of spaces are presented as alternates to traditional domestic life, with aspects of the local environment beautified in ways akin to how someone might decorate a home. For example, the path the women take to the factory is described in a way that signals aesthetic pleasure: "The exhaust makes wavy patterns in the still air" and "Little tufts of yellow flowers push through the dusty smelling concrete" (1988: 38–9). Such details make it easy to lose sight of the fact that the environment depicted is essentially a slum—war-torn with dilapidated, bombed-out buildings and others abandoned, left to rot. The women of *Up the Junction* revitalize such spaces, not through physical transformations, per se, but through a reshaping of what spaces such as these represent in their own minds. This process is done in a manner that accentuates the value of community, even when the physical community is in ruins. Upon explaining that he cannot take her home because "me mum's pawned all the furniture," Rube's date, Dave, underscores the magnetizing effect of the local urban space: "This is where we lived till it got demolished—slum clearance. They moved us out to lousy Roehampton" (1988: 32). As one of the more notorious council estates built in the postwar period, Dave's rejection of Roehampton in favor of what remains of the Clapham Junction is a telling rebuke of modern housing programs. In essence, Dunn's text envisions a working-class community as full of life, despite its dereliction, to explore concerns of gentrification while also demonstrating how space can be reclaimed by residents and viewed in meaningful ways.

That the factory does not appear in the text until after the reader has been introduced to the protagonists' social and domestic lives suggests that work is devalued in terms of its capacity to shape identity. Furthermore, when it is introduced, it is deemed distinct from other representations of factory labor in prior kitchen sink texts. For example, whereas Arthur's lathe in *Saturday Night and Sunday Morning* is a symbolic stand-in for both rugged individualism and the status quo, the workbench featured in Dunn's text is more jovial—a source of camaraderie and a space where the novel's protagonists express themselves freely without judgment. Although the factory itself is presented as cold enough to make the workers' fingers red and swollen, the space is warmed by friendly jibbing in which "twenty-five women hunched over three long tables, packing cheap sweets for Christmas" laugh and offer to trade each others' husbands (1988: 19). The harbinger of the dying patriarch is repurposed in Mrs. Smith ("an old woman spits into a rag and wipes her hands over" [1988: 20]), yet she still participates in the gossip engaged by the other workers. While the building lacks the most basic amenities, and the conditions are less than satisfactory, the women support one another by sharing tips on how to sustain themselves within the workspace (1988: 23). Dunn's representation of the factory is hardly utopian, but it demonstrates a shift away from the representations of male labor in earlier kitchen sink texts, suggesting that such spaces can be transformed into social hubs of community.

Yet it is the workspace that fuels the narrative in that the protagonists' camaraderie extends beyond the factory with the three women spending much of their free time together. The general area that surrounds the workplace is in a continual state of demolition ("We turn a corner past a giant bulldozer crashing through the slums" [1988: 14]), but such descriptions are momentary, almost instantly overlooked or countered by a more appealing description. The transformation of the community is well underway, and the novel is set against a continual barrage of demolition and reconstruction. Yet, the characters simply step over the piles of rubble and steer clear of potholes. The effect is that Dunn is able to capture a community in the process of remaking, while also demonstrating the working-class motif of "making-do" in that the characters exist within their world while not letting their world dictate their actions.

As the protagonists navigate the sites of demolition and redevelopment, there is a distinct sense that gender roles are also undergoing similar renovation. From the opening scene in which the three protagonists loom over the men in the pub, Dunn's text promotes a form of collective agency to match changes taking place regarding the social status of women in mid-century Britain. In the text, the factory provides an outlet for such attitudes to coalesce and for women to form connections, expressed through the use of vernacular and explicit language that continues out into the local community. As Adrian Henri writes in his introduction, "One suspects that [Dunn's] symbolic crossing of the River Thames was in search of something more real and somehow satisfying, even at worst, than Chelsea's fashionable bohemia" (1988: XIV). Accordingly, the nature of something "more real" is linked to a spatial boundary that designates certain class associations and behavioral patterns. As Henri continues, the area depicted in the text "lacked many of the basic amenities, but their very proximity had given rise to a dense web of family and neighborhood relationships" (1988: XIV). Noted in the previous chapter, the enclosed nature of the spaces like those depicted in *Up the Junction* confirms notions of class policing and prescribed social status. But Dunn's text also reveals the way spaces such as these can be transformed in a productive manner. For example, the temperature of the factory requires the workers to operate in close proximity to sustain heat—a gesture that doubles as both pragmatic and metaphorical in a manner similar to the way the protagonists navigate their local environment. Similarly, the protagonists' capacity to manipulate subjugated social positions also stems from their proximity as a group. In this respect, the repressive confines and limitations of space are restructured in a manner that results in mutual support. But, whereas in the past such spaces might be attributed to the sustenance of a mass working-class body, Dunn's text highlights the disarticulation of class-consciousness and its fragmentation into subdivided units.

Up the Junction matches verisimilitude with didacticism in that it portrays the limits of classed space while also suggesting how such limits can be overcome. The use of vernacular—perhaps the text's most salient indicator of social rank—highlights the regional and dialectical bordering of classed spaces in Britain. Given the relative proximity of Chelsea to Battersea, the distinction in dialect creates a boundary for the protagonists to question. Lily is othered in such a space, outed by Rube early in the narrative as "an heiress from Chelsea" (1988: 2), leading a local man to ask "What's it like havin' a ton of money?" (1988: 2).[6]

By focusing on vernacular, Dunn defines working-class spatial boundaries otherwise indistinct amidst the urban sprawl of the capital. Just as Jo in *A Taste of Honey* reinvents the sites she occupies to suit a new class consciousness, Dunn's text presents a community long abandoned to rot but resuscitated in a manner that makes it appealing to non-community members. The period's authors and their characters' ability to recognize the way spatial limitation informs lived experience—and then imagine alternate forms of class expression in response—are perhaps kitchen sink realism's most-salient effect. Whereas the early kitchen sink texts emphasized space as a way to articulate links between environment and identity, texts like Dunn's respond with alternative ways of existing. Like Delaney's Jo, the characters of *Up the Junction* reclaim and transform the spaces they inhabit, from the workplace, to the domestic environment, to social spaces such as pubs in which gender norms are challenged and inverted. Despite other texts from the period exploring the potential of rethinking spatial experience in ways that transform class understanding, texts like *Up the Junction* can be read as forthright in their efforts to portray an active resistance to spaces that would ordinarily shape and define class through the imposition of behavioral norms designed to uphold the status quo.

Subterranean Space and Diasporic Demimondes in *City of Spades*

Like Dunn's *Up the Junction*, Colin MacInnes's *City of Spades* focuses on the urban metropolis but features social demimondes created as alternative communities. As part of MacInnes's London trilogy, which also includes *Absolute Beginners* and *Mr Love and Justice*, *City of Spades* narrates the events that led up to the 1958 Notting Hill Race Riots while offering an on-the-ground depiction of the colonial immigrant experience in mid-century London.[7] Taken as a whole, the trilogy indexes urban movement in the form of gentrification but also the renegotiation of British identity in the light of imperial decline. The three narratives provide windows into mid-century Britain through their use of diasporic voices presenting unique perspectives on current events otherwise difficult to parse. MacInnes's personal investment in such voices is intriguing in that, throughout his career, his dedication to marginalized people, youth subculture, and the working-class rarely wavered.[8] Yet, as Nick Bentley has pointed out, MacInnes's work is consistently overlooked in relation to the period (2003: 150), and he is rarely coupled with the work of the Angry Young

Men—the reason being, perhaps, that his elevated class, professional training in writing, and open bisexuality present him more as an outsider to writers like Sillitoe or Osborne who, in many ways, embraced the overt masculinity linked to the movement.

City of Spades uses a dual narrative format that MacInnes would further explore in *Mr Love and Justice*, shifting the narrative voice back and forth between two central characters: Montgomery Pew, a social worker with the recently acquired title of Assistant Welfare Officer; and Johnny Fortune, an eighteen-year-old Nigerian meteorology student from Lagos. The narrative places Montgomery as the caseworker for Johnny, allowing for an exploration of racial tension in mid-century Britain. It also considers the intersection of race and class in terms of space and environs. Even through his comparatively elevated status as a student scientist, Johnny is relegated to the veritable basement of society, living first in a hostel on "Immigration Road" (MacInnes 2005: 113) before moving in with a drug dealer and then dealing drugs himself. The notion of downward movement is palpable throughout *City of Spades*—specifically in how subcultural spaces are forced to exist beneath the city. Because *Absolute Beginners* traces movement through and out of the city, and *Mr Love and Justice* registers movement upward into peripheral high rises, trajectory can be seen to play a key role in MacInnes's exploration of social advances taking place within the urban metropolis. The contrasting characters illuminate shifts in British identity through such movement, with white, middle-class characters coming to terms with the inevitable transformation of the postcolonial landscape through their interactions with the marginalized characters. The unnamed narrator of *Absolute Beginners* offers a hopeful, open-minded outlook on cultural diversity whereas *Mr Love and Justice* demonstrates how white, middle-class government workers and poor, Black pimps become culturally homogenized in housing designed to sequester. *City of Spades* depicts how the city itself is broken up into regions dedicated to specific communities. Similar to the way the industrial areas depicted in *Up the Junction* are defined by their proximity to factories and railroads, the spaces inhabited by the characters of *City of Spades* are identified in an analogous manner. Immigration Road, named after the hostels established in the 1950s to deal with the waves of colonial immigration, resembles the makeshift living arrangements found in the East End's Brick Lane region. The city's subdivision and territorialization captured throughout the London trilogy illustrate Lefebvre and Harvey's conception of spatial production—not just as planned sites, but as regions that develop and exist through social interactions and temporal events.

While MacInnes's novels were perhaps overshadowed by the cult appeal of Julien Temple's 1986 film adaptation of *Absolute Beginners*, *City of Spades* offers a pertinent analysis of the way subculture came about out of a necessity expressed through spatial limits.⁹ For a character like Johnny, the spaces he inhabits are so repressive that he becomes desperate to move into more comfortable spaces, even if that means placing himself into precarious social situations. In this regard, MacInnes outlines the way criminality arises as the result of environments acting upon an individual in damaging ways. But, as argued by Bentley, texts like *City of Spades* do not simply center on the nature of restrictive space and its impact on individuals; they simulate a transformation underway in what constitutes Britishness and citizenship: "The text enters a cultural debate concerned with defining a national identity that has been loosened from its traditional certainties, one that is no longer the property of the dominant cultural institutions, but is in the process of being reconstructed from below" (2003: 160). Such a "reconstruction from below" is indicative of a working-class imaginary in which new conceptions of identity arise as the upshot of spatial limitations and top-down ideological forces. Therefore, a novel like *City of Spades* can be read not only as analysis of the impact of urban reconstruction and gentrification in light of immigration, but also as a model of resistance in a manner that reiterates Lefebvre, Harvey, and Soja's emphasis on spatial reclamation.

MacInnes was one of few white writers at the time directly engaged with issues of race and colonial repatriation. To that end, he speaks to the housing crisis to show how anxieties faced by white working-class people in the postwar years were deflected onto racial and ethnic minorities. This, of course, nods to the political value of an interchangeable underclass for those who benefit from such formations. *City of Spades* contours the frustrations present in texts like Osborne's *Look Back in Anger* but introduces intersectional complexity in that the text focuses on dialect as well as a journalistic approach to the recounting of significant events in British culture. According to Bentley, MacInnes adopts this strategy in response "to what he considered to be a misrepresentation of youth and black subcultures in both the mainstream media" with narratives "driven by an imperative to record previously unrepresented voices" (2003: 150). While this is certainly true, and MacInnes covers a lot of territory throughout the London trilogy, the most dominant themes of his text are race relations, youth and racial subculture, as well as shifts in the urban makeup of the city.

In addition to the topical themes, a key factor of MacInnes's style is the use of contrast to grant definition to his subjects. Given that the narratives of the London trilogy are so grounded in specific environments in which working-class and minority experiences dominate, MacInnes introduces middle-class characters to stress difference. His fiction tends to underscore the chasm between social classes, the forces and mechanisms that keep such distinctions in place, and the increased likelihood that middle-class characters will be reduced to working-class statuses rather than working-class positions seeing social elevation. However, MacInnes's characters tend to recognize such limits and form new kinds of communities in response. The quixotic tone perceptible throughout much of MacInnes's work—especially identifiable in *Absolute Beginners'* unnamed narrator—speaks to the excitement and vivacity accompanying new outlooks and imaginings of class identity. Despite the adversity experienced by characters such as Johnny, *City of Spades* illuminates the potential for class insurrection through a reorganizing of social position and the repurposing of spaces designated as derelict or socially bankrupt.

Similar to *Up the Junction*, characters in *City of Spades* reshape the urban territory as a field of potentiality, transforming spaces in ways to better meet their needs. The novel begins with the dueling narrators placed into new environments—Montgomery into his new office and role, and Johnny to the Piccadilly Circus tube station where he tries to run up a downward-moving escalator, earning him the ire of the ticketing official and setting the metaphorical tone for the upward battle he faces. Set in contrast from the start, the spaces Montgomery and Johnny inhabit are distinct but become increasingly intertwined as the story progresses. Johnny's first place of residence, a "Brixton house [that] stood all by itself among ruins of what I [Johnny] suppose was wartime damages, much like one tooth left sticking out in an old man's jaw" (2005: 26) stands in contrast to that of Montgomery. Montgomery's flat "two odd rooms and a 'kitchenette', most miscellaneously furnished" is literally and metaphorically elevated "on the top floor of a high, narrow house near Regent's Park with a view on the Zoological Gardens" (2005: 33). Yet, despite this elevation, Montgomery's status is precarious in that "A year ago, the property changed hands, and notices to quit were served on all tenants" (2005: 33), rendering the building largely vacant in hopes of redevelopment. After seeking legal action, Montgomery was able to secure his home, leaving him as the sole tenant blocking the landlord's redevelopment plans—a gesture that swiftly aligns him with Johnny's circumstances in that he exists in a space in which his presence is resented. Thus, MacInnes establishes domestic space as hostile and precarious early in the text, causing both narrators to seek out more substantial and supportive ways of being in the city.

Spaces like The Moorhen—a pub that belies "the legend of the gaiety, the heart-warming homeliness" by undermining the idealized myth of the British institution through its "grim spectacle of 'regulars' ... sitting morosely eyeing one another, in private silence" (2005: 42)—stand in contrast to the makeshift dance halls like The Cosmopolitan that Johnny characterizes as "the nearest proximity I've seen yet in London to the gaiety and happiness back home" (2005: 49). The narrative continues to contrast traditional British institutions with counterhegemonic, subcultural sites of refuge. It concludes with a unification of the two men's worlds in a courtroom described as "damaged in the Hitler war" and then "redecorated in a 'contemporary' style—light salmon wood, cubistic lanterns, leather cushions in pastel shades—that pleased none of the lawyers, officials or police officers who worked there" (2005: 207). By reflecting on the unpopularity of postwar redevelopment plans, MacInnes considers the impact of such spaces on the psyche, remarking that those who did work there "injected into their behavior an additional awesome formality to counteract the lack of majesty of their surroundings" (2005: 207). As the novel closes with Johnny losing his battle against the metaphorical downward-moving escalator in terms of his legal state, MacInnes employs various spatial images to show the pernicious oppression of environment on the emergence of subculture and cultural difference.

City of Spades provides one of the better examples of how the period's texts confront the social implications of space, granting insight into the way class limitation can be circumvented through new understandings of spatial production. It should be noted that MacInnes was estranged from other writers of the period in that his embrace of youth subculture and racial diversity was paramount in his work, moving his representations away from the ubiquitous and instantly recognizable working-class environments of writers like Sillitoe or Osborne. *City of Spades* is a unique example in that MacInnes's Johnny provides a perspective relatively overlooked within kitchen sink realism—that of the colonial immigrant. All the same, parallels can be drawn between Dunn's embrace of working-class women in society since both writers explore articulations of space that challenge traditional working-class roles.

Devin McKinney has raised concern that MacInnes's novels border on naïveté in their optimism. McKinney also claims that MacInnes tends to undermine any optimism with moments of bleakness that are then replaced once more by optimistic events (2006: 38). The result, the author claims, is a loop in which hope and resignation are held in perennial tension. Be that as it may, it is perhaps more helpful to think of MacInnes's texts as performing two distinct roles: the narrative representation of a working-class world and a particular mindset or approach that stands in opposition to the limits and restrictions of such a world. The former veers toward pessimism as the spaces and events depicted within a text like *City of Spades* are bleak, but the latter is idealized in ways that reframe the former. From this perspective, *City of Spades* does not lay out a tangible method by which to transform physical space but suggests a different way of conceiving of space instead, reshaping the relations that can occur within such environments.

The most intentional repurposing of space in the text is the underground club, a practice that MacInnes establishes in *City of Spades* and develops further in *Absolute Beginners*. Such spaces also exist in Dunn's *Up the Junction*, revealing how, in working-class and poor communities of the time, the practice of reimagining social life was already underway. At the core of MacInnes's text is the supposition of cultural difference. Johnny, for example, finds that his naively upbeat persona is no match for a culture that seeks to deny his presence, and the underground clubs he frequents exist as a subterranean diaspora. Whereas Lefebvre and Harvey's conception of the way space is produced implies a somewhat fixed nature—once a space is established, it remains relatively static. The clubs in *City of Spades* are more vibrant, opening and closing with expediency to evade the law. In this regard, Foucault's heterotopic space—a space that challenges homogenic, fixed space through contingency—recalls the nature of the underground spaces depicted by MacInnes in that such sites necessitate a new mode of urban citizenship. While Foucault's mirror revealed a replica of space subject to its own laws and regulations, the club exists as a place within a space, but one underscoring the inequitable nature of mid-century London through its heterotopic potentiality. As illegitimate spaces that shunned dominant society (Montgomery has to ask the right people in order to find the space), there is an implicit awareness of one's momentary self-exile, represented by MacInnes as a subterranean descent.

Whereas Dunn's *Up the Junction* offers a vision of a working-class community in which the unequal balance of gender is reinscribed, *City of Spades* demonstrates how Black immigrants transgress spatial limitations through alternative spaces. The illicit nature of the underground club—especially with regard to its mobility and dynamism—responds to the shifting nature of Britain as a whole, accentuating the disconnect between a dynamic populace as well as structures and institutions that remain static. MacInnes's opening image of Johnny's efforts to run up the downward-moving escalator illustrates the kinds of opposition faced by the waves of immigrants arriving in England following the decline of imperial power. But it also demonstrates the way characters in texts of the era attempt to rethink the limits of space and push back against the forces acting on them. Reading *City of Spades* through the lens of spatial production reiterates the value of underground clubs and illicit space as a counterhegemonic strategy. As McKinney reminds us, the narrative ends on a somewhat bleak note as represented in the title of the final chapter, "Johnny Fortune leaves his city." Yet, what the novel successfully emphasizes is how the city is becoming a multicultural center in that newly arrived immigrants place demands on the space by challenging its present structure and reshaping it to meet their needs. Like Dunn, MacInnes's optimism is based less on the state of the working-class community itself; instead, it celebrates the potential for working-class and marginalized subjects to imagine alternative modes of being and initiate such practices through spatial transgression.

Differential Space and Inversion in *The Loneliness of the Long Distance Runner*

Similar to *Up the Junction* and *City of Spades*, Alan Sillitoe's novella *The Loneliness of the Long Distance Runner* illustrates the way classed environments can be repurposed from their intended role as a form of counterhegemonic engagement. Published in 1959 and compiled from the collection of vignettes that also led to *Saturday Night and Sunday Morning*, the novella provides a parochial take on similar concerns outlined in MacInnes's text: the impact of spatial restrictions placed on individuals leading to desperate acts. But whereas MacInnes's text sketched the importance of subcultural space as a counter to a society ill-equipped to handle the needs of a shifting populace, Sillitoe explores the way assumptions about dominant institutional spaces can be undermined to produce specific effects that benefit people otherwise assumed powerless. Although critics tend to gravitate toward Tony Richardson's 1962 film version that Sillitoe helped to develop, the novella has generally been read through the lens of class and class limitation. Anthony Daniels, for example, has approached the text as a way to understand the actions of the protagonist: "Crime for him is class war, the inevitable consequence of social injustice and the irreconcilable conflict of economic class interest" (2008: 25). Alexis Tadié (2015) considers the text in terms of the title, exploring the metaphorical significance of running and its relationship to cultural identity. For Tadié, the image of the cross-country runner is an apt paradox for confined space such as that of the borstal, yet it is clear that Sillitoe's investment in such an image speaks to the novella's championing of transformed space.

The novella tells the story of Colin Smith—a working-class young man who shares a cramped back-to-back home with his family. His destiny as a laborer in the local factory is laid out for him in the example of his father who, as the story reveals, dies from a fatal illness developed (presumably) as the result of his labor. As with Arthur, Colin finds himself at turning point: to succumb to the consigned life of his father or to strike out and make a change. Given the apparent limitations of his working-class environment, Colin turns to petty crime, stealing money from a local bakery and is inevitably caught by the authorities. Despite attempts to brandish power over the "copper" by denying his involvement, Colin's plan is foiled when a rainstorm washes the stash of hidden money out of a drainpipe in clear view of the questioning officer. The novel clarifies that Colin's intention was not to get caught, but the initial assertion of power over authority forms a central theme that is at the root of Sillitoe's narrative. In this regard, the social production of space can be seen to incorporate the subjective responses of individuals made to inhabit disaffecting spaces such as these, allowing for a degree of relative freedom in spaces ordinarily understood as repressive. While in the borstal, Colin discovers ways to wield power over the authority that exists there, using his athletic prowess as a form of labor to win a national cross country competition and help the borstal gain national recognition. As the novel ends, we learn that while Colin has the capacity to win, he throws the race intentionally to announce his agency and rebuke those who would exploit his labor. His ability to humiliate the Governor and discredit the borstal grants him momentary power over an environment that would otherwise seek to strip him of agency.

The text uses flashback sequences, inviting back and forth comparisons between the working-class region Colin inhabits and the borstal that posits an alternative to that existence. Although the text's politics are fairly transparent, Sillitoe drafted a follow-up narrative, much of which appears to be a vehicle through which to articulate Colin's next move. Set eight years later, Colin is seen to meet with members of a nationalist party and spends copious time researching class warfare in a local library.[10] The original narrative is certainly political, but its success relies upon its allegiance to a fairly traditional structure that keeps the text from devolving into outright propaganda. Although incomplete and therefore never released, Sillitoe's attempted follow-up appeared to take a far more overt political position.

But as a more typical "Angry" text than either *Up the Junction* or *City of Spades*, the novella recounts the thematics affiliated with the genre more readily. In this narrative, the "Angry Young Man" motif is sustained while the text also considers aspects of spatial transgression. Like *Up the Junction*, the text is better known through Richardson's adaptation. The novella and the film are closely aligned since—as was true of *Saturday Night and Sunday Morning*—Sillitoe wrote the screenplay alongside the director. The themes that run throughout are the standard themes associated with the kitchen sink movement: frustration, limitation, and a setting in which such effects are compounded. But, in contrast to Sillitoe's other famous protagonist, Arthur—or even Osborne's Jimmy—Colin turns to crime. So, a pivotal element of this text is its willingness to interrogate the level of desperation possible by young, disenfranchised working-class men.

Sillitoe has remarked that Arthur's position in *Saturday Night and Sunday Morning* is due to a "spiritual lack." Gillian Mary Hanson posits that, in the case of Colin, spiritual deficiency can be interpreted as an inability to cope with external realities, turning instead to superficial solutions such as consumerism and material acquisition. According to Hanson, characters like Colin and Arthur feel trapped until they realize that change must come from within (1999: 31). But Colin is perhaps one of the better examples of a character who faces his predicament and takes action to change it. Consequently, *The Loneliness of the Long Distance Runner* both adopts and develops themes of rebellion, exploring the way that the protagonist not only conceives of himself as transforming classed space, but actively undermines and upends the social contract in the process. Such an act of defiance is not merely an antisocial gesture, however; instead, it calls out social inequity by inverting power structures.

The Loneliness of the Long Distance Runner limits its setting to intensify contrasts in power and social position. The bulk of the narrative takes place between the working-class community where Colin and his family reside and the borstal where he serves his sentence. The state of the home community is the result not just of neglect and war damage, but a general malaise of the postwar era in which social plans aimed to help the impoverished failed to materialize. Colin recalls the time as "autumn and the night foggy enough to set me and my mate Mike roaming the streets when we should have been rooted in front of the telly or stuck into a plush posh seat at the pictures" (2010: 28). While it might be assumed that television and visits to the cinema should work to pacify disenfranchisement, it has failed in the case of Colin who "was restless after six weeks away from any sort of work" following his father's recent death from throat cancer, presumably from the same kind of labor Colin was already familiar with: "I sweated my thin guts out on a milling-machine with the rest of them" (2010: 28). The text presents an area of Nottingham indistinguishable from many northern industrial communities with requisite terraces punctuated by pubs and chip shops; the antisocial urge entering Colin's mind is presented more as a response to boredom and frustration than of necessity.

In contrast, the borstal appears in the text as a lavish space—one that perhaps stems from Sillitoe's momentary fascination with British street crime. As mentioned in the previous chapter, Sillitoe would order texts through the British Council Library while living in Majorca, becoming interested in the nature of social justice and the recidivism of prison inmates (Sillitoe 1995: 226). Therefore, the borstal in *The Loneliness of the Long Distance Runner* was born not from personal experience (as was mostly the case in *Saturday Night and Sunday Morning*) but from a more imaginative position. With that said, the idealization of the borstal in the text serves to clarify the state of working-class environments in Nottingham through narrative contrast. Whereas a generalized sense of malaise led Colin to seemingly random criminality, the borstal is both relaxing and instructive. At several points, it is described as "wasn't so bad" (2010: 12), "supposed to be good" (2010: 9), and even a space that offers "a good life" (2010: 11). Colin also points out that he "didn't suffer in Borstal at all" and that he "was nearly eighteen months in Borstal before [he] thought about getting out" (2010: 15). For him, the space grants clarity to the nature of power and class within culture: "But in another way Borstal does something to me … What it does is show me what they've been trying to frighten me with" (2010: 16). That is to say Sillitoe's description of the borstal sounds more like a retreat with time set aside for labor, education, and (most often for Colin) exercise in the surrounding countryside. The freedom depicted in the space sharply contrasts the lack of freedom present in the supposedly free working world. As idealistic as Sillitoe's depiction is, its function is to draw attention to and enunciate the state of working-class environments by suggesting that imprisonment is a better option than the kinds of imprisonment associated with a disenfranchised working-class life.

Where *Up the Junction* and *City of Spades* explore the way urban environs as a whole can be transformed, Sillitoe's text takes a simpler perspective by restricting the represented spaces to that of a binary and showing with greater clarity how the undercurrent of power within such spaces can be inverted. Following Lefebvre, it is possible to conceive of Colin's home environment as a space of apparent freedom, despite the dire circumstances of his family life. This, of course, is in opposition to the borstal which, given the punitive nature of such institutions, signifies tangible restraint and control in the form of a disciplinary system. Yet, Sillitoe's text undermines such assumptions by portraying the outside world as the space of restriction while showing how sites of institutional incarceration can be recast as sites of transgression. The text's radical inversion of social power structures represented in the two spaces suggests that similar reversals of power can be actioned across a variety of spaces by emphasizing the subjective component associated with spatial production. According to Lefebvre's thinking, a space like the borstal exists as a combination of three components: its physical and conceptual structure (both of which can be understood as objective), as well as its social structure grounded in assumed power. In other words, the borstal is imprisoning as the result of its naturalization in society as a space of penance. Sillitoe's text challenges the subjective construction of such spatial codes through a protagonist who flips the power dynamics on their head, undermining the wishes of the governor and controlling his fate through his own skills.

The dynamics that Sillitoe engages within the text are established in relation to space but are also represented as sources of power to be weaponized:

> It's like me rushing up to thump a man and snatch the coat off his back when, suddenly, I pull up because he whips out a knife and lifts it to stick me like a pig if I come too close. That knife is Borstal, clink, the rope. But once you've seen the knife you learn a bit of unarmed combat … You see, by sending me to Borstal they've shown me the knife, and from now on I know something I didn't know before.
>
> (2010: 16)

Colin's time at the borstal reveals that it is more than merely the physical structure; it is the production of space tacitly acknowledged between those who occupy the site in addition to its social and ideological coding. Therefore, the belief of the borstal as carceral is more reliant upon the maintenance of a hierarchy of control than the physical structure as, after all, the borstal has no perceptible walls; its disciplinary nature is the result of the social and relational components of spatial production. Sillitoe's ability to convey this particular narrative stems from the contrast established between the two main spaces of the narrative: the binary of inside and out, a metaphorical mirror of "them and us." The physical makeup of the "outside"—the space of supposed freedom—is considered imprisoning through a home linked to the space of labor, streets that offer no refuge, and the incipient promise of the kind of death experienced by his father. The "inside," however, is a space without such walls—one in which inhabitants can (literally) run free with access to education and forms of labor unavailable outside. Such contrasts, of course, speak to Lefebvre's spatial production in that "outside" represents the tangible experiences of classed space whereas "inside" reflects a working-class imaginary or a new state of being in classed space. Furthermore, there is a shared camaraderie between the inmates that is most perceptible when it is revealed that Colin intends to throw the race. For Colin, the ability to redirect power is revealed to him by the judge who sentenced him to the borstal in the first place:

> We want to trust you while you are in this establishment … If you play ball with us, we'll play ball with you … We want hard honest work and we want good athletics … And if you give us both these things you can be sure we'll do right by you and send you back into the world an honest man.
>
> (2010: 9–10)

For Colin to agree to the judge's request would be tantamount to following the state's demands, thus accepting the imbalance of power that sustains the space of the borstal. However, his willingness to challenge what is clearly a dishonest promise on the part of the judge positions him as outside of the implied contract, allowing him to reimagine the circumstances for his own benefit.

While the physical structures represented in Sillitoe's text are vital to the narrative action, they establish the paradox that the narrative engages: the imposed limitations of the outside world are cast in relief by the expansive, open space of the borstal. Such components certainly align with the objective components of Lefebvre's produced space, but it is also the novel's manipulation of socially created space that is at play. Whereas both Lefebvre and Harvey suggest that identifying the social component of produced space is challenging, Sillitoe's text puts forth a perspective on the way such concepts can be recognized. And, of course, once such productions are identified and understood, they can then be reimagined in new ways that are ultimately subjective. In the words of Colin, "They can spy on us all day to see if we're pulling our puddings and if we're working good or doing our 'athletics' but they can't make an X-ray of our guts to find out what we're telling ourselves" (2010: 10). *The Loneliness of the Long Distance Runner* reveals how imaginative writing can help contour the subjective and elusive "lived" component of Lefebvre's triad in a manner that recalls Westphal's geocritical analysis, specifically the way cultural texts can act as a hinge to transform an individual's conception of spatial production, granting the individual both agency and a new way to conceive of their social position.

Conclusion

Recalling once more the Warwickshire County Council's effort to restrict the release of *Saturday Night and Sunday Morning*, I suggested that group's real anxiety was more likely the way such texts facilitate insubordinate frames of mind. If kitchen sink realism does indeed advance new and transgressive ways of expressing working-class identity through negotiations of space, then perhaps the County Council was right to worry. What this chapter has demonstrated is that the elevated significance of space in kitchen sink realism is far from decorative; it serves as a motif across media forms, allowing for an authentic and mimetic portrayal of working-class life (the aesthetic factor of social realism) and a didactic, instructive component in which the reader is invited to question their own class articulation through interactions with the environment (the ethical factor of social realism). Colin's awareness of the borstal's reliance on socially driven narratives of power is what allows him to confront the space and transform it for his own purposes. When he is restrained for his crimes and made to function under state management, he realizes that it is his own mindset that offers the most powerful tool he has in that he is able to undermine the foundation of the borstal by inverting the hierarchy of control. Although Sillitoe's example is specific to the story and is clearly not a programmatic model of how an individual might confront carceral situations, the text underscores the reciprocal qualities of classed space—specifically the way repressive operations rely, in part, on the tacit acceptance of inequality. Furthermore, it performs Lefebvre's notion of the spatial triad by proving that spatial comprehension can never be truly imposed on an individual without their permission. Correspondingly, *Up the Junction* and *City of Spades* show how a social group can, collectively, undermine assumptions and therefore transform classed space into something that suits its needs more readily. Although certainly not the only trope of kitchen sink realist aesthetics, spatial negotiations are likely the most consistent and impactful. As such, the following chapter will consider how this advance—what I suggest is a reconfiguration of the realist mode—sustains a legacy of class portrayal. Furthermore, I suggest that if kitchen sink aesthetics can be read as an apex of working-class representation, then the strategies and motifs advanced by the movement can potentially function as a way to gauge and evaluate subsequent portrayals of working-class life.

Notes

1. It is worth mentioning that this online repository of Sandford's writing is drawn from an archive held at the Herefordshire Archive and Records Centre. The website is commandeered by George Miles with a footnote proclaiming "Almost all of the content of these webpages is copyright of the estate of Jeremy Sandford, RIP. They are provided here for your private research, and as a tribute to Jeremy." The online repository can be found at: www.jeremysandford.org.uk.
2. While Dunn worked on *Up the Junction* during their time in Battersea, Sandford wrote what would become 1966's *Cathy Come Home*, shown as part of the BBC's *The Wednesday Play* series. Directed by Ken Loach, the quasi-documentary film considers the plight of the homeless and parental rights. It is often considered one of the most influential plays ever produced for British television.
3. As is true of a number of geographers after Lefebvre, Westphal's approach signals attempts to think beyond positivist representation, drawing instead on notions of imagined and potential approaches to space.
4. Although Harvey would develop these ideas further across several texts, his essay "Space as a Keyword" (2006a) summarizes them with great clarity.
5. As mentioned in this book's introduction, MacInnes is rarely spoken of in relation to kitchen sink texts. While there is a certain tonal shift in that the London trilogy veers more boisterous whereas kitchen sink texts are routinely characterized by the prosaic, I would argue that their parallels—documentary-style motifs, an emphasis on youth subculture, class, and spatial negotiations—is what aligns them. It might be argued that what has kept them separate from other texts of the era is that they feature postwar immigrant communities rather than a northern white working-class.
6. It is important to note here that the character of Lily is named Polly in Peter Collinson's 1968 adaptation, played by Suzy Kendall. In Ken Loach's TV adaptation from 1965, the main character is named Eileen and played by Vickery Turner.
7. For this particular study, I am referencing the 2005 Allison & Busby Omnibus Edition of MacInnes's three texts, referred to here as "the London trilogy."
8. MacInnes's seeming dedication to progressive positions regarding race and sexuality has been read by certain critics as a fetishization of the young, Black men whom MacInnes was romantically interested in. Furthermore, Lawrence

Phillips has suggested that a vocal embrace of the cultural other should be viewed with a degree of skepticism in that "The problematic result of this positive, liberal enthusiasm when coupled with desire, is the (re)creation, at best, of an updated version of the noble savage, and at worst stereotyping" (2006: 109). Phillips continues to note that "This was a dilemma prevalent among white intellectuals of the period in response to the changing city" (2006: 109). Characters in MacInnes's work such as *City of Spades*'s Montgomery, the unnamed narrator of *Absolute Beginners*, and Edward Justice from *Mr Love and Justice* are reflective of such complicated world views.

9   It is worth noting that the film was not critically successful, but its cult status was likely driven by David Bowie's popular theme song.

10 The manuscript of the follow-up text is both messy and arduous. It adopts a heightened political tone that reads more as propaganda, including references to the British National Party and unsophisticated critiques of television as well as the state of the nation. Although the follow-up was never completed, aspects of it can be determined in the film version of the initial script with the family's television broadcasting propaganda. It can be found in the same typescript of *The Deserters* alongside the early vignettes for *Saturday Night and Sunday Morning* and *The Loneliness of the Long Distance Runner* (Mss. II, box, folder 15, tab 12, the Lilly Library, Indiana University, Bloomington, Indiana).

4

Against Class Fetishism: The Legacy of Kitchen Sink Realism

Returning to this book's guiding premise—that the kitchen sink era represents a formal and stylistic apogee—this final chapter surveys attempts by scholars to totalize tropes linked to the movement, questioning the efficacy of doing so given the relative mutability and definitional flexibility of class-conscious writing. In response, it advances a spatial aesthetics of class representation—a summation of the way kitchen sink texts accentuate environment and settings as part of their political and aesthetic program. The aim of this chapter is to suggest a framework by which to evaluate representational veracity and to consider the function of portrayals of working-class life across media forms—particularly their capacity to present alternative modes of class articulation that counter imposed class structures and social positions. Needless to say, such an endeavor is not to affix a definitive schema to class analysis since doing so would likely reduce a diverse swathe of texts to a single "type"; instead, it unpacks characteristics used in a specific body of work as a point of reference by which to assess subsequent texts employing similar strategies. In light of my earlier claim that working-class writing of the kitchen sink era sought to reunite political and aesthetic objectives in order to reconsider the basis of British citizenship, such a framework offers a path by which to weigh the efficacy of contemporary working-class representation against the transgressive intentions of the movement. Given the commercial imperative to commodify classed identities through the fetishization of "grittiness," the chapter reviews a number of contemporary texts to gauge the legacy of and proximity to kitchen sink objectives in contrast to class tourism and egregious exploitation. Put differently, it asks whether the texts of the movement can and should be read as an aesthetic and ethical benchmark. Picking up where my introduction's sweeping audit of the literary field left off, the chapter presents a series of brief spatial analyses of contemporary working-class cultural texts from literature, theater, film, and television shows to illustrate the value of such comparisons. In doing so, I reiterate the debt owed to the spatial tropes developed during the kitchen sink era, noting how subsequent working-class representation frequently cites—knowingly or unknowingly—motifs advanced by the movement's writers. What this evaluation also reveals is that when motifs do diverge, they tend to do so for reasons of commercialization by exploiting classed environments and elevating the aesthetic over the political through egregious shock effects and sensationalism. Yet, as this chapter submits, for every representational attempt to commodify classed identities, a new form of portrayal arises in protest, certifying working-class cultural production as perennially subversive, contingent, and imminently countercultural.

A Genealogy of the Realist Mode: Form versus Function

Given the movement's emphasis on spatial interaction, it is advantageous to consider how such aesthetic choices inform the realist mode—in particular, the mode's prior use of space and environment relative to mid-twentieth-century developments. In *Realism and Space in the Novel*, Rosa Mucignat (2013) shows how attention to spatial dimensions and descriptors bolstered the expansion of the novel in the late eighteenth and early nineteenth centuries. For Mucignat, a precise focus on spatial representation in a text signals a narrative shift away from the idea of the text as fantastical escape toward a more concrete materiality with spatial representations acting as an "organizational framework" that grounds the novel's more abstract components (2013: 1). Mucignat proposes three analytical foci relative to spatial depiction: visibility, depth, and movement. Visibility simply indicates how spatial references are positioned throughout the narrative structure. This may be extended to include considerations of detail and perception, but such an approach also reflects kitchen sink realism's dedication to patterns of repetition, the steady sequencing of spatial descriptors that work to remind the reader of their overdetermined role in the narrative. Depth, as Mucignat has it, designates the effect of depicted space on other aspects of the text such as characters and behavior. My own discussion of spatial negotiations—specifically the way classed space engenders certain behaviors—describes a similar mode of thought. Movement—Mucignat's third analytical consideration—is more complicated, referring to the way spatial representation itself is informed by "an increased heterogeneity of locales" (2013: 2). Whereas visibility and depth certainly seem like crucial components to address in terms of spatial references in literature, homogeneity (as opposed to heterogeneity) is apt—especially in light of narratives that call for a sense of limitation imposed by types of space. As mentioned, a characteristic of kitchen sink's spatial representation is the emphasis on sameness; places depicted act as a portrait of many different towns, most conspicuously in northern industrial communities in which urban planning and industrialization showed little concern for character or idiosyncrasy. But what is uniquely helpful in Mucignat's argument is the focus on the way realist authors embrace representations of space as superfluous. In kitchen sink texts, such effects intensify space but also act as a device that replicates the mechanical repetition of factory labor.

The steady, rhythmic repetition of signifiers is taken up in Roland Barthes's 1968 essay, "The Reality Effect," in which he argues that superfluous effects akin to recurrent depictions of space break the realist illusion. Barthes refers to these instances as "insignificant notation"—extraneous detail which he considers to be "a kind of narrative luxury" (1968: 141). Such regular intrusions, Barthes claims, "halt the vertigo of notation" (1968: 145) in that the realist text seeks not to cast a spell but to remind the reader that they are indeed reading a text in which the goal is to signal reality rather than simply supersede it. In other words, "the reality effect" can be read as a technique used in realist texts to shift the reader's attention away from the presumed central focus—be it the character or the plot—toward self-referentiality through details once considered peripheral or background. In terms of kitchen sink texts, plot lines are rarely complicated and are fairly interchangeable. In this respect, the reality effect produced is one of awareness of spatial types—the rhythmic, systematic repetition of signifiers that remind the reader of the novel's industrial nature. Yet, where the characters of Victorian social novels—texts equally dedicated to ensuring the reader is aware of industrial plight—often operate as archetypes, working-class characters in kitchen sink realism demonstrate greater psychological depth which, in turn, grants the reader a better comprehension of the way space and identity collide.

It is perhaps most appropriate to consider kitchen sink realism as a refinement of prior realisms rather than as a retort, a correction, or a break. Texts of the movement tend to expose the limits of aesthetic realism by taking an active turn toward the political. It is, of course, too reductive to suggest that prior realisms centered on aesthetics in such a way that they reduced texts to a state of purely institutional or academic interest. The chief characteristics associated with realism—a shift away from the sensational toward something like documentary-style objectivity—are characteristics that parallel the development of the modern novel. Yet, the texts of the kitchen sink era do seem to view such realisms skeptically. Arguably, these texts are elevated and cerebral, but written with a working-class audience in mind rather than a more academic readership or as texts that simply feature working-class characters. Whereas realist novels of the past aimed for maximal narrative objectivity, kitchen sink realism's politicization of the aesthetic mode grants the text a more subversive mien.

The growth of realism is generally read as a response to dominant romantic tropes. However, the evolution of the mode implies a continued effort to recalibrate aesthetic and political imperatives by merging form with function. While the early British Romantics such as William Wordsworth sought to democratize representation through the use of vernacular and a heightened focus on the ordinary, the Victorian period can be seen as an elaboration rather than a break. It was more the propensity for detailed storytelling seen in the popularity of serialized fiction and the dramatic monologue—rather than a concerted effort to dethrone the Romantic tradition—that helped define realist fiction. Since both the Romantics and the Victorians saw literary texts as didactic and utilitarian, any aesthetic progress between the two is best read as a desire to improve the social function of imaginative writing. Therefore, the social novel's dedication to realism can be read as an evolution of the Romantics' celebration of the ordinary, and kitchen sink realism can be viewed as a further evolution of this same thought.

As Mucignat indicates, spatial representation in realist novels was used more to serve the plot which held primacy. In kitchen sink realism, spatial details and descriptions surpass narrative function, moving closer to Barthes's notion of superfluous. This is due, in part, to the fact that a number of the key kitchen sink texts were conceived as vignettes—short pieces that, by design, would necessitate discreet, regular mentions of setting and environment. But it is likely also because kitchen sink texts are of their moment—they do not project into the past or the future, emphasizing instead their world as experienced in the contextual present. The result is a steady, rhythmic pattern of environmental detail. So, it is possible to consider how kitchen sink's heightened emphasis on spatial representation acts in a manner similar to Barthes's superfluous—a feature designed to bring about the reality effect through self-referentiality. That is to say, representations of space and place in kitchen sink texts surpass mere formalities; instead, they signal the important role of environmental details as part of the movement's aesthetic program. By moving away from the idea that depicted space is little more than a stage for the story, the effect is that characters engage with spaces more readily—space shifts from a formal feature to an active, functional component of the realist technique. Such a development can be understood as part of the evolutionary process of realism, to naturalism, to social realism, and, eventually, to kitchen sink realism.

Questioning the value of the realist mode, Barthes asks why imaginative writing should seek to capture experiences already available in the world at all. Ultimately, he concludes that the purpose of traditional realism is to obfuscate ideology by claiming to present a direct, unmediated depiction of reality. This simulation of the real, he suggests, masks the subjective nature of cultural production, especially as it relates to class and authentic experience. For Barthes, realism is a trick by which the dominant class can sustain the social order that suits their needs through "the disintegration of the sign" which he claims to be "modernity's great affair" (1986: 148). In this sense, even the most socially conscious texts are mired by an aesthetic that exceeds the ethical: altruism and social change. Such concerns are at the root of realism's continued evolution—specifically in the way kitchen sink texts navigate the problem of aesthetics. In the British consensus era—a time when working-class people saw new degrees of public recognition—the limits of the original realist mode are cast in stark relief, leading to the need for writers and artists to rethink its goals relative to the form's utility.

The turn toward naturalism signifies a similar evolution, demonstrating a move away from the aesthetic impulse of traditional realism by broadening depictions of landscapes in ways that permit a more recognizable set of relations. The kind of naturalism pioneered by Émile Zola, and the kind also identifiable in the work of writers such as Thomas Hardy, was driven more by the cultural impact of Darwinism and social factors related to environment rather than the social problems stemming from industrialization. Naturalism, then, can be read as consideration of cause and effect in which characters negotiate particular sites with responses operating in a manner that suggests sociological inquiry. Although Romantic principles undergird this gesture—specifically regarding the meditative impact of nature on the psyche—naturalism frequently sidestepped the idyllic, centering instead on the rise of industry and the impact of factory life on the worker. The naturalism of Hardy and other writers like George Gissing, advanced the aesthetic of the Victorian social novel through a more nuanced integration of setting, depicting a malevolent environment in which characters' responses suggested new forms of identity. Despite this evolution of intent, naturalism was still very much an institutional affair in which emphasis on form surpassed function. The question remains as to whether or not naturalist authors sought to illuminate conditions worthy of social change, or whether they used such imagery as aesthetics for aesthetics' sake.

Speaking generally, both social realism and naturalism use similar strategies of representation—specifically the environment's impact on the human psyche. Distinctions between the two modes are identified through the project's aims in which political objectives compete with aesthetic modes of representation. As Samantha Lay has remarked, pinpointing differences between naturalism and social realism is challenging since social realism "is both politically and historically contingent" (2002: 8)—meaning that definition requires revision as time goes on. Given this, the way to identify a work of social realism as opposed to traditional realism or perhaps naturalism is to focus on a writer's intent and to discern the degree of political aspiration involved. For example, a text by Hardy in which working-class conditions are depicted with relative authenticity might still appear to prioritize bourgeois aesthetics when contrasted with a text by the Chartists whose writing was unambiguously political. As such, twentieth-century social realism politicizes the formal tendencies of traditional realism. Indeed, kitchen sink texts recalibrate the political and the aesthetic yet maintain tension between the two. Hence, the period's texts should be read as a high point of realist representation.

Critical Approaches to Kitchen Sink Aesthetics

Critical attempts to totalize the movement's aesthetics underscore the fact that the term "movement" is itself inelegant with regard to capturing the nature of postwar writing. Despite this, a number of critics have made claims about its relative success or failure. As I have suggested throughout, a study of the period is perhaps better served by focusing on particular tropes, partly because the texts vary in terms of content, but also because the movement exists across media formats. As this book has demonstrated, engagement with space and detailed depictions of classed environs is perceptible in the novels, the plays, and the films. Peter Kalliney has argued that the texts of the movement fail to accurately convey the kind of spaces inhabited by working-class people. Referencing John Osborne and Kingsley Amis, Kalliney states that "most Angry texts were not written by working-class writers" (2006: 113). As discussed in the first chapter, Osborne's case is indeed unusual in that his background can be read more as a synthesis of experience—much of which can be categorized as transitory, producing within him a degree of social delinquency and radical distrust of authority that draws parallels to Hoggart's notion of "us" in relation to "them." This is also true of other writers like Nell Dunn (who came from significant means but found vitality in working-class spaces) and Colin MacInnes (whose work is rarely discussed in relation to the writers of the kitchen sink era). Kingsley Amis is perhaps better considered a precursor to the movement rather than a member of it, and *Lucky Jim* certainly anticipates the figure of the outsider codified in many of the kitchen sink protagonists. While *Lucky Jim* reflects the insouciance of the prototypical "angry young man," the novel bears little resemblance to kitchen sink structures. In fact, as mentioned in the introduction, Keith Waterhouse's *Billy Liar* reconceptualizes *Lucky Jim* in a way that is more aligned to the kitchen sink movement. In its place, I would suggest that texts by a figure such as Sid Chaplin put forward a more likely precursor in that Braine and others cited Chaplin as an inspiration, and Chaplin himself would go on to adopt the very motifs he inadvertently inspired, especially in texts like 1961's *The Day of the Sardine* and 1962's *The Watchers and the Watched*. Aside from this, prominent figures of the movement such as John Arden, Stan Barstow, Edward Bond, Nell Dunn, Alan Sillitoe, David Storey, and Arnold Wesker were all born and raised in working-class environments, and others associated with the movement were familiar with working-class life and customs. That said, Kalliney offers effective pointers about the writers of the period, mentioning that "most Angry texts display a sense of acutely conflicted, highly ambivalent class consciousness" (2006: 113). He references *Look Back in Anger*, drawing on Jimmy's equivocal stance on class politics. But this example can also be read as somewhat of an anomaly in relation to other texts of the time. Jimmy's conflicted status stems more from his frustration—the result of what he perceives to be a failure of the Welfare State. This point is made apparent throughout the play by the fact that, despite his educated status, he had no real access to social mobility. As mentioned in Chapter 2, the deficiencies of the eleven-plus and Education Act only served to sustain the persistence of class divisions. Jimmy may appear conflicted and he struggles to articulate the nature of his oppression, but Osborne himself was clearly attuned to such concerns.

Kalliney raises questions of aesthetic consistency within the movement as a whole, echoing voices of prior critics while characterizing the key figures as "leftist dissidents who use social realism as a means of protesting against the affectations of the experimental, high modernist literature that flourished between the wars" (2006: 112). He notes how virtually all of the period's texts use domestic interiors as "a trope for capturing the social atmosphere of the 1950s" (2006: 115). Once more, the proximity of the titular kitchen sink rings true. But Kalliney's critique centers on the role of masculinity, particularly the way such authors tend to place amplified forms of masculinity into traditional domestic spheres to hypothesize the results. While this is certainly true of the two texts that he examines (*Look Back in Anger* and *Saturday Night and Sunday Morning*), it is arguably less true of texts like *A Taste of Honey* or *Up the Junction*. Consequently, it is possible to acknowledge that the domestic space is a common theme, but it is less plausible to suggest that its main role is that of an arena for the contestation of masculinity. Furthermore, Kalliney claims that the movement's portrayal of provincial domestic space acts as a reclamation of nationalistic pride but also as a shifting of the focus away from London and its assumed centrality in high-brow writing. Again, this is certainly arguable in relation to the two texts that he considers but is less the case in texts like *Up the Junction* or *Billy Liar* in which the former's narrative is entirely set in South London and the latter discusses London as a desired destination. Although the domestic environment is central to these texts, forming a common thread through virtually all of them, I would harbor that its role is more along the lines of what I discuss in Chapter 1: that the domestic state of the immediate postwar years reiterates the ways in which class was imposed in a prescriptive manner, acting more as a mechanism of stratification than as a necessary solution to the housing crisis.

David Castronovo's 2009 text *Blokes: The Bad Boys of English Literature* provides a similarly rich analysis. It opens with a terse statement pathologizing the protagonists generally linked to kitchen sink texts: "Aggression, self-assertion, the pursuit of pleasure, the generating of mischief and transgressive humor, the flight from traditional disciplines and codes, the contempt for institutions, the boredom with routine, the struggle to live vitally" (2009: 1). This certainly reflects of a number of characters associated with the movement—Osborne's Jimmy and Sillitoe's Arthur in particular. But such a perspective overlooks the causal effects behind such positions which, I suggest, is an essential component of the era. Castronovo does touch on genre tropes that extend beyond the laddish behavior of the protagonists. In his concluding chapter, he discusses texts like John Wain's *Hurry on Down* (1953), emphasizing the novel's reliance on space and environs to show how its protagonist toys with existential class-crises: "The story begins in Stotwell, a nondescript place in the Midlands"—the kind of place that allows the protagonist to explore a "grubby, seedy world that wasn't lowlife but wasn't interested in a better life or a more meaningful life" (2009: 134). The space that Castronovo describes here is a space that acts as a backdrop for a number of kitchen sink texts—an environment marked by resignation and acquiescence, presented in ways that stress its ubiquity and repetition. Furthermore, Lichtenstein and Schregenberger's *As Found: The Discover of the Ordinary* draws a number of connections between art movements and kitchen sink aesthetics, providing an instructive introduction to the general ideas across different media forms. Here, the authors note the consistent referencing of social taboos and issues rarely discussed in public, arguing that the embrace of difficult topics and the prevalence of coarse language played a key role in the abolition of censorship during the 1960s. The authors also recount the profound effect the movement had on the arts more broadly, claiming that "The change of location from London to the industrial landscape, and the change of subject matter from the haves to the have-nots" was instrumental in the movement's lasting impact (2006: 266). Kenneth Tynan contends that the era was driven by a generational nihilism stemming from the rise of nuclear armament: "What distinguished the modern English 'young angries' is that they all came of age around the time that their elders invented the hydrogen bomb. How could they revere 'civilization as we know it' when at any moment it might be transformed into 'civilization as we knew it?'" (1961: 192). Although I would disagree that nihilism is a consistent thread woven throughout these works, the impact of generational tension and conflict is sustained throughout all of the texts of the period—chiefly due to reasons of confinement and shared habitation outlined in the first chapter. In general, it can be said that the central tenets of the movement revolve around a disenfranchised character whose embitterment is the result of rigid class definitions and failed social policy. The subject matter is often gritty and visceral, with settings designed to amplify emotional states. While such details do indeed appear across the novels, plays, and films, there are subtle distinctions worth addressing.

Multimedia Motifs and Kitchen Sink Thematics

Declaration, the 1958 volume edited by Tom Maschler, is the closest document to a manifesto that the movement ever had. The text challenges the "Angry Young Men" appellation by presenting a broader range of voices than that of the standard "angries," with essays from Doris Lessing, Colin Wilson, and Kenneth Tynan. Furthermore, the text also offers more specific coverage of discrete media forms with Bill Hopkins discussing novels, John Osborne on drama, and Lindsay Anderson on film. Tynan's essay "Theatre and Living" grants insight into the impact of the movement on the world of theater, focusing in particular on the formal attributes that distinguish an "angry" play from others at the time.

Tynan opens his essay by assuring the reader that any formal labels applied to the movement are tenuous at best, declaring that "From definitions everything follows, so with a definition I shall begin this ragbag of an aesthetic credo in which, very probably aesthetics will not be mentioned at all" (1958: 91). Following an irreverent dismissal of drawing-room-style theater, he then underscores the movement's emphasis on states of anguish—the kind most readily perceptible in *Look Back in Anger*: "Where there is no desperation, or where desperation is inadequately motivated, there is no drama; characters, for instance, who scream when their noses are tickled or commit suicide the day after falling in love are bad cases of inadequately motivated desperation" (1958: 91). For Tynan, as with others, the crucial component of the movement in theater was an emphasis on social issues mostly ignored by the theater arts. Such issues, it is worth noting, read like a list of the problems associated with the Beveridge Report: "poverty, ignorance, oppression and the rest—are theatrically shunned" (1958: 92). Furthermore, his characterization of the writers of the period is exacting in that he claims them to be "a flourishing bunch, worth more than a passing word" but "different from the radical intelligentsia of the thirties in one vital respect: they are not engaged in a filial revolt against the class from which they sprang" (1958: 94). He claims that plays aiming for social change are often clumsy (1958: 93) whereas the kitchen sink writers' aims, in his evaluation, broadened perspectives to present a more granular vision of British culture (1958: 94). From this, it is evident that Tynan believes the most-prominent attribute of kitchen sink drama is authenticity—the depiction of the working-class subject and the social concerns faced.

In recent years, critics have looked back to the movement in order to refine tropes and motifs, commonly drawing on Osborne's play as the blueprint. For instance, Stephen Lacey writes:

> All the qualities are there, qualities one had despaired of ever seeing on the stage—the drift towards anarchy, the instinctive leftishness, the automatic rejection of "official" attitudes, the surrealist sense of humor … the casual promiscuity, the sense of lacking a crusade worth fighting for.
>
> (2002: 18)

In addition to representing issues pertinent to the working classes, critics generally felt that kitchen sink theater was best understood through its desire to shock the establishment. On the one hand, a play like Osborne's builds on Antonin Artaud's "Theatre of Cruelty"; on the other, such plays can also be comprehended as a precursor to the In-Yer-Face movement of the 1990s. But the desire to shock and upset is perhaps also the reason why kitchen sink plays felt at home in Joan Littlewood's Theatre Workshop. As Nadine Holdsworth notes, Littlewood rose to prominence through reinterpretations of classic plays but quickly became known as a champion of writers who sought to present "vibrant depictions of life on the fringes of society that captured the public's imagination and the interest of West End producers keen to capitalize on a successful product" (2006: 25). That said, Littlewood was less enthused by some of the dramatists that Tynan tended to elevate, claiming her protégé Shelagh Delaney to be "the antithesis of London's Angry Young Men" in that "She knows what she is angry about" (Ellis 2003). Stage design was of utmost importance to Littlewood—especially in light of the plans she imagined with Cedric Price for 1961's "Fun Palace"—a stage designed as an interactive space for communities and the shared celebration of theatrical arts. Littlewood was known for maximizing set design while working with minimal budgets. So, productions of kitchen sink plays—in which the setting played such an instrumental role—were felt to be in good hands. For instance, Littlewood's production of Delaney's play was sensitive to the impact of spatial confinement, but paid notable attention to the use of symbolic lighting to convey Jo's capacity to transform spaces to fit her needs. Theatrical productions of kitchen sink drama clearly respected the writers' desires to elevate the environment as a decisive factor in the narrative, emphasizing the shock of dismal spaces as well as the ways in which the characters constructed their identity relative to the places they inhabit.

As with the plays produced at the time, salient themes and motifs can be identified within the novels in a manner that suggests continuity across forms. Most identifiable in the novel is the use of regional vernacular with linguistic nuance heightened by the phonetic form. As Stuart Laing argues, until 1955, there were few genuine representations of working-class people in literature—a point Laing links to the decline of social realism due to associations with WWII. So, fiction featuring grim, gritty spaces fell out of fashion as it failed to compete with the grim, gritty conditions that much of the country faced as a lived reality. Laing registers this trend's impact on publishing, specifically the closure of presses known for documentary-style work (1986: 60). He also discusses the general dearth of working-class representation and regional voices, especially in the period leading up to the rise of the kitchen sink era, citing Clifford Tolchard's rebuke of the British writer John Lehmann's claim of sustained working-class representation: "there *was* a kind of lack of journals which were prepared to welcome working-class writing" (1986: 60, emphasis original). In this sense, the reality of the postwar years created an environment in which representations of poverty would hardly be considered marketable or appealing. Given the popularity of working-class texts during the 1930s, it can be seen how such a shift might produce a vacuum predisposed to a new set of working-class voices in the postwar era.

Reminiscent of the movement's plays, the novels used setting and environment as part of their aesthetic program. As explained in previous chapters, depictions of working-class space act less as a backdrop for the action and more as a problem in need of a solution. Novelistic descriptions of setting are surprisingly repetitious in a manner that recalls Barthes's superfluousness, with industrial environs marked by filth and grime. Escape from such sites is experienced through periodic retreats into nature that recall the work of the Romantic poets which also suggest escape as a necessity. But kitchen sink texts tend toward a form of realism grounded in consensus through the tacit recognition of a quasi-mythical working-class community—homes and industrial communities usually presented as appendages to the local factory. Through their relative anonymity, novelistic representations of working-class environs serve as a reminder of the sameness of industrial spaces.

In addition to geographic detail, the novels also deploy spatial signifiers that extend the use of setting to describe the impact of space on identity. Tropes associated with the movement's novels suggest the use of spatial metaphors as a way to augment direct references to spatial limits and confines. One notable device is the prevalence of the dying patriarch—a harbinger of the younger generation's future in the industrial environment. Such emblems, perhaps most clearly rendered in texts like Sillitoe's *The Loneliness of the Long Distance Runner* or MacInnes's *Absolute Beginners*, position the patriarch as confined to the home, commonly hidden from view. The reader is granted knowledge of their situation, and the home is—once more—cast less as a sanctuary and more as a grave. The dying patriarch generally serves as a warning for the protagonist, forcing them to respond by revolting against the status quo or succumbing to a life of acquiescence. The home becomes a floating signifier—less of a site of respite, and more as compulsory constituent of the means of production.

In *British Social Realism: From Documentary to Brit Grit*, Samantha Lay compiles tropes of the British New Wave film movement, situating the cinematic adaptations of kitchen sink writing within a genealogy of cinema. But as a movement with remarkable crossover into other media forms, many of the tropes that Lay identifies are also identifiable within plays and novels of the time. Central to Lay's schematizing of tropes is the assertion that social realism, as a movement, demonstrates its commitment to the cultural moment in terms of history as well as politics (2002: 8). Similar to Kalliney, Lay claims that a vital component of the movement is the exploration of taboo topics and themes alongside authentic depictions of character types in working-class settings (2002: 9). However, Lay also draws distinctions between social issues and the themes that emerge to suggest a genre-specific pattern of commonalities. She begins by isolating key factors, maintaining that social realism in film tends to focus on "characters who are inextricably linked to place or environment" in tandem with the effects that place has on them (2002: 19). Furthermore, she maintains that the topics engaged must be timely—the content reflecting the world as experienced in the contextual present. The upshot, she submits, is that such films seek to move underrepresented or marginalized groups further into the spotlight. This is accomplished, in part, by a heightened verisimilitude, with the films of the time merging fiction with documentary (2002: 20). Lay also insists that the intent of the text should be apparent, and such an intent should not prioritize financial gain but serve a political purpose. In addition, she speaks to the requirement of elevated verisimilitude, with filmic adaptations walking the line between fiction and documentary (2002: 20). Last, Lay argues that, counter to traditional narrative arcs with neat resolutions, social realist films resist definitive outcomes, although she adds that this component is open to interpretation (2002: 21).

Lay also touches on issues of style, a factor perhaps more readily understood through film yet still evident in the novels and the plays. The use of gritty images, she claims, results in an "observational style of filming which tends to produce a distance between text and spectator" as well as a "tension between 'sociological realism'—which privileges a documenting of situations and events—and a style of social realism sometimes referred to as 'poetic realism'" (2002: 22). Lay clarifies that poetic realism is ultimately a romanticization of working-class culture—one that Roger Manvell has called "industrial romanticism," most recognizable in contrasting images of factories against sweeping landscapes or bombed-out buildings against pristine blue skies (1946: 100). Similarly, Lay references Andrew Higson's brief but noteworthy essay "Space, Place, Spectacle, Landscape and Townscape in the 'Kitchen Sink' Film" (2016b) in which he describes the concept of "That Shot of Our Town from That Hill"—a cinematic technique in which the protagonist is temporarily removed from the community and granted the ability to look down from above, gaining objectivity and clarity. I would note that such cinematic details predate the films of the New Wave as texts like *Saturday Night and Sunday Morning* and *This Sporting Life* also feature similar motifs, with Sillitoe placing Arthur outside of the town to weigh up his choices, and Storey placing Frank on the rugby field—momentarily removed from the factory. This is, of course, a romantic gesture of retreat in which nature offers clarity about urban life through contrast. Hence, the stylistic attributes most commonly discussed in terms of the films of the time are not restricted to the medium and can indeed be identified within the novels and the plays, suggesting that the movement shares tropes and motifs across formats with specific effects in mind. In other words, if kitchen sink realism could ever be codified, it is through the effects used rather than the content or by characteristics tied exclusively to a specified media type. To read a kitchen sink text, arguably, is to read motifs across a variety of forms.

Toward a Spatial Aesthetics of Class

If, as has been suggested, the texts aligned with the kitchen sink movement offer a refinement of the original tenets of realism—in particular, through the intensification of spatial interaction—then a general review of the main aesthetic devices is in order. Doing so helps provide a well-defined sense of how the era elevates both form and function to recalibrate the aesthetic with the ethical. This invites a new way of thinking about working-class life as represented in cultural production more broadly, positioning the kitchen sink movement as a touchstone or as a benchmark by which to gauge subsequent depictions of working-class life. While kitchen sink texts are most known through their monikers or their embrace of taboo topics, they are less known by their use of spatial metaphors or depicted negotiations with working-class space. And yet, this component serves as consistent trope, one that validates authorial authenticity and a commitment to representing the under-represented with veracity. So, aside from characterization and plot, setting is of crucial significance in these works, and the following review of components catalogs the methods and motifs central to the movement's spatial aesthetics.

Represented spaces are depicted as "gritty," rendered as such through the impact of industry on communities. As noted, comprehension of what constitutes "gritty" is shaped by one's own perspective and surroundings. Furthermore, it is a term which, as of late, has been used to fetishize working-class life along the lines of neoliberal bootstrapping (Lee 2021). Yet, the term is multivalent, warranting careful analysis. Additionally, texts that feature grit in its various forms demand attention to the way the motif is utilized. For example, the environments featured in Sillitoe's texts tend to be matter-of-fact with little editorial commentary; they reconstruct the streets and factories of industrial Nottingham through an objective, unwavering lens to capture the general filth and despondency of the area. This representation of grit connotes industrial pollution, persistence and tenacity, as well as impressions of risk and survival; in other words, the aesthetic and the political work in tandem. By contrast, John Braine's *Room at the Top* tends to magnify grim working-class spaces, focusing specifically on war damage as if to remind the reader that working-class locales are commensurate with impoverishment and lack. Here, grit is primarily aesthetic, acting as a surface-level signifier of working-class life that stands in opposition to the sites of middle-class life the protagonist hopes to access. Shelagh Delaney, on the other hand, underscores the inhospitality of her environs but seeks to find value in them. Her environments are cast as unmistakably bleak, but she challenges the negative valence of "gritty" by suggesting the inherent comfort in grit and grime. In the texts of the period, environments are universally "gritty," but the concept can be explored through the multivalent nature of language.

Despite the notion of gritty space as contaminated by industrial debris, environments depicted convey a mysterious appeal. A goal of the movement, I suggest, is to center the impact of space on an individual's conception of social status, and working-class spaces associated with industrial environs are generally presented as appealing in spite of their repressive nature. Even in cases of abject poverty, the period's texts highlight value in shared struggle as well as identities marked by tenacity. Given this, kitchen sink texts' depictions of space tend to vacillate between depictions of grime associated with industry and familiarity represented in social environs. Representations of space in kitchen sink realism are rarely linear, rarely nostalgic, and rarely engage pathos. Instead, they focus on recognition; working-class people will recognize characteristics of the depicted space immediately.

As such, the spaces are authentically reproduced rather than fabricated as textual worlds or cast in an idealized, romanticized form. In a manner that recalls the premise of social realism, kitchen sink authors draw attention to gritty environments of northern industrial areas but reframe them by uncovering the extraordinary within the ordinary. This is accomplished through interactions with space or by stressing the value of a particular site within an environment. In this sense, the documentary-style motifs borrowed from social realism are reiterated and enlarged for a broader audience. On the one hand, the work of Sillitoe or Delaney demonstrates a commitment to replicating areas surrounding both Nottingham and Salford with care; on the other, a text like Braine's *Room at the Top* turns to fictional spaces like Dufton and Warley through the use of representational blueprints—working-class and middle-class spaces rendered instantly decipherable through details such as cleanliness and resources available.

Yet, such recognition is a paradox. While emphasizing the extraordinary, the spaces depicted in kitchen sink texts remain ordinary, bordering on anonymous. Even in cases in which a region or area is made identifiable, kitchen sink texts generally do not take the position of venerating or promoting a designated region; the emphasis on *types* of space takes precedence to specific places. Although the texts of the period reached broad audiences, the spaces spoke directly to individuals most likely to occupy the kind of regions and settings depicted. Furthermore, depictions of working-class sites rarely extend beyond a handful of standard institutions: the home, the school, the workplace, and the pub. A traditional kitchen sink drama would struggle to exist in a coastal or entirely pastoral setting; industry and its attendant monotony serve as key requirements. In this manner, the sites depicted are simultaneously familiar yet indistinct.

Kitchen sink texts also tend to describe the same environment multiple times, allowing the notion of repetition to function as rhythmic pauses in the narrative. In addition, such sites are often presented from multiple angles, offering manifold perspectives and viewpoints while sidestepping specificity or idiosyncrasy. This is perhaps more apparent in the novels than in the plays and films where, it can be assumed, setting is omnipresent. Yet, plays like *Look Back in Anger* and films like Ken Loach's 1967 adaptation of Nell Dunn's *Poor Cow* from 1967 use repetition by either drawing attention to the setting through stage directions or cinematic cuts that force recognition of the backdrop. Repetition can also be read as a stylistic device meant to fragment the narrative, allowing for a degree of aesthetic experimentation without abandoning realism or accessibility. Given that a number of kitchen sink texts grew out of shorter fiction pieces, the repetition of spatial details and movement through space helps unify the narrative.

The depicted space regularly impacts the individual, and the texts tend to highlight such interactions in a manner that calls to mind Lefebvre's spatial triad. In other words, the setting is rarely just decorative; emphasis is given to the way characters navigate through, interact with, and are impacted by the spaces they inhabit. Arguably, this trope requires critical acuity in order to determine such details, but the texts frequently highlight the way spaces produce certain moods or actions. The effect is accomplished through, and can be identified by, characters' associative responses. For example, domestic spaces generally lead to a sense of limitation and restriction; any comfort or security they might provide is contingent and momentary. Factory settings, by contrast, can bring about a sense of security through perceived freedom and independence. Even though work sites can symbolize drudgery and exploitation, they endow working-class characters with a sense of identity and value. Spaces outside of designated working-class environs can generally be read as contingent, transgressive sites that prompt reverie, reflection, or crises. Such moments are usually featured in texts as fleeting breaks from the central narrative with the capacity to act as heterotopic sites of potentiality. The spaces of kitchen sink realism are ultimately spaces of confinement in which characters strive to renegotiate and articulate new ways of expressing classed subjecthood. Therefore, the texts are rarely set in open spaces or spaces that symbolize freedom of movement. Closed confines (be it rooms or institutions) are met with closed environs (collections or groupings of spaces that appear to be physically confined or confining). Kitchen sink texts, by their very nature, magnify social limits represented by space, and the novels, plays, and films of the period perform this function consistently through depicted space as well as spatial metaphors that help enunciate class.

In terms of working-class writing and the representation of working-class characters and environments in British fiction, the texts of the kitchen sink period act as a watershed moment in their fine-tuning of the formal aesthetics of class-conscious cultural production. Texts related to the movement demonstrate a particular sensitivity to spatial representations of social class, using such references to imagine new modes of belonging. Considering this, the period's texts can serve as a benchmark for subsequent working-class portrayals and weighing ethical allegiances. Three aspects should be considered in relation to the way space is represented. The first is that the heightened emphasis on spatial representation as superfluous can be viewed as an evolution of realism in that such a technique pushes naturalism toward a mode of representation in which political capacity is featured while sidestepping propaganda. That is to say that, following Barthes's logic, there is a persistent breaking of the narrative frame that moves the reader back and forth between the fictional and documentary-style motifs designed to simulate the real. Second, that such methods add rhetorical ethos in that working-class spaces represent environments that working-class people interact with, elevating the function of spatial representation from mere backdrop to that of an operative element. Third, that the increased presence of space and its significance is characterized by a number of components specific to the period. Such texts, then, are in direct conversation with the contextual moment—a gesture that balances the aesthetic (by increasing verisimilitude) with the ethical or the political (by raising awareness of social conditions). This balance is precarious, and the potential commodification of working-class identity runs throughout. What follows are brief case studies of the way texts that build on the aesthetics developed during the kitchen sink era adhere to or veer away from the principles I have suggested above. Evaluating such aesthetic effects—specifically, effects driven by the use of spatial metaphors and spatial negotiations—reveals how representation turns toward fidelity and allegiance while also revealing instances in which such techniques are applied with more commercial and potentially exploitative intentions in mind.

Coronation Street as Commodified "Kitsch-en" Sink

The long-running British soap opera *Coronation Street*—affectionately referred to as "Corrie"—played an instrumental role in popularizing representations of working-class life. Written by Tony Warren, and first broadcast in December of 1960, *Coronation Street* sustained the kitchen sink aesthetic through the remainder of the century and established the blueprint for a host of other popular TV dramas. Although set in the fictional town of Weatherfield, the show was filmed in Manchester with Weatherfield based on Salford. The bulk of the narrative is centered around the titular street, named after the 1902 coronation of King Edward VII, Queen Victoria's successor. Accordingly, the name of the show connotes a modern spin on industrial British life, focusing on twentieth-century realities as they were experienced by many working-class people. Although much of the action takes place on indoor sets, the street serves as the central hub of the community, with local meeting places such as The Rovers Return—a pub established alongside the street—operating as an iconic symbol of community. The significance and familiarity of *Coronation Street* in British culture cannot be understated, its popularity and dissemination largely the result of the advent of home television in the years preceding the show combined with the relative dearth of programming. Furthermore, the success of Granada Television and subsequently Independent Television (ITV) stems, at least in part, from the popularity of *Coronation Street*. Originally conceived as a kitchen sink-inspired drama, the show demonstrates how the spatial aesthetics of the era were commodified and repackaged for mass consumption. Stridently different from soap operas that promote aspirational fantasies, *Coronation Street* is unabashedly working class, reflecting ideals and experiences far more commonly understood by postwar Britain.

The show's enduring success begs the question as to why low-budget representations of the mundane sustain attention relative to more escapist drama. According to Judith Jones, the show's astounding longevity can be understood as the result of "its cast of strong characters, its northern roots and sense of community … combined with skillfully written and often amusing scripts" (Jones). Nick Couldry adds that *Coronation Street* provides escape through recognition in that the show "has offered a continuous fictional reality, operating in parallel to viewers' lives" (2000: 76). Couldry argues that the show's appeal to viewers stems from its ability to operate as "a mnemonic system for events in their own life" (2000: 76) in which a shared experience produces "social memory through acts of repetition" (2000: 75). To a degree, this is the function of the soap opera: to dramatize and commodify social interactions in a manner that might draw a small but dedicated viewership. Couldry points out that the ritualistic phenomenon of viewership is aligned to the identifiable and relatable qualities associated with kitchen sink realism, recalling Kenneth Tynan's initial comment on *Look Back in Anger* as a play written in a voice familiar to the lives it represents. Furthermore, the show "has a temporal depth" in that viewers aligned events in their own lives to events that took place "on the street" (2000: 76). Such factors develop the show's appeal beyond the boundaries of the show itself, demonstrating the degree of culture-shaping effects possible through television.

Be that as it may, *Coronation Street*'s content was hardly gripping. The set—a cheap build housed at the Granada Studios in Manchester—provides the kind of accidental wall shaking that gives low-budget soap operas their camp charm. It was the collective endorsement of the viewership that elevated the street from its transparently fictional setting to something more like a tangible, recognizable reality; the street was so universally identifiable, even in its relative anonymity, that it became a place as real for many British people as a material address. Temporal connections made by viewers in relation to their own lives, amplified by the shared experience of mass consumption, elevated the show from a fictional narrative to something closer to a consensus of lived experience. When the set was opened to the public and sold as a kind of pilgrimage, it elicited an emotional response from visitors that Couldry remarks was "hardly trivial" (2000: 77). Visitors treated the space as though it were real and fully operational, taking pleasure in "the apparently banal things people do on the Street set to connect up with the outside, non-fictional world: posting cards in the Street pillar-box or using the telephone box" (2000: 77). Though nobody would ever mistake Coronation Street as existing within the real world, the emotional and cultural investment in the show is profound.

Coronation Street denotes a uniquely British approach to the soap opera through its ability to romance monotony in ways commensurate with kitchen sink narratives. As Christine Geraghty suggests, the appeal is augmented by issues of identity: "While soaps have always had a tendency to deal with the everyday and the mundane even in their most extreme moments, in British soaps this emphasis on the quotidian inevitably intertwined with issues of class and religion" (2000: 66). Geraghty continues to suggest that the show's monotony is what makes it so relatable: "The working class, as a specific group, not just as ordinary people, was represented in *Coronation Street* so that the drama of personal relationships so characteristic of a soap was placed within a homogenous community living in the backstreets of a town in northern England" (2000: 66). The heightened emphasis on the mundane presented through spatial negotiations of identity situates *Coronation Street* as a seemingly legitimate heir to the foundational kitchen sink aesthetic. Furthermore, the emphasis on the ordinary recalls David Sylvester's essay in *Encounter* which, it is worth recalling, was meant as disparaging.

Coronation Street differs from both the original kitchen sink texts and the burgeoning New Wave film movement in that the displays of rugged individualism associated with the foundational texts are replaced by an emphasis on community. Whereas kitchen sink texts are infused with frustration channeled into aggression and violence, *Coronation Street* tends to favor the nostalgic sentimentality suggested in the work of Hoggart and Orwell. This reveals an important distinction in the commercial capacity of kitchen sink aesthetics in which emphasis on community makes for a more palatable and, therefore, more salable product than the kind of individualism and new modes of class articulation championed by the early kitchen sink sequence. At the core of this distinction is my aforementioned assertion of recalibrated aesthetic and ethical dynamics. The original kitchen sink texts tended to use their aesthetic program for political means while *Coronation Street* thrives on the aesthetic, rarely adopting a political stance that might trouble easy digestion. In fact, one possible criticism leveled at the show is that its romanticizing of working-class culture minimizes the day-to-day struggle of workers by substituting them with day-to-day monotony. As Olwen Terris writes, "while retaining a strong regional identity and an unthreatening sense of working-class community, 'the street' has largely preferred to entertain rather than engage in contemporary realism" (Terris). So, *Coronation Street* draws on the aesthetics of kitchen sink realism while attenuating the ethical and the political dimensions. In doing so, it became one of the most successful and resilient British TV shows in history. Clearly, *Coronation Street* epitomizes a process of commodification—not just of kitchen sink principles, but of working-class identities.

The show places the original kitchen sink movement into stark relief by emphasizing the ethical intentions absent in the commodified aesthetic. While the films of the British New Wave certainly turned more toward commercial viability than the novels and plays, *Coronation Street* represents one of the first and most perceptible transformations of kitchen sink aesthetics into a popular commodity. Made for an audience to watch after a day's work, it was no accident that the show minimized portrayals of labor beyond that of the bar staff at The Rovers Return, cementing its viability as a ritualized and, ultimately, pacifying example of commodified working-class life.

Representations of space in *Coronation Street* can be read as mirrors of the intended audience's own inhabited space. That said, spaces presented are mediated in a manner that, on the one hand, calls to mind the spatial metaphors of the kitchen sink era and, on the other, helps to construct a consumable product free of kitchen sink's ideological heft. First, the spaces depicted in the show are commensurate with the kitchen sink motif of spaces portrayed as conventional and ubiquitous. The bulk of the sites are restricted to domestic interiors (with minor variations between them), the interior of The Rovers Return, a community shop, and, much less frequently, the local factory. The ubiquity is further emphasized by the iconic title sequence, preserved over the show's lifespan albeit with minor updates that signal film innovation rather than any tangible changes in the street itself. From the first episode to the present, an overhead camera pans row after row of chimney pots to establish a landscape composed entirely of industrial housing terraces. When paired with the similarly iconic and morose theme music from composer Eric Spear, the effect combines repetition with familiarity in ways that render the space immediately knowable despite its fictionality. The early Granada TV title page that claimed "From the North" is communicated through the use of spatial references that code working-class communities as "northern." Even the most current version of the sequence still focuses on chimney pots despite their relatively outmoded function in contemporary British society. This image signals both the warmth of the community and the domestic space that the chimneys help to heat, but it also triggers a nostalgic effect central to the commodification process.

As Nicola Wilson has discussed, the regularity and repetition seen in the physical sets and environments of *Coronation Street* also serve to offset the anxiety of community upheaval taking place through the continuation of slum-clearance projects and the gentrification of urban working-class communities (2015: 145). The symbolic attributes of the domestic sanctuary critiqued through kitchen sink texts—as well as the domestic ordering established in the work of Hoggart—are perceptible in the homes of *Coronation Street*'s various residents and are therefore worthy of inquiry. Although interior decor responds to shifting tastes in culture, the spaces romanticize the working-class terraced housing known to encapsulate notions of community through sameness. For example, the first episode broadcast in 1960 features a scene from the multi-generational home of Ken Barlow (played by William Patrick Roache, who has starred in the role consistently since the show began) in which he eats dinner with his parents in a manner that mimics scenes from Sillitoe's *Saturday Night and Sunday Morning*. The scene serves to establish the generational divides central to Sillitoe's work in that the space is clearly decorated to reflect an older generation's sensibilities through the presence of knick-knacks and Victorian figurines. While less antagonistic than the intergenerational motifs central to kitchen sink texts, Barlow announces his more modern sensibilities by discussing the latest record he purchased and remarking to his mother that she probably would not understand the music he likes. The gesture parallels several prominent kitchen sink texts circulating at the time, and links would likely be drawn by the viewing public but without the movement's more pressing agenda. Put differently, the trope of the cramped multigenerational domestic space is softened but without losing any of its connotative power. Of note is a now-famous scene from 2016 in which Barlow suffers a debilitating stroke. Following this, the generational roles are reversed as Barlow argues with his own son before falling ill. The scene offers a metatextual nod to the first episode by replicating details. For instance, the floral print fabrics seen on the curtains of the 1960 dining room, as well as those on the housecoat of his mother, Ira, are repeated in the wallpaper and the curtains of the 2016 space. Also, the tiled grid of the 1960 fireplace is reincarnated as wallpaper in the 2016 version, and the same overall confinement is expressed through the layout of the terrace floor plan which remains unchanged not just from the 1960s episode, but from the Victorian era—the period when such a home was likely constructed. Such connections are not accidental; they exist to sustain a sense of familiarity and repetition through signification that ensures the program's longevity.

As the second most featured space, The Rovers Return has also remained fairly static as a representation of the cultural role of drinking in working-class communities. The pub is so well-recognized in Britain that it is not a stretch to assume that most British people would list it as one of the country's most famous institutions. Despite its cultural fixity, the interior has been revamped several times to respond to the natural progression of other pubs in England throughout history. When changes occur, though, they certainly do not go unnoticed. For instance, in an episode broadcast on June 18, 1986, The Rovers Return suffered an electrical fire that incinerated much of the space and left it in need of refurbishment. The fire made national newspaper headlines, and the episode's usual closing credits were extended as a kind of eulogy. In fact, throughout its history, The Rovers Return has used spatial design to represent changes in culture as well as changes in the social climate. For instance, in the show's early years, the pub communicated the devalued position of women in society through the "The Snug"—a small room with access to the main bar—the only room where women were permitted to purchase alcohol for themselves.[1] The 1986 fire and subsequent rebuild signified a kind of overhaul of old social norms associated with public houses in that the refurbishment saw the removal of "The Snug" and a general redesign of the interior. Aside from "The Snug," "The Public" was the section that saw the most community spirit and dialog. The post-1986 bar expanded "The Public" section of the bar in a manner that promoted a more egalitarian community, but long after British society had accepted such changes. In addition, more than simply serving the needs of the local community, regular attendance at The Rovers Return can be interpreted as a door to the community in that for a resident of the street to not frequent the pub would mark them as somewhat suspicious outsiders. Once more, this demonstrates the subtle difference between the way spatial representation was engaged in kitchen sink texts in which the individual was elevated, emphasizing how *Coronation Street*'s success was grounded almost entirely in the sentimentalizing of an idealized working-class culture—one that romanticized solidarity and community spirit in an era in which such aspects of working-class life were on the decline. To this day, the show is still heralded as a fixture of British culture. Yet, given the heightened realism and social impact of kitchen sink aesthetics, it can be argued that the show is a commodification of working-class life that has, in turn, become a simulacrum.

This is all to say that *Coronation Street* is one of several examples in which the spatial motifs of kitchen sink realism are mobilized for commercial intent. The ethical and political facets that made the kitchen sink sequence an apogee for formal realism are subjugated to sentimental nostalgia that is commodified and sold as pacifying. That said, the significance of *Coronation Street* cannot be overlooked in terms of cultural import and the representation of working-class culture in Britain. Nonetheless, such use of rhetorical devices to appeal to specific emotional needs—mostly structured on anxiety around shifts in what constitutes postwar working-class life—suggests an adaptation of the methods developed in the late 1950s. Rather than rebalancing the aesthetic with the ethical to counter the more propagandist working-class writing from decades prior, *Coronation Street* turns instead toward an aesthetically driven approach in which the political is diminished in favor of consumerism. Despite criticism aimed at the show's sepia-hued representation of working-class life, it would be disingenuous to say that *Coronation Street*'s primary contribution to television is that it bankrolled an otherwise insurgent identity. In fact, it follows the lead of the British New Wave which can also be seen to move from some of the more antagonist tendencies of the novels and plays of the kitchen sink era to something akin to a mainstream spectacle. So, rather than malign the impact of *Coronation Street* in British culture, the show can be read as a response to the need for a more complete representation of working-class life, appealing to a much wider audience than the New Wave films, and serving as a consistent source of entertainment for more than half a century.

Channel 4 and Commodified Class Aesthetics

Although *Coronation Street*'s embrace of kitchen sink spatial motifs denotes the first tangible extension of the movement's influence, it was far from the only one. Since the original movement was indeed a multimedia enterprise, the rise of television and commercial film can be contrasted against the relative balkanization of novels and theater. Another salient example of the way the multimedia nature of the aesthetic is sustained is through media corporations that demonstrate a significant predilection for working-class identities.

Channel 4—the most class-aware TV network in Britain—emerged from the margins of broadcasting, providing a publicly owned alternative to the nation's three existing TV stations. Prior to 1982, the two BBC license-funded channels (BBC1 and BBC2) and the commercial channel, ITV, were the only stations on offer. Channel 4's development opened debates about content since ITV initially envisioned the channel as equivalent to BBC2, a station meant as a vehicle for more special-interest and culturally sophisticated programming. BBC1 and ITV prioritized consumer-centered broadcasting, both with a profit motive in mind as BBC1's funding stemmed from basic licensing whereas ITV was a commercially driven endeavor. As Dorothy Hobson has shown, initial discussions relating to the inception of Channel 4 sought to counter what was felt to be a commercial domination of the airwaves. As the BBC already monopolized viewership through its two channels, and ITV sought to expand their advertising capacity, public need dictated that Channel 4 should serve as an alternative to corporate endeavors (Hobson 2008: 2). The new channel illuminated distinctions between programming-as-commodity-product and more culturally minded efforts. The leading proposition for the station, presented in September of 1972 by home secretary William Whitelaw, established basic tenets: that the new station should be accountable to the public through full transparency of accounting and finances, that it should aim for national programming with the option of more regional programming to follow, that it should provide a platform for comprehensive and extended news coverage of topical matters, and that content should be open to educational and independent producers otherwise distanced from the more commercial platforms (Hobson 2008: 5–7). Curiously, the station's first CEO, Jeremy Isaacs, had put forth a similar set of principles the month prior, insisting that the channel should cater to "substantial minorities presently neglected" with "broad educational purposes" (Hobson 2008: 8). Isaacs's proposal matched those of Whitelaw, underscoring the new station's emphasis on culture and social betterment. However, as Hobson declares, the 1981 Broadcasting Act—an act targeting programming that "offends against good taste or decency or is likely to encourage or incite to crime or to lead to disorder or to be offensive to public feeling"—read as a warning (qtd. in Hobson 2008: 14). Despite intentions of autonomy and free expression articulated as part of the channel's formation, strict broadcasting rules pertinent to content would likely pose a problem.

The first TV show to air on Channel 4 was the long-running quiz show, *Countdown*, followed by the equally enduring low-budget *Brookside*—a soap opera set in Liverpool which ran for twenty-one years. Building on *Coronation Street*'s success, *Brookside* drew from the kitchen sink movement's embrace of taboo topics by addressing a number of social issues head-on. The show focused on the challenges of social elevation experienced by several working-class families following their arrival into the middle-class Brookside Close. The first evening's programming also included the first British hour-long news broadcast and concluded with *In the Pink*—a show in which the feminist collective Raving Beauties (Sue Jones-Davies, Dee Orr, and Fan Viner) hosted a cabaret of women's writing, performed as poems and songs. The Channel 4 logo itself—a series of rainbow-colored blocks, seemingly inspired by the 1978 Pride flag—connoted diversity relative to the largely heterodox BBC1 and ITV stations. Early programming did indeed represent diversity, with content aimed at Asian audiences (*Eastern Eye*, *Bandung File*), Black audiences (*Black on Black*, *Bacchanal*), and, later, gay-specific programming (*Out on Tuesday/*

Out). Also, in contrast to more commercial programming, Channel 4's early endeavors featured shows commandeered by members of the communities they represented. The first published report on Channel 4 placed lesbian documentaries like *Veronica 4 Rose* (1983) alongside children's programming such as the animated adaptation of Raymond Briggs's *The Snowman* (1982). Working-class concerns and issues surrounding labor in the era of Thatcher were also well-covered in programming like the 1984 documentary *People to People: Just Like Coronation Street* that "traced the history of an Oldham community uprooted by wholesale slum clearance" (Annual Report 1985: 8), and attention was given to young voices in current affairs programming like *Ear to the Ground* (1983) and *Our Lives* (1983) that narrated "the experiences of various young East Enders through a novel mixture of documentary and fiction" (Annual Report 1984: 11).[2] In recent years, however, Channel 4 has come under fire from key figures associated with the station's inception, such as *Brookside*'s creator Phil Redmond who, in January of 2016, commented that "What's needed on British TV is different voices, working-class voices, something more than elites recruiting from the elites and making TV that doesn't understand the issues affecting ordinary people" (Jeffries 2016). Redmond remarks that Channel 4 "was supposed to be for alternative voices. It's not for anything now" (Jeffries 2016). Nevertheless, for much of the 1980s and the 1990s, Channel 4 stuck to its original goals and offered genuinely alternative perspectives almost entirely unmediated by commerce or ratings.

In addition to providing a platform for unique TV programming, Channel 4 is also responsible for the inception of Film4 Productions, originally known as Channel Four Films or Film on Four. With more than 500 productions to date, Film4 has proven monumental with regard to shaping British culture, featuring work by directors like Ken Loach, Lynne Ramsay, Mike Leigh, Ben Wheatley, Derek Jarman, and many others. The first film produced by the company, Stephen Frears's *Walter* (1982) set the tone for representing class issues, with Ian McKellan's depiction of mental illness resulting in his award of The Royal Television Society's Performer of the Year. To cover the impact of Channel 4 films' contribution to culture is beyond the purview of this chapter, but films like Frears's *My Beautiful Laundrette* (1985), Neil Jordan's *Mona Lisa* (1986), and Alan Clarke's *Rita, Sue and Bob Too* (1987) all embraced taboo subject material in thoughtful ways. That said, Edmund Dell—a founding chairman of Channel 4—expressed hesitation over some of the films' content. Dell signaled his appreciation of the film series—specifically those produced under the guidance of David Rose (the commissioning editor)—by calling them "a credit to Channel 4." However, he adds that:

> Sometimes I felt that some films, not from the David Rose stable, were being shown more to startle and to prove that Channel 4 had the courage to do what no other channel had dared to do than because of any intrinsic merit. Jeremy [Isaacs] would say of such films that only ten people had complained but that a million had enjoyed them. But there was no evidence that anyone had enjoyed them and sometimes such evidence as we had suggested that no one had enjoyed them.
>
> (1998: 8–9)

Dell's comments are revealing, suggesting that certain depictions—specifically depictions of gritty cultural identities—were deployed for shock value, pointing toward the commercial imperatives of commodified kitchen sink aesthetics. Despite concerns raised about the efficacy of Channel 4's output today as expressed by figures such as Phil Redmond, there is no question that the impact of the programming and a significant portion of Channel 4's content owes a debt to the kitchen sink movement's aesthetic sensibilities.[3] Much of the programming adopts gritty representational strategies as well as a clear and direct emphasis on space and spatial negotiations.

In terms of TV programming and representation of class and space, three examples are worth consideration in relation to their allegiance to kitchen sink aesthetics and distinctions between ethical and commercial intent: the aforementioned *Brookside*, *Skins*, and *Benefits Street*. As an inaugural drama, *Brookside* (1982–2003) exemplifies Channel 4's objectives by exploring the dynamics of class through a spatially driven lens. In an effort to heighten verisimilitude, the series was set in real houses in a Liverpool suburb constructed and used specifically for the show's production. Following production, the set was abandoned and left to rot until developers purchased the homes then leased them out. The cul-de-sac is relatively anonymous and inconsequential; a space replicating a number of lower-middle-class housing development projects seen in city suburbs nationwide. Focusing on six revolving households, the narrative explores the often-unacknowledged challenges associated with upward mobility by merging social classes in a homogenous arena. Despite being hamstrung by low-budget production, questionable acting, and formulaic plot lines, the series addressed topical social issues by constructing the cul-de-sac as a petri dish of socioeconomic difference. Whereas kitchen sink texts signaled social limits through claustrophobic spaces and communities with minimal resources, Brookside Close acts as hermetic ecosystem in that the action rarely leaves the confines of the titular cul-de-sac. *Brookside's* real innovation, though, was the fully constructed set. It leant the show a heightened level of verisimilitude in that the spaces occupied by the show's residents mirrored the kind of spaces occupied by the viewer with greater credibility. As Stuart Borthwick has mentioned, the close was somewhat unorthodox in its range of housing types, with "small 'two up, two down' working-class accommodation placed next to large detached houses for wealthier occupants" that "set the stage for confrontation between classes, with politically contentious issues dealt with in an upfront manner" (2004: 356). In this sense, *Brookside's* appeal was as ethnographic as it was entertaining in that it spoke to challenges of upward mobility and class in the Thatcher era through spatial negotiations. Furthermore, the show recounted the pressures of home ownership in which Thatcher's conservative government promoted "right to buy" schemes while systematically destabilizing work opportunities and increasing unemployment. In a sense, Brookside Close served as a microcosm of shifts underway in British culture, allowing the show to act as a critical reflection of the state of working-class England as well as Channel 4's commitment to class politics and diversity.

Skins (2008–2013), on the other hand, benefitted from a substantially larger budget than *Brookside* and saw wider commercial appeal as the result. The show's popularity in the UK would spawn an ill-conceived American remake for MTV that advertisers quickly abandoned due to challenging subject matter and poor ratings. In this regard, *Skins* can be parsed as an example of the way certain aesthetics derived from the kitchen sink era were commodified and sold as "gritty." Written by Bryan Elsley and Janie Britain, the show takes place in Bristol and depicts a diverse group of teenager's final years of high school. While the content is topical and pertinent to the show's depicted demographic—concerns over eating disorders, learning disabilities, and domestic abuse—the main draw was its controversial depiction of teenage sexuality. The setting recalls a number of representational devices seen in earlier class-conscious texts, particularly the depiction of generational difference as the upshot of confined multigenerational households. *Skins* is a drama in which teenagers abandon their homes to transform the local environment into habitable spaces and spaces of transgression. Just as Brookside Close served as a crucible for different class demographics, the high school in *Skins* brings together different backgrounds in a relatively homogenous and recognizable setting. Class and racial divides are cast in stark relief when characters leave their self-created sanctuaries and return to their respective domiciles. For example, the Stonem House—one of the prominently featured locations in the series—is a middle-class household, situating Tony Stonem as privileged relative to other characters. Thomas Tomone stands in contrast to Tony as a recent immigrant from the Congo Republic who squats in an abandoned estate nearby. The racialized nature of this arrangement recalls early waves of Black immigration outlined in the work of writers like MacInnes, most notably in the way MacInnes depicts diasporic communities and the necessity of subversive space. In *Skins*, the school acts as a unifier in which class and racial differences are far from irrelevant but lessened in contrast to the larger community. The narrative underlined the necessity of transgressive sites as alternates of domestic space, yet the show's commercial imperatives raise questions about its efficacy in terms of posing solutions in that commodified grittiness informs the show's commercial viability.

Benefits Street is quite different and worthy of critical scrutiny as, for many, the show reads as an abdication of the Channel's inaugural remit and as an example of the way kitchen sink aesthetics can be mobilized for exploitation. Filmed as a documentary over the period of a year, *Benefits Street* claimed to capture the lives of the residents of James Turner Street in Birmingham. The featured street comprises standard Victorian terraced housing and was originally intended for the more aspirational or "respectable" working-classes seeking social elevation. However, the terraces were built prior to the advent of housing byelaw renovation, placing several into a state of developmental purgatory akin to the domestic spaces seen in Delaney's *A Taste of Honey*. Despite such concerns, the majority of the street's residents—and residents from neighboring streets—enjoyed relative prosperity during the postwar years while employed by local industry. Deindustrialization and neoliberal policies of the 1980s sank the region into mass unemployment, with more than 200,000 manufacturing jobs lost. The show's premise was to offer an objective look at the lives of a community dependent on unemployment benefits, but the show centered more on sensationalism and the reinforcement of certain stereotypes associated with deindustrialized communities. As such, the show prompted tangible social reforms and initiated political debate despite astonishment that Channel 4 would commercialize poverty and suffering with such willing enthusiasm. In some ways, the show marked a return to an aesthetics pioneered by the kitchen sink movement: unencumbered depictions of industrial decline and the residue of commerce. All the same, *Benefits Street* sidesteps the poetic realism of kitchen sink texts through questionable editing techniques that seek to align the residents themselves with trash and refuse. Camera angles and visual choices would often stage residents in close proximity to images of decay or waste for maximum rhetorical impact. The show aired five initial episodes and drew swift critical condemnation as exploitative "poverty porn." Those involved with the production claimed to have been misled, noting how they believed the show would emphasize the value of community in impoverished spaces. Whereas past representations of working-class people seeking to pinpoint gritty communities would focus on characteristics and affectation, *Benefits Street* used the space itself to align—and metaphorically link—residents to trash. The result was that identities were linked to spaces—which, in turn, were linked to rampant stereotypes and generalizations about poverty.

Similar to the way Channel 4 TV programming embraced space as part of its class rhetoric, the films produced by or in conjunction with Channel 4 have adopted similar approaches as well. For instance, directors such as Mike Leigh and Stephen Frears use environment and spatial metaphors to accentuate working-class realities in ways that recall the calibration of political and aesthetic objectives relative to the kitchen sink movement. Leigh's *Life is Sweet* (1990) and *Naked* (1993)—films with stridently oppositional aesthetics—saw significant support from Channel 4 films as they represented the kind of work that the channel was interested in producing. *Life is Sweet* portrays the struggles of a working-class family in a North London estate, recounting their various schemes and plans to escape from poverty and their immediate environment. Despite the characters' frustrations, the film conveys an unmistakable optimism—chiefly due to Leigh painting the environment in whimsical, pastel hues with a persistent presence of sunlight throughout. Depicted environs are instantly identifiable as types in what appears as a working-class London suburb with none of the cosmopolitan flare of the capital. Yet Leigh still manages to frame the space as illuminated and beaming. When frustration overwhelms—as it does for several of the characters—their pessimism is countered by the space itself. In this regard, *Life is Sweet* irradiates grim environs in a manner that reveals community spirit generally overlooked in modern-day representations of working-class life, especially in light of deindustrialization and its effects. Leigh adapts the kitchen sink motif of recognizably anonymous space by flooding it with color to act as a metaphor for shared struggle and sustenance.

Although *Life is Sweet* remains buoyant throughout, *Naked* is dark in terms of content, outlook, and setting. The film sheds pastel hues for bruised black and blue tones, as if the environment has succumbed to violence. Literally and metaphorically dark, *Naked* casts a shadow over the working-class themes of *Life is Sweet*, exchanging optimism for aggressive nihilism. Where the latter amplified the value and support of local communities—even in spaces of shared suffering—*Naked's* spatial aesthetics suggest an urban demimonde that characters struggle to navigate and survive. While the story begins and ends in a sinister flat owned by an equally sinister landlord, the setting is more expansive, moving through various back alleys and uninhabited spaces of London. It exists as a series of shadows through which the central character, Johnny, maneuvers. By inhabiting such spaces, Johnny meets other alienated characters living meager existences in similarly shadowy sites. The film's complexity resists easy interpretation, but Leigh's characters reflect class-based destitution, specifically in a post-Thatcher environment in which community and human connection is replaced by a form of decomposing individualism. Although the film is filled with disturbing, visceral violence, the environment itself is the most haunting, bordering on apocalyptic—a gesture well-suited for the post-Thatcher years.

Stephen Frears's 1985 *My Beautiful Laundrette*, based on Hanif Kureishi's screenplay, offers one of the clearest perspectives into the Thatcher era—specifically regarding minority and queer representation. Set in the South London area of Wandsworth, the narrative pits left-wing political positions against the mounting right-wing nationalism of the latter part of the twentieth century. Originally produced for television and emblematic of the kitchen sink style associated with Channel 4 programming of the time, the film won international accolades and was nominated for an Academy Award. In the screenplay's introduction, Kureishi signals the media-rich nature of the work, commenting that as "I was primarily a playwright, I wrote each scene of the film like a little scene for a play, with action written like stage directions and with lots of dialogue. Then I'd cut most of the dialogue and add more stage directions, often set in cars" (1996: 3). Kureishi adds how, during his preliminary discussions with Frears, they opted to film in February because "England looks especially unpleasant" then (1996: 4). The writer's desire for a gritty, gloomy texture was also evidenced by the film's low-budget production: "There were no commercial pressures on us, no one had a lot of money invested in the film who would tell us what to do. And I was tired of seeing lavish films set in exotic locations" (1996: 5). Furthermore, the balance between the aesthetic and the political was made clear in that "the film was to be an amusement, despite its references to racism, unemployment, and Thatcherism. Irony is the modern mode, a way of commenting on bleakness and cruelty without falling into dourness and didacticism" (1996: 5). In this sense, *My Beautiful Laundrette*—both the screenplay and the film—adopts the kitchen sink approach in which gritty environments and a charged context strike a balance between the aesthetic and the political.

This is perhaps made most apparent through the setting, but the screenplay is usually overlooked in relation to the film's success. Kureishi's stage direction leaves room for artistic license yet still resembles the more pointed stage direction as seen in the kitchen sink plays of the 1950s. The opening scene's "large detached house" is quickly registered as a squat by the political signage across the boarded-up windows, reading, among other things, "Your greed will be the death of us all" (1996: 9). The squat is deemed a multicultural space of refuge, yet most of its inhabitants are racial and ethnic minorities. The stage direction draws connections to the paradoxical appeal of dereliction developed in kitchen sink representation, most clearly in the scenes in which the central character navigates the city: "OMAR walks along a South London street, towards NASSER's garage. It's a rough area, beautiful in its own falling-down way" (1996: 13). Such flourishes should come as no surprise as Kureishi was well-versed in kitchen sink motifs having served an apprenticeship at the Royal Court Theatre where he would become the official Writer in Residence in 1982. From this vantage point, the aesthetic touches that Kureishi uses can be seen to position him as one of the most-likely ambassadors of the original movement while also allowing for new critical perspectives based on cultural advances. The decision to make the film when "England looks especially unpleasant" underscores the screenplay's social critique of working-class life in the Thatcher era. Although the film was contentious—especially so in the British Asian community—it is generally heralded as groundbreaking in its depictions of race and sexuality. More specifically, it was also recognized for its commentary on the entrepreneurialism and greed promoted by Thatcher's conservative policies during the period, set against a backdrop in which working-class and diasporic communities shared space. Frears's drive to shade the represented environs as classed casts the text's concerns about social mobility and identity in stark relief.

Despite the kind of missteps seen with the production of shows like *Benefits Street*, Channel 4 is perhaps the most obvious heir to kitchen sink's aesthetic and ethical intent. Its unambiguous and open embrace of cultural margins replicates mid-century determination to insert working-class voices into the arts. Furthermore, the Channel's transparent finances, and its commitment to the initial remit, situate it as a network not only invested in productions inspired by a kitchen sink realist aesthetics of space but by the ethical impulse to increase access and representation. Its status as a network with a range of programming interests, especially given Film4's success, helps position it as a vehicle to sustain the kitchen sink legacy.

Theaters of Anger and Aggression

Late twentieth-century developments in British theater also reveal advances in spatial motifs and devices traceable to kitchen sink realism. For the period in question, Aleks Sierz's *In-Yer-Face Theatre: British Drama Today* insists on the use of the label "In-Yer-Face" in a manner that recalls the application of labels like "kitchen sink" and "angry young man." In a 2002 issue of *New Theatre Quarterly*, Sierz argues that titles such as "Neo-Jacobeanism" are too aligned to tradition, that "New Brutalism" infers only violence and brutality, and that "Theatre of Ennui" suggests a misplaced boredom (2002: 18). For Sierz, "In-Yer-Face" is fitting since it encompasses the confrontational, discomforting manner associated with the post-Thatcher era's revival of aggressive drama. Sierz's title is apt given the nature of the performances—particularly the way the audience is implicated. While this body of work is hardly "proletarian" in a traditional sense, it does embrace an aesthetics of grit while using shock effects to upend conventions. As such, it can be read as a reverberation of kitchen sink realism's legacy.

Sierz defined a set of thematics for his label, arguing for work that pushes kitchen sink drama's embrace of the taboo to the extreme. This was, according to Sierz, the kind of drama "that takes the audience by the scruff of the neck and shakes it until it gets the message" (2001: 4). He aligns this change with the era of "Cool Britannia," forging direct links to the past by claiming how "New writing had rediscovered the angry, oppositional and questioning spirit of 1956, the original Angry Young Man" (2001: xii). In doing so, he provides a productive way to consider lineages of working-class representation at the turn of the century. What he deems to be "new writing" is characterized by provocation and shock that "taps into more primitive feelings, smashing taboos, mentioning the forbidden, creating discomfort" (2001: 4). For Sierz, the key characteristics of In-Yer-Face Theatre: "language is usually filthy, characters talk about unmentionable subjects, take their clothes off, have sex, humiliate each other, experience unpleasant emotions, become suddenly violent" (2001: 5). The use of extreme shock effects is, apparently, because these writers "have something urgent to say" and such tropes are best expressed in drama that uproots the audience from familiar theater experiences to produce outrage expressed as "walkouts, letters to the press, leader articles denouncing a 'waste of public money', calls for bans or cuts in funding, mocking cartoons, questions in parliament, or even prosecution on charges of obscenity or blasphemy" (2001: 5). Good theater, for Sierz, is measured by its ability to offend, and it goes without saying than many of the results listed mirror the reception of the kitchen sink plays in the postwar period.

Sierz also puts forth a comprehensive genealogy of the role of shock in British theater, demonstrating how the plays of the late 1990s extended ideas established in earlier decades. Of certain interest is the way that such approaches build on thematics advanced in relation to classed space. In his introduction, Sierz posits that the theater of the 1990s privileges the author over the production, putting "writers, as opposed to directors, designers or performers, center stage, not only because the writer is central to the process of play-making but also because they have a wider significance: the writer defines the Britishness of British theatre" (2001: xi). In this regard, In-Yer-Face theater echoes kitchen sink drama in that plays such as *Look Back in Anger* conveyed an autobiographical charge. The kind of plays central to this movement—plays such as 1993's *Penetrator* by Anthony Nielson, 1995's *Blasted* by Sarah Kane, and 1996's *Shopping and Fucking* by Mark Ravenhill—are emblematic of the tropes that Sierz sketches. This turn toward unusually aggressive theater of the 1990s, Sierz argues, offered an opportunity "to explore the way we live and feel" (2001: 30), inferring that the decade served as a moment in which frank discussions of topics became permissible. Yet, the texts of the kitchen sink era do the same. For instance, when In-Yer-Face productions use depictions of infanticide, Edward Bond's 1965 play *Saved* comes to mind. In fact, Bond's discussion of "aggro-effects" acts as a precursor for late-1990s shock theater, linking the In-Yer-Face aesthetic to that of the kitchen sink movement.[4] Although such texts suggest parallels and departures from mid-century class-conscious drama, they certainly emphasize space and setting in a manner that connotes class and classed identities.

Case in point, Kane's *Blasted* draws attention to the role of setting early on, and the narrative uses the stage to consider the fragility of the human body. The space is repeatedly violated by representations of the state in the guise of the military and, of course, the mortar bomb tied to the play's title. Of note is the way Kane depicts space such as to recall the paradoxical contrasts associated with earlier drama. The play is set in a single room that progressively deteriorates, but the opening stage direction appears as a commentary on kitchen sink's repetition of anonymous space: "A very expensive hotel room in Leeds—the kind that is so expensive it could be anywhere in the world" (1996: 3). The discord of "a very expensive hotel room" in a northern city known more for its industry than its wealth is compounded by the first line of dialog delivered by Ian who quips "I've shat in better places than this" (1996: 3). While the function of space in Kane's play is one of abject disruption, social stratification is insinuated by dialect and classed behavior. The play mocks theatrical traditions by offering a set that would not be out of place in a Terence Rattigan production. Yet, the explosive dismantling of the room—combined with the explosive violence displayed by the characters—reflects what Helen Iball has described as a play that "tears apart the domestication of mimesis, the 'kitchen sink' realism that has been perceived as the dominant dramatic mode of the Royal Court Theatre in the post-war era" (2008: 4). In this sense, while Kane's play might be read as an attempt to usurp the theater of the late-1950s, it relies on the same spirit of radicalism that pried theater from the elite and introduced new working-class voices.

Ravenhill's *Shopping and Fucking* references multiple settings, often characterless in a manner that suggests the clinical sterility of a supermarket. The opening scene is set in a flat, "once rather stylish, now almost entirely stripped bare" (1996: 3) in which the minimal decor functions as a blank canvas upon which the protagonist can vomit, copiously. This, of course, recalls the notorious opening sequence of Sillitoe's *Saturday Night and Sunday Morning* in which Arthur vomits—figuratively and literally—on the older generation from which he seeks to distance himself. Ravenhill's play begins and ends in a setting that signals domestic sanctuary. Yet, the flat is furnished not with furniture or personal items but with commercial packaging like pizza boxes, plastic forks, and microwave meals. Just as the Porter's flat in *Look Back in Anger* is permeated by ideological detritus, the spaces of Ravenhill's play are as—if not more—susceptible to cultural onslaughts, only this time in the form of commerce and commodity. Ravenhill claimed how his characters are "just trying to make sense of a world without religion or ideology" (qtd. in Sierz 2001: 130), so domestic sites stripped of personal touch or identity act as backdrops against which unadulterated commodification can occur. In a way, *Shopping and Fucking* updates the conspicuous consumption of texts such as *Saturday Night and Sunday Morning* for the contemporary moment, suggesting that gritty, working-class subjecthood is today marked by a steady flow of consumer waste.

The title of Neilson's *Penetrator* implies a similar kind of sensibility seen in both Kane and Ravenhill's work, which is indeed a motif of the genre. The penetration, in question, is not merely tied to the play's sexual violence, but how spaces are penetrated in a way that resembles Osborne's *Look Back in Anger*. Following the opening sequence, the action moves into a rented flat: "It is cheaply furnished, though someone with an eye for interior design has made the best of it. A coffee-table, however, overflows with junk. Posters of various icons on the wall. In this space, the credibly masculine fights with a softer influence. Damp on the walls near the roof, and the sound of distant traffic outside" (2013: 62).

While critics were quick to acknowledge the homoerotic signifiers of what is essentially a cross between a bachelor pad and a boxing ring, the emphasis on trash, pop culture, and insubstantial resources recalls the spaces inhabited by Jo and her mother in Delaney's *A Taste of Honey*. However, Delaney used the space as an opportunity for characters to recreate their social position while the characters in *Penetrator*—and, arguably, the bulk of the plays of the In-Yer-Face grouping—confer an absence of agency as well as a notable inability to assert control over their own lives. Whereas the spaces of the kitchen sink era offered transgressive potential, these plays depict a world in which identity is written through space as a one-way transaction. Class lines are considerably more difficult to identify in these works as the worlds they conjure are cloistered and dystopian, preventing any possible vision of an existence beyond grit, oppression, and violence.

Although the plays aligned with Sierz's definition of late twentieth-century theater are not explicitly classed, the debt owed to mid-century drama is unmistakable. Representative of a post-industrial turn—especially in the wake of 1980s conservative governance—these plays tell of a growing ambiguity about the very existence of a recognizable working-class culture. The most tangible throughline to kitchen sink texts, then, is the emphasis on space as a marker of identity—environments functioning as triggers to the play's action. Such theatrical writing, in part, reproduces the kind of spatial confines seen in Osborne or Delaney's work—primarily due to the physical limitations of set design. But it is this sub-genre's emphasis on gritty sensibilities that render In-Yer-Face productions as classed and part of a lineage of realist aesthetics.

Class and Space in Contemporary Fiction

In terms of fiction, the aesthetics of the kitchen sink era extend well into the present, with work such as Barry Hines's *A Kestrel for a Knave* (1968), David Storey's *Saville* (1976), and Pat Barker's *Union Street* (1982) acting as examples of the kind of texts that demonstrate an allegiance to mid-century motifs. But contemporary class-conscious writing—especially work driven by a designated cultural moment—is also worthy of inquiry. For instance, Irvine Welsh's 1993 novel *Trainspotting* underlines the way space and environment inform identity. Welsh relies on heavy-hitting, visceral images, calling to mind some of the more aggressive representations seen in the In-Yer-Face movement. Kim Duff has argued that the novel's hostile barrage-effect is the result of cultural trends dominant at the time, responding, she suggests, to the vestiges of punk subculture and the drug-fueled hedonism of 1990s raves (2014: 52). Duff maintains that the characters in *Trainspotting* are products of their surroundings—the Muirhouse housing estate of the text—relegating them to types commonly associated as working-class (2014: 53). As was true of the kitchen sink writers, Welsh's text is highly autobiographical in that he grew up in the same estate as his characters, raised by two working-class parents. The plot revolves around a series of estate dwellers, with several actively addicted to heroin. Written as a loose collection of vignettes linked together by the main character Mark Renton, the novel calls to mind Sillitoe's mid-century writing—narratives held together by a memorable protagonist whose identity is threaded throughout. Even though there is a palpable plot, the novel operates as a sequence of spatially driven sketches—specifically the interactions associated with council estates, emphasizing such sites' tendency to inscribe social worth. What propels the novel is the steady stream of violence, the sense of alienation, and the use of coarse language meant to signify class. In this regard, the novel reads as an extension of the spatially inflected motifs associated with the kitchen sink era while also underscoring such effects in a manner consistent with class representation of the mid-1990s.

In addition to the repetition of visceral content, the novel is structured around engagements with the local environment—a space that remains constant even when the narrative moves from one vignette to the next. Here, the tropes affiliated with mid-century working-class texts are activated, including the seemingly ubiquitous "view of the factory" acting as a persistent reminder of social position and labor. For instance, when Begbie tells of his wife's efforts to sign up for new housing, a sense of resignation is expressed as the upshot of space:

> The wifey goes up tae the council fir a hoose ... The council sais tae her, hair's it ye want tae fuckin stay, like? The woman said, ah want a hoose in Princes Street looking ontay the castle ... Instead ay a view ay the castle, she's goat a view ay the gasworks. That's how it fuckin works in real life, if ye urn a rich cunt wi a big fuckin hoose n plenty poppy.
>
> (1993: 115–16)

Furthermore, the space is figured as restrictive and limiting in that each estate tends to resemble the rest, with Renton describing Leslie's futility: "they say she's in the Southern General in Glesgie life-support. Paracetamol joab. She went through tae Glesgie tae git away far the smack scene in Muirhoose n ended up movin intae Possil wi Skreel n Garbo. There's nae escape fir some fuckers.

Hari-kiri wis Les's best option" (1993: 204). Despite the grim prognosis of life in these environments, Welsh's text is mostly read by critics as one that pushes back against social limits through depictions of strategic, intentional delinquency. That said, given the discussion of "behavioral sink" outlined in the first chapter, it is clear that *Trainspotting* also reads as a reflection of vicious cycles: sites of alienation and disenfranchisement engender responses that only serve to perpetuate alienation.

Claire Elliot, citing the beneficial role of patient narratives in augmenting hard scientific data, has argued that texts like *Trainspotting* can help health care professionals better understand the world of the addict (2003: 126). Following this logic, a novel like *Trainspotting* can also help gauge a range of social ills pertinent to the contextual moment and the kind of environments depicted—fiction acting as fact through the use of social realist techniques. For instance, 2014 saw the release of Garry Fraser's documentary, *Everybody's Child*—a documentary deemed the real-life version of *Trainspotting*. It depicts the struggles of growing up on council estates such as Muirhouse while also delivering worrying statistics: during the time in which *Trainspotting* was set, more than half of the infamous estate's residents had contracted HIV from IV drug use. Central to the documentary is the notion that spaces like Muirhouse are figurative prisons in which working-class people are cordoned off from the rest of society. Fraser reported, in an interview with Vice, how drug use and violence were normalized on the infamous estate, commenting that "I grew up expecting that my life was jail ... Muirhouse was an area that was completely cut off, and I don't think the government gave a fuck if anyone dies there" (Fraser 2015). Welsh has spoken similarly of Edinburgh, proclaiming that "Drugs were part of the normal landscape when I was growing up" (Wintle 2015). Most telling is the way that both Fraser and Welsh describe drug addiction relative to geography and space—a sentiment captured in the text, suggesting how classed space does indeed produce behavioral responses and that spaces such as these are, themselves, constructed specifically for such a purpose.

Welsh's attention to environmental details underscores the way certain spaces actively marginalize and alienate individuals. Muirhouse echoes the kinds of social impact seen in much postwar mass housing where corners were cut to maximize profit without much concern for the residents' basic well-being. Similar to Clare Elliot, Judy Hemingway has shown how authors like Welsh offer unique insights into tangible social problems through what she refers to as the use of "reconstructive geographies" (2006: 325). Hemingway focuses on the text's engagement with high and low culture, specifically how it stages a battle between the world of the council estate and the more high-brow Edinburgh Festival that opens the novel. In doing so, Hemingway claims that Welsh emphasizes the impact of the Thatcher years in which "lines of demarcation were drawn between those who were valued and those who were not" (2006: 328). Yet Hemingway's argument is structured upon signifiers of cultural difference rather than the depicted spaces themselves, specifically the difference between the vernacular of the main characters and the more refined speech of background characters who indulge in more culturally sophisticated practices (2006: 329). Similarly, Lewis MacLeod has declared that *Trainspotting*, in addition to being a novel about Edinburgh, is a novel about "the construction and transgression of boundaries" (2008: 89). For MacLeod, Renton's transgression of the oppressed estate is mostly geographical in nature, contingent upon his ability to physically cross the boundary that renders the space as classed (2008: 104). MacLeod rightly clarifies that such transgression is also metaphorical through Renton's ability "to reconcile subordination with resistance" (2008: 104)—a gesture that replicates the conflict faced by Arthur in *Saturday Night and Sunday Morning*, and one that suggests a personal choice over class and cultural solidarity. Nevertheless, *Trainspotting* is also a text that lifts from 1950s working-class writing in other ways, yet does so without exploiting what came prior.

To consider the criteria outlined as part and parcel of spatial representation within working-class writing, *Trainspotting* borrows heavily from mid-century aesthetics, but amplifies the effect for the contextual present. The miserable, run-down environments usually seen in working-class fiction are exploded in the opening scene in which the Edinburgh festival—a space metaphorically designated for high-brow culture—is contrasted against what is now recognized as the notorious "worst toilet in Scotland" scene of the novel. Here, every possible violation of sanitation and cleanliness is mobilized in graphic detail, suggesting that a character like Renton has no place in civil society and is relegated to the basement, slipping and falling in puddles of human waste. Given that this scene takes place early in the text, Welsh introduces the theme of social ostracism that the novel develops throughout. Whereas mid-century texts' spaces are infused with poetic realism, in contemporary work such as *Trainspotting*, spaces are cast more as abject, underscoring the severity of division in society. While Muirhouse is no different from any other estate developed in the 1950s and abandoned by municipal support soon after, Welsh draws attention to the ubiquitous role of council housing but amplifies the harm social neglect causes its residents. As the result, he brings the concerns associated with spaces like

Muirhouse to the forefront of cultural discourse. To this end, Welsh's work balances the aesthetic of chaos and disorder with the political imperative of illuminating its effects on the population. His point, it seems, is that by creating spaces that harm residents in such a manner, the country at large is harmed through the spread of violence, drug abuse, and the spread of HIV.

Conclusion

That said, a question can be raised as to how extreme texts like *Trainspotting* differ from the kinds of representation in a text like *Benefits Street*. The main difference, arguably, is the engagement with space and the way individual characters navigate their worlds. Although *Trainspotting* is a visceral, aggressive text, it invites consideration of how characters engage with their surroundings to renegotiate their identity. *Benefits Street*, on the other hand, uses space primarily as backdrop, with characters depicted more as the inevitable outcome of their environment. As this text has argued, kitchen sink realism elevated representations of working-class space in order to stage problems and potentially work out solutions. The result is that a text like *Trainspotting* illuminates space as a pivotal component of the narrative. What this chapter has aimed to outline is the way that spatial representation and metaphors affiliated with kitchen sink realism persist in the present. In addition, if kitchen sink realism offers a moment in which previously discreet aesthetic and ethical imperatives come into momentary alignment, then perhaps the thematics central to the movement can serve as a general guide to portrayals of working-class life and as a benchmark of aesthetic and ethical credibility.

This study of postwar writing—particularly writing linked to the kitchen sink realism movement—sought to accomplish three main goals: to suggest that the texts associated with the movement are not simply cult-classics or museum pieces tied to their era, that the dynamism and spirit of the movement produced representational strategies and methods that advanced the realist mode, and that such aesthetic strategies and techniques are liable to be exploited through identity fetishism and the commodification of a romanticized monolithic culture. As Prunetti posits in his *Jacobin* essay, "we need to think about the possibility that the middle class will appropriate our stories and use them for purposes we didn't intend." This book insists that our concerns are perhaps better centered on industries associated with cultural production willing to exploit identity to sell a product. More pointedly, the book questions what happens when such narratives flood the market and influence the nature of the identity in question. As discussed in the introduction, Linkon warns against efforts to police authorial voices based on social position or working-class credentials (2020: 25). Whereas Prunetti expresses skepticism about who gets to tell certain stories and in what ways, Linkon indicates that authorship and legitimacy are more complex. Class-centric essay collections such as Nathan Connolly's *Know Your Place* from 2017 and Kit de Waal's *Common People* from 2019 demonstrate how writing about working-class life and culture comes from a wide range of positions and perspectives. Furthermore, the very idea of the working-class itself has changed significantly over time, and the notion that a fixed, monolithic identity persists denies the reality of what it means to be working-class today. This book submits that a moment in cultural production, one in which working-class voices of the time dominated, led to a high point of representational aesthetics understood through spatial and environmental motifs. This is not to say, though, that contemporary working-class writing must revolve around characters resembling Jimmy Porter or Arthur Seaton. In fact, as Prunetti rightly adds, "the testosterone level of proletarian stories is dropping; and class is becoming more and more intertwined with other forms of oppression, like gender and race. The narrative of the 'fight outside the pub' is dropping away, and toxic masculinity is questioned even in working-class settings." Forms of working-class life signify in vastly different ways today than in the 1950s and the 1960s, and we would be well-advised to remain open to the possibility that a working-class text or a working-class voice need not adhere to any demarcated themes or motifs; rather, that such connections emerge from the reader rather than the text itself. What this study shows is that, although brief, kitchen sink realism was no mere blip on the aesthetic radar. Similarly, it was no mere cult phenomenon. Instead, it altered the tenets of realism in a manner that transformed representations of class through the use of active spatial strategies, in terms of both identity articulation and metaphors for the shifting nature of class. That the aesthetics of the movement are identifiable in work today emphasizes not simply the legacy of the period, but its investment in realigning aesthetic and ethical goals.

So, what is the path forward for assessing the veracity and motivation of working-class cultural production? If, as Owen Jones advises in *Chavs: The Demonization of the Working-Class*, that class bias, polarization, and exploitation through populist rhetoric are traceable to a media-fueled set of ideas and stereotypes about working-class life, then a logical response is to analyze the nature of the representation through critical tools and practices that serve not to sustain or police the contours of identity but to detect and question intent. As this book has argued, the intent of the kitchen sink period was to augment representation—to recalibrate aesthetic motifs with ethical and political goals in mind. While the films of the British New Wave certainly embraced mainstream appeal and wide distribution—potentially positioning them as part of the problematic practice of commodifying marginal identities—it is worth keeping in mind Tony Richardson's claim following the success of the *Look Back in Anger*'s stage production. As Gardner recounts, Richardson capitalized on commercial film's burgeoning interest in "gritty identities" and used that interest as a way "to worm himself and his old Free Cinema buddies into the film industry" (2006: 102). But, doing so suggests a similarly subversive maneuver commensurate with the actions discussed in Chapter 3—a knowing, calculated attempt to shift representation and alter power dynamics. Such a move sums up much of what kitchen sink realism sought to accomplish, and this text offers just one way of considering such a move.

Notes

1 For the first year of production, a sign can be seen on the bar instructing women to return to their seats soon after being served.
2 Upholding its dedication to transparency, Channel 4 still makes all of its annual reports available to the public: https://annualreport.channel4.com/.
3 Attempts to privatize the channel have been repeatedly thwarted by the British government. A report published in May of 2016 by Patrick Barwise and Gillian Brooks outlines the central concerns of privatization, warning that the most immediate threat would be a reduction in independent production—a key factor upon which the channel was founded. However, as of 2022, Channel 4's future is in grave danger. Conservative politicians such as Nadine Dorries have pushed for privatization, arguing that the station cannot compete with media conglomerates such as Netflix or Amazon in its current form. Such sentiments, of course, run counter to Channel 4's entire legacy and function. The channel has opposed such proposals, emphasizing integrity over corporate profit. In addition, countless media figures have publicly stated their opposition to privatization as well.
4 Bond felt that prior portrayals of working-class life amounted to a "philosophy of the rich which required the poor to live" (2001: 31) in a certain way that satisfied

need of aesthetics. In other words, he felt that prior explorations of the working class in literature veered more toward fetishism or class tourism. This he called a true "act of violence." He referred to "difficult" images and scenes as "aggro-effects—effects designed to make the audience question what they normally accept," cautiously adding "but this isn't to shock them pointlessly" (2001: 32).

References

Abbott, Paul. 2004. *Shameless*. London: Channel 4.
Adams, Ann Marie. 2007. "Looking Back in Realism: The Making and Unmaking of Dramatic Form in the Reception of the British New Wave." *The Journal of the Midwest Modern Language Association* 40 (1): 75–86. https://doi.org/10.2307/20464211.
Alcalá, Roberto del Valle. 2016. *British Working-Class Fiction: Narratives of Refusal and the Struggle Against Work*. London and New York, NY: Bloomsbury.
Aldridge, Meryl. 1979. *The British New Towns: A Programme without a Policy*. London and Boston, MA: Routledge.
Alexander, Anthony. 2009. *Britain's New Towns: Garden Cities to Sustainable Communities*. London and New York, NY: Routledge.
Allen, Trevor. 1953. *We Loved in Bohemia*. London: Christopher Johnson.
Amis, Kingsley. 1954. *Lucky Jim*. London: Victor Gollancz, Ltd.
Anderson, Lindsay. 1958. "Review of A Taste of Honey." *Encore* 5 (2): 42–3.
Atha, Christine. 2012. "Dirt and Disorder: Taste and Anxiety in the Homes of the British Working Class." In *Atomic Dwelling: Anxiety, Domesticity, and Postwar Architecture*, edited by Robin Schuldenfrei, 207–26. London and New York, NY: Routledge.
Augé, Marc. 2009 [1992]. *Non-Places: An Introduction to Supermodernity*. Translated by John Howe. London: Verso.
Bachelard, Gaston. 1994 [1964]. *The Poetics of Space*. Translated by Maria Jolas. Boston, MA: Beacon Press.
Bakhtin, Mikhail. 1981. "Forms of Time and of the Chronotope in the Novel: Notes Toward a Historical Poetics." In *The Dialogic Imagination: Four Essays*, edited by Michael Holquist, translated by Caryl Emerson and Michael Holquist, 84–258. Austin: University of Texas Press.
Barker, Pat. 1997 [1982]. *Union Street*. London: Virago.
Barstow, Stan. 1964. *Joby*. London: Michael Joseph.
Barstow, Stan. 2010 [1960]. *A Kind of Loving*. Cardigan, UK: Parthian.
Barthes, Roland. 1989 [1968]. "The Reality Effect." In *The Rustle of Language*. Translated by Richard Howard. Berkeley, CA: University of California Press.
Barwise, Patrick, and Gillian Brooks. 2016. "The Consequences of Privatising Channel 4." *Channel 4*. https://www.channel4.com/media/documents/press/news/Desktop/Barwise_final%204May'16.pdf.
"Battersea Power Station." n.d. Battersea Power Station. Accessed December 11, 2021. https://batterseapowerstation.co.uk/.

Beaven, Brad. 2005. *Leisure, Citizenship and Working-Class Men in Britain, 1850–1945*. Manchester, UK: Manchester University Press.

Bentley, Nick. 2003. "Translating English: Youth, Race and Nation in Colin MacInnes's *City of Spades* and *Absolute Beginners*." *Connotations: A Journal for Critical Debate* 13 (1–2): 149–69.

Bentley, Nick. 2007. *Radical Fictions: The English Novel in the 1950s*. Oxford, UK: Peter Lang.

The Birmingham Post. 1961. "County Ban on Film Described as 'Shocking,'" January 14, 1961.

Blishen, Edward. "Carry on up the Zeitgeist: Look Back in Anger." 1992. London: BBC Radio 4 FM.

Bond, Edward. 2001 [1993]. *Letters: Volume 5*. Edited by Ian Stuart. London and New York, NY: Routledge.

Borsay, Peter. 2006. *A History of Leisure: The British Experience since 1500*. Basingstoke, UK: Palgrave Macmillan.

Borthwick, Stuart. 2004. "Brookside." In *Encyclopedia of Television*, edited by Horace Newcomb, 2nd ed., 356–7. New York, NY and London: Fitzroy Dearborn.

Bottomley, Maurice. 2012. "Clubs—Ham Yard." *Cocktails with Elvira* (blog). February 11, 2012. https://elvirabarney.wordpress.com/tag/hambone-club/.

Bourdieu, Pierre. 1990 [1980]. *The Logic of Practice*. Translated by Richard Nice. Stanford, CA: Stanford University Press.

Bourke, Joanna. 1993. *Working Class Cultures in Britain, 1890–1960*. London and New York, NY: Routledge.

Brady, Mark. 1986. "Looking Back at the Language of Anger." In *Four Fits of Anger: Essays on the Angry Young Men*, edited by Mark Brady, John Dodds, and Christopher Taylor, 150–70. Pasian di Prato, IT: Campanotto Editore.

Braine, John. 1980 [1957]. *Room at the Top*. New York, NY: Methuen.

"British New Wave: *Up the Junction*." 2013. Interview. *Author Nell Dunn on What Inspired Her to Write Up the Junction*. BBC Radio 4 FM. https://www.bbc.co.uk/programmes/p01g4mzf.

Brooke, Stephen. 2012. "'Slumming' in Swinging London? Class, Gender and the Post-War City in Nell Dunn's *Up the Junction* (1963)." *Cultural and Social History* 9 (3): 429–49. https://doi.org/10.2752/147800412X13270753069000.

Bullock, Nicholas. 2002. *Building the Post-War World: Modern Architecture and Reconstruction in Britain*. London and New York, NY: Routledge.

Calhoun, John B. 1962. "Population Density and Social Pathology." *Scientific American* 206 (2): 139–49.

Carpenter, Humphrey. 2002. *The Angry Young Men: A Literary Comedy of the 1950s*. London and New York, NY: Allen Lane.

Castronovo, David. 2010 [2009]. *Blokes: The Bad Boys of British Literature*. London: Continuum.

Chait, Melanie. 1982. *Veronica 4 Rose*. London: Channel 4.

"Channel Four Television Company Limited: Report and Accounts for the Year Ended 21st March 1984." 1984. https://assets-corporate.channel4.com/_flysystem/s3/2017-06/annual_report_1984_1.pdf.

"Channel Four Television Company Limited: Report and Accounts for the Year Ended 21st March 1985." 1985. https://assets-corporate.channel4.com/_flysystem/s3/2017-06/annual_report_1985_1.pdf.

Chansky, Dorothy. 2015. *Kitchen Sink Realisms: Domestic Labor, Dining, and Drama in American Theatre*. Iowa City, IA: University of Iowa Press.

Chaplin, Sid. 1961. *The Day of the Sardine*. London: Eyre & Spottiswoode.

Chaplin, Sid. 1962. *The Watchers and the Watched*. London: Eyre & Spottiswoode.

Chapman, Stanley D., Ed. 1971. *History of Working-Class Housing: A Symposium*. Newton Abbot, UK: David & Charles Ltd.

Cherrington, Ruth. 2012. *Not Just Beer and Bingo! A Social History of Working Men's Clubs*. Bloomington, IN: AuthorHouse.

Clarke, Alan. 1987. *Rita, Sue, and Bob Too*. London: Channel 4.

Cohen, David, Greg Lanning and Roger Thomas. 1985. *Bandung File*. London: Channel 4.

Collins, Tony. 2009. *A Social History of English Rugby Union*. London and New York, NY: Routledge.

Collinson, Peter. 1968. *Up the Junction*. Hollywood, CA: Paramount Pictures.

Colquhoun, Ian. 2008. *RIBA Book of British Housing: 1990 to the Present Day*. 2nd ed. Amsterdam, NL and London: Architectural Press.

Connolly, Nathan. 2017. *Know Your Place: Essays on the Working Class by the Working Class*. Liverpool, UK: Dead Ink.

Couldry, Nick. 2000 [1999]. *The Place of Media Power: Pilgrims and Witnesses of the Media Age*. London and New York, NY: Routledge.

Daniels, Anthony. 2008. "Lessons of the Long-Distance Runner." *The New Criterion* 27 (1): 23–8.

Darley, Gillian. 2003. *Factory*. London: Reaktion Books.

Davies, Colin. 2005. *The Prefabricated Home*. London: Reaktion Books.

Delaney, Shelagh. 1958. *A Taste of Honey*. New York, NY: Grove Press.

Dell, Edmund. 1998. "Controversies in the Early History of Channel Four." *Contemporary British History* 12 (4): 1–52.

Derkow, Barbara. 1981. *In the Pink*. London: Channel 4.

Dickson, Paul. 1947. *Country Homes*. Films of Fact.

Downes, David. 2013 [1966]. *The Delinquent Solution: A Study in Subcultural Theory*. Abingdon, UK and New York, NY: Routledge.

Dugan, Emily. 2009. "Britain's Estates Are 'Social Concentration Camps.'" *The Independent*, May 3, 2009. https://www.independent.co.uk/news/uk/home-news/britain-s-estates-are-social-concentration-camps-1678127.html.

Dunn, Nell. 1967. *Poor Cow*. London: MacGibbon & Kee.

Dunn, Nell. 1988 [1963]. *Up the Junction*. London: Virago Modern Classics.

Dunn, Nell. 2013a. "British New Wave: *Up the Junction*." Interview. *Author Nell Dunn on What Inspired Her to Write Up the Junction*. BBC Radio 4 FM. https://www.bbc.co.uk/programmes/p01g4mzf.

Dunn, Nell. 2013b. "The Writer Nell Dunn on 'Up the Junction' and 'Poor Cow.'" 2013. Radio Interview. *Woman's Hour*. BBC Radio 4 FM.

Dunn, Nell. 2016a. "'It Was Such a Laugh!' Writer Nell Dunn in Conversation." Interview by Selina Robertson. *The F-Word* (blog). https://thefword.org.uk/2016/06/it-was-such-a-laugh-writer-nell-dunn-in-conversation/.

Dunn, Nell. 2016b. "Playwright and Author Nell Dunn in Conversation about Her Career." Interview by Philip Fisher. Theatre-Voice: Radio Interview. http://www.theatrevoice.com/audio/interview-nell-dunn/.

Durkheim, Émile. 1984 [1893]. *The Division of Labor in Society*. Translated by W.D. Halls. New York, NY: The Free Press.

Elliot, Claire. 2003. "Mainlining with *Trainspotting*: Using Literature to Enter Other Worlds." In *The Healing Environment: Without and within*, edited by Deborah Kirklin and Ruth Richardson, 125–36. London: Royal College of Physicians.

Ellis, Samantha. 2003. "*A Taste of Honey*, London, May 1958." *The Guardian*, September 10, 2003.

Engelhart, Katie. 2014. "Britain's Working Men's Clubs Succumb to Modern Life." *The New York Times*, April 15, 2014. https://www.nytimes.com/2014/04/20/travel/britains-working-mens-clubs-succumb-to-modern-life.html.

Feldman, Gene, and Max Gartenberg, Eds. 2012 [1958]. *The Beat Generation and the Angry Young Men*. Eureka, CA: Stark House Press.

Finnimore, Brian. 1985. "The A.I.R.O.H. House: Industrial Diversification and State Building Policy." *The Construction History Society* 1: 60–71.

Foucault, Michel. 1986. "Of Other Spaces." *Diacritics* 16 (1): 22–7. https://doi.org/10.2307/464648.

Fraser, Garry. 2014. *Everybody's Child*. Documentary. Surrey, UK Journeyman Pictures.

Fraser, Garry. 2015. This Guy from Edinburgh's Estates Made a "Real-Life Trainspotting" About His Youth. Interview by Daniel Dylan Wray, February 19, 2015. https://www.vice.com/en/article/jmbwdp/an-interview-with-the-star-and-director-of-the-documentary-version-of-trainspotting-291.

Frears, Stephen. 1982. *Walter*. London: Channel 4.

Frears, Stephen. 1985. *My Beautiful Laundrette*. London: Mainline Pictures.

Friedan, Betty. 2010 [1963]. *The Feminine Mystique*. New York, NY: W. W. Norton & Company.

Gardner, Colin. 2006. *Karel Reisz*. Manchester, UK: Manchester University Press.

Gay, Paul. 2007. *Skins*. London: E4.

Geraghty, Christine. 2000. *British Cinema in the Fifties: Gender, Genre, and the 'New Look.'* London and New York, NY: Routledge.

Gibson, Tony. 1993. "Delinquency Then and Now." *The Raven: Anarchist Quarterly* 6 (2): 100–113.

Gidley, Ben, and Alison Rooke. 2010. "Asdatown: The Intersections of Classed Places and Identities." In *Classed Intersections: Space, Selves, Knowledge*, edited by Yvette Taylor, 95–115. Farnham, UK and Burlington, VT: Ashgate.

Gieseking, Jen Jack, William Mangold, Cindi Katz, Setha Low, and Susan Saeger, Eds. 2014. *The People, Place, and Space Reader*. New York, NY and London: Routledge.

Gilleman, Luc. 2014 [2002]. *John Osborne: Vituperative Artist*. New York, NY and London: Routledge.

Gilroy, Paul. 2002 [1987]. *There Ain't No Black in the Union Jack: The Cultural Politics of Race and Nation*. Abingdon, UK and New York, NY: Routledge.

Gindin, James. 1962. *Postwar British Fiction: New Accents and Attitudes*. London: Cambridge University Press.

Gindin, James. 1987. "Lawrence and the Contemporary English Novel." In *The Legacy of D. H. Lawrence: New Essays*, edited by Jeffrey Meyers, 30–53. New York, NY: Palgrave Macmillan. https://doi.org/10.1007/978-1-349-08308-4_3.

Goldthorpe, John H., David Lockwood, Frank Bechhofer, and Jennifer Platt. 1967. "The Affluent Worker and the Thesis of Embourgeoisement: Some Preliminary Research Findings." *Sociology* 1 (1): 11–31. https://doi.org/10.1177/003803856700100102.

Goodall, Derek. 1982. *Countdown*. London: Channel 4.

Gössel, Peter, and Gabriele Leuthäuser. 2001. *Architecture in the Twentieth Century*. Cologne, DE: Taschen.

Greer, Germaine. 2008 [1970]. *The Female Eunuch*. New York, NY: Harper Perennial Modern Classics.

Guyan, Kevin. 2016. "Masculinities, Planning Knowledge and Domestic Space in Britain, c. 1941–1961." PhD Dissertation, London: University College London.

Hammond, Matthew Brown. 1919. *British Labor Conditions and Legislation During the War*. New York, NY: Oxford University Press.

Hampton, Trevor. 1982. *Black on Black*. London: Channel 4.

Hanley, Lynsey. 2007. *Estates: An Intimate History*. London: Granta.

Hanson, Gillian Mary. 1999. *Understanding Alan Sillitoe*. Columbia, SC: University of South Carolina Press.

Harvey, Andy. 2010. "Staging the Sixties, *This Sporting Life* by David Storey." Paper presented at Masculine Identifications Conference, University of Huddersfield, July 2010.

Harvey, David. 2006a. "Space as a Keyword." In *David Harvey: A Critical Reader*, edited by Noel Castree and Derek Gregory, 270–93. Maiden, MA: Wiley-Blackwell.

Harvey, David. 2006b [1982]. *The Limits to Capital*. London and New York, NY: Verso.

Harvey, David. 2012. *Rebel Cities: From the Right to the City to the Urban Revolution*. London: Verso.

Harwood, Elain. 2010. *England's Schools: History, Architecture, and Adaptation*. Swindon, UK: English Heritage.

Haslam, Dave. 2015. *Life After Dark: A History of British Nightclubs and Music Venues*. New York, NY: Simon & Schuster.

Heilpern, John. 2002. "The World's Only Expert On Hobson's Choice Speaks!" *Observer* (blog). January 21, 2002. https://observer.com/2002/01/the-worlds-only-expert-on-hobsons-choice-speaks/.

Heilpern, John. 2007. *John Osborne: A Patriot for Us*. New York, NY: Alfred A Knopf.

Hemingway, Judy. 2006. "Contested Cultural Spaces: Exploring Illicit Drug-Using Through *Trainspotting*." *International Research in Geographical and Environmental Education* 15 (4): 324–35. https://doi.org/10.2167/irg198.0.

Higson, Andrew, Ed. 2016a [1996]. *Dissolving Views: Key Writings on British Cinema*. London and New York, NY: Bloomsbury.

Higson, Andrew. 2016b [1996]. "Space, Place, Spectacle: Landscape and Townscape in the 'Kitchen Sink' Film." In *Dissolving Views: Key Writings on British Cinema*, edited by Andrew Higson, 133–56. London and New York, NY: Bloomsbury.

Hines, Barry. 2000 [1968]. *A Kestrel for a Knave*. London: Penguin Classics.

Hobson, Dorothy. 2008 [2007]. *Channel 4: The Early Years and the Jeremy Isaacs Legacy*. London and New York, NY: I.B. Tauris.

Hoggart, Richard. 1971 [1957]. *The Uses of Literacy: Aspects of Working-Class Life with Special Reference to Publications and Entertainments*. London: Chatto & Windus.

Holdsworth, Nadine. 2006. *Joan Littlewood*. London and New York, NY: Routledge.

Hopkins, Eric. 1991. *The Rise and Decline of the English Working Classes, 1918–1990: A Social History*. London: Palgrave Macmillan.

Hutchings, William. 1987. "The Work of Play: Anger and the Expropriated Athletes of Alan Sillitoe and David Storey." *Modern Fiction Studies* 33 (1): 35–47. https://doi.org/10.1353/mfs.0.1323.

Hutchings, William. 1988. *The Plays of David Storey: A Thematic Study*. Carbondale, IL: Southern Illinois University Press.

Hutchings, William. 1993. "Proletarian Byronism: Alan Sillitoe and the Romantic Tradition." In *English Romanticism and Modern Fiction: A Collection of Critical Essays*, edited by Allan Chavkin, 83–113. New York, NY: AMS Press.

Iball, Helen. 2008. *Modern Theatre Guides: Sarah Kane's Blasted*. London and New York, NY: Continuum.

Imrie, Rob. 2004. "Disability, Embodiment and the Meaning of the Home." *Housing Studies* 19 (5): 745–63. https://doi.org/10.1080/0267303042000249189.

Ironside, Virginia. 2003. "Nell Dunn." *The Independent*. May 17, 2003. http://www.independent.co.uk/arts-entertainment/theatre-dance/features/nell-dunn-i-never-used-to-think-about-death-until-i-was-50-i-was-never-going-to-die-i-was-immortal-105000.html.

Jackson, Dianne. 1982. *The Snowman*. London: Channel 4.

Jeffries, Stuart. 2016. "Brookside Creator Phil Redmond: 'Northern Powerhouse? Northern Slaughterhouse, More Like.'" *The Guardian*, January 13, 2016.

Jennings, Paul. 2011. *The Local: A History of the English Pub*. Cheltenham, UK: The History Press Ltd.

Jennings, Paul. 2016. *A History of Drink and the English, 1500–2000*. London and New York, NY: Routledge.

Jordan, Neil. 1986. *Mona Lisa*. London: Film4 Productions.
Jones, Judith. n.d. "The Museum of Broadcast Communications—Coronation Street." Museum of Broadcast Communications. Accessed December 21, 2017. https://web.archive.org/web/20150702082801/http://www.museum.tv/eotv/coronationst.htm.
Jones, Owen. 2020 [2011]. *Chavs: The Demonization of the Working Class*. London and New York, NY: Verso.
Kaika, Maria. 2004. *City of Flows: Modernity, Nature, and the City*. New York, NY and London: Routledge.
Kalliney, Peter J. 2006. *Cities of Affluence and Anger: A Literary Geography of Modern Englishness*. Charlottesville, VA: University of Virginia Press.
Kane, Sarah. 1996 [1995]. *Blasted & Phaedra's Love*. London and New York, NY: Bloomsbury Methuen Drama.
Kitchin, Laurence. 1960. *Mid-Century Drama*. London: Faber & Faber.
Kureishi, Hanif. 1996. *My Beautiful Laundrette and Other Writing*. London: Faber & Faber.
Lacey, Stephen. 2002 [1995]. *British Realist Theatre: The New Wave in its Context 1956–1965*. London and New York, NY: Routledge.
Laing, Stuart. 1986. *Representations of Working-Class Life, 1957–1964*. London: Palgrave Macmillan.
Lay, Samantha. 2002. *British Social Realism: From Documentary to Brit Grit*. London: Wallflower Press.
Lee, Simon. 2021. "Lit Grit: The Gritty and the Grim in British Working-Class Cultural Production." In *The Routledge International Handbook of Working-Class Studies*, edited by Michele Fazio, Christie Launius, and Tim Strangleman, 371–80. New York, NY: Routledge.
Lefebvre, Henri. 1991 [1974]. *The Production of Space*. Translated by Donald Nicholson-Smith. Malden, MA: Wiley-Blackwell.
Leigh, Mike. 1991. *Life Is Sweet*. London: Palace Pictures.
Leigh, Mike. 1993. *Naked*. London: First Independent Films UK.
Lichtenstein, Claude, and Thomas Schregenberger. 2006. *As Found: The Discovery of the Ordinary: British Architecture and Art of the 1950s, New Brutalism, Independent Group, Free Cinema, Angry Young Men*. Zurich, CH: Lars Müller Publishers.
Linkon, Sherry Lee. 2021. "Class Analysis from the Inside: Scholarly Personal Narrative as a Signature Genre of Working-Class Studies." In *The Routledge International Handbook of Working-Class Studies*, edited by Michele Fazio, Christie Launius, and Tim Strangleman, 20–31. New York, NY: Routledge.
Littlewood, Joan. 2016. *Joan's Book: The Autobiography of Joan Littlewood*. London and New York, NY: Bloomsbury Methuen Drama.
Loach, Ken. 1967. *Poor Cow*. Vic Films Productions.
Loach, Ken. 1965. *Up the Junction (The Wednesday Play)*. TV Film. London: BBC1.
Loach, Ken. 1966. *Cathy Come Home*. TV Film.
Loach, Ken. 1967. *Poor Cow*. London: Vic Films Productions.

MacInnes, Colin. 1961. *England, Half English*. London: MacGibbon & Kee.
MacInnes, Colin. 2005. *The London Novels: City of Spades, Absolute Beginners, and Mr Love and Justice*. London: Allison & Busby.
MacLeod, Lewis. 2008. "Life Among the Leith Plebs: Of Arseholes, Wankers, and Tourists in Irvine Welsh's *Trainspotting*." *Studies in the Literary Imagination* 41 (1): 89–106.
MacLeod, Lewis. 2012. "'Various Pubs Give Signs of Life': Of Drink and Time in Alan Sillitoe's *Saturday Night and Sunday Morning*." *Yearbook of English Studies* 42: 113–31. https://doi.org/10.5699/yearenglstud.42.2012.0113.
Mansfield, Jane. 2010. "The Brute-Hero: The 1950s and Echoes of the North." *Literature & History* 19 (1): 34–49. https://doi.org/10.7227/LH.19.1.4.
Manvell, Roger. 1946 [1944]. *Film*. Harmondsworth, UK: Pelican.
Marwick, Arthur. 2003 [1982]. *British Society since 1945: The Penguin Social History of Britain*. London: Penguin Books.
Maschler, Tom, Ed. 1958 [1957]. *Declaration*. London: MacGibbon & Kee.
Mass Observation. 1943a. *An Enquiry into People's Homes: A Report Compiled by Mass Observation*. London: Advertising Guild Services. https://www-massobservation-amdigital-co-uk.libproxy.txstate.edu/Documents/Details/Publication-Peoples%20Homes.
Mass Observation. 1943b. "People and Homes." File Report 1651. University of Sussex. Mass Observation Archive. https://www-massobservation-amdigital-co-uk.libproxy.txstate.edu/Documents/Details/FileReport-1651.
Mass Observation. 1946. "Second Report on the Modern Homes Exhibition." File Report 2363. University of Sussex. Mass Observation Archive. https://www-massobservation-amdigital-co-uk.libproxy.txstate.edu/Documents/SearchDetails/FileReport-2363?thumbnailIndex=1.
McKerrow, Richard. 2014. *Benefits Street*. London: Channel 4.
McKinney, Devin. 2006. "The Flesh Failures." *The Believer* 4 (2): 31–8.
Mellor, Leo. 2011. *Reading the Ruins: Modernism, Bombsites and British Culture*. Cambridge, UK: Cambridge University Press.
Morgan, John, and Michael Toppin. 1982. *Eastern Eye*. London: Channel 4.
Mucignat, Rosa. 2013. *Realism and Space in the Novel, 1795–1869: Imagined Geographies*. Surrey, UK and Burlington, VT: Ashgate.
Neaverson, Peter, and Marilyn Palmer. 1994. *Industry in the Landscape, 1700–1900*. London: Routledge.
Neilson, Anthony. 2013 [1998]. *Plays:1*. London and New York, NY: Bloomsbury Methuen Drama.
Nethersole, Reingard. 1990. "From Temporality to Spatiality: Changing Concepts in Literary Criticism." In *Space and Boundaries: Proceedings of the XIIth Congress of the ICLA*, edited by Roger Bauer and Douwe Fokkema, 5:59–63. München, DE: Iudicium.
Nottingham Evening Post. 1961. "City MP Hits at 'Saturday Night' Film." February 4, 1961.

Orwell, George. 2014 [1937]. *The Road to Wigan Pier*. London: Penguin Classics.
Osborne, John. 1956. *Look Back in Anger*. London: Penguin Plays.
Osborne, John. 1981. *A Better Class of Person: An Autobiography Vol 1: 1929–1956*. London: Faber & Faber.
Osmond, Humphry. 1957. "Function as the Basis of Psychiatric Ward Design." *Mental Hospitals* 8 (4): 23–7. https://doi.org/10.1176/ps.8.4.23.
Patterson, Michael. 2003. *Strategies of Political Theatre: Post-War British Playwrights*. Cambridge, UK: Cambridge University Press.
Paul, Ronald. 1982. *"Fire in Our Hearts": A Study of the Portrayal of Youth in a Selection of Post-War British Working-Class Fiction*. Gothenburg, SE: Acta Universitatis Gothoburgensis.
Perks, Jeff. 1983. *Our Lives*. London: Channel 4.
Phillips, Lawrence. 2006. *London Narratives: Post-War Fiction and the City*. London and New York, NY: Continuum.
Pittock, Malcolm. 1990. "Revaluing the Sixties: *This Sporting Life* Revisited." *Forum for Modern Language Studies* 27 (2): 97–108. https://doi.org/10.1093/fmls/XXVI.2.97.
Power, Anne. 2007. *City Survivors: Bringing Up Children in Disadvantaged Neighbourhoods*. Bristol, UK: Policy Press.
Prieto, Eric. 2011. "Geocriticism, Geopoetics, Geophilosophy, and Beyond." In *Geocritical Explorations: Space, Place, and Mapping in Literary and Cultural Studies*, edited by Robert T. Tally Jr., 13–27. Basingstoke, UK: Palgrave Macmillan.
Proshansky, Harold M., Abbe K. Fabian, and Robert Kaminoff. 1983. "Place-Identity: Physical World Socialization of the Self." *Journal of Environmental Psychology* 3 (1): 57–83. https://doi.org/10.1016/S0272-4944(83)80021-8.
Prunetti, Alberto. 2022. "Workers Telling Their Own Stories Can Rebuild Working-Class Pride." *Jacobin*. January 7, 2022. https://jacobinmag.com/2022/01/didier-eribon-retour-a-reims-movie-class.
Ravenhill, Mark. 2005 [1996]. *Shopping and Fucking*. Edited by Dan Rebellato. London and New York, NY: Bloomsbury.
Ravenscroft, Alan. 1983. *Ear to the Ground*. London: Channel 4.
Redhead, Steve. 2007. "This Sporting Life: The Realism of The Football Factory." *Soccer & Society* 8 (1): 90–108. https://doi.org/10.1080/14660970600989525.
Redmond, Phil, and Colin McKeown. 1982. *Brookside*. Channel 4.
Reisz, Karel. 1960. *Saturday Night and Sunday Morning*. Woodfall Film Productions, British Lion Films, Bryanston Films.
Richardson, Tony. 1961. *A Taste of Honey*. Iver Heath, UK: British Lion Films.
Richardson, Tony. 1962. *The Loneliness of the Long Distance Runner*. Iver Heath, UK: British Lion Films.
Robertson, Seona, and Dianne Tammes. 1984. *People to People: Just Like Coronation Street*. London: Channel 4.
Rosen, Andrew. 2003. *The Transformation of British Life 1950–2000: A Social History*. Manchester, UK: Manchester University Press.

Rosenfield, Orna, Judith Allen, and Teri Okoro. 2011. "Race, Space and Place: Lessons from Sheffield." *ACE: Architecture, City and Environment* 4 (17): 245–92. http://dx.doi.org/10.5821/ace.v6i17.2536.

Russell, Ken. 1960. *Monitor: Shelagh Delaney's Salford*, London: BBC.

Salwak, Dale. 1984. *Interviews with Britain's Angry Young Men*. San Bernardino, CA: Borgo Press.

Sandford, Jeremy. 2006. "Battersea Night (3)." www.jeremysandford.org.uk. 2006. https://www.jeremysandford.org.uk/jsarchive/warp-battersea-night-3.html.

Schofield, Camilla. 2013. *Enoch Powell and the Making of Postcolonial Britain*. Cambridge, UK and New York, NY: Cambridge University Press.

Sierz, Aleks. 2001. *In-Yer-Face Theatre: British Drama Today*. London: Faber & Faber.

Sierz, Aleks. 2002. "Still In-Yer-Face? Towards a Critique and a Summation." *New Theatre Quarterly* 18 (69): 17–24. https://doi.org/10.1017/S0266464X0200012X.

Sierz, Aleks. 2008. *John Osborne's Look Back in Anger*. London and New York, NY: Continuum.

Sillitoe, Alan. 1962. "I Reminded Him of Muggleton." *Shenandoah*, 13: 47–50.

Sillitoe, Alan. 1982. "Writing and Publishing." *London Review of Books* 4 (6): 8–10.

Sillitoe, Alan. 1995. *Life Without Armor*. London: HarperCollins.

Sillitoe, Alan. 2010 [1958]. *Saturday Night and Sunday Morning*. New York, NY: Alfred A Knopf.

Sillitoe, Alan. 2010 [1959]. *The Loneliness of the Long Distance Runner*. New York, NY: Vintage.

Sillitoe, Alan. n.d. "A.Y.M. Note." Note. The Lilly Library, Indiana University, Bloomington IN. Mss. II, box 12, folder 27. The Sillitoe mss.

Sillitoe, Alan. n.d. "The Deserters." Unpublished Typescript. The Lilly Library, Indiana University, Bloomington IN. Mss. II, box 3, folder 15, tab 3. The Sillitoe mss.

Sillitoe, Alan. n.d. "Wider Spiritual Horizons." Unpublished Article. The Lilly Library, Indiana University, Bloomington IN. Mss. II, box 22, no folder. The Sillitoe mss.

Skeggs, Beverley. 2004. *Class, Self, Culture*. London and New York, NY: Routledge.

Skilton, Brian. 1984. *Bacchanal*. London: Channel 4.

Skovmand, Michael, and Steffen Skovmand, Eds. 1975. *The Angry Young Men*. Copenhagen, DK: Akademisk Forlag.

Smithson, Norman. 1969. *The World of Little Foxy*. London: Victor Gollancz.

Soja, Edward W. 1996. *Thirdspace: Journeys to Los Angeles and Other Real-and-Imagined Places*. Malden, MA: Wiley-Blackwell.

Storey, David. 2000 [1960]. *This Sporting Life*. London: Vintage.

Storey, David. 2013 [1963]. *Radcliffe*. Richmond, VA: Valancourt Books.

Storey, David. 2013 [1976]. *Saville*. Richmond, VA: Valancourt Books.

Sutherland, John. 2011. *Lives of the Novelists: A History of Fiction in 294 Lives*. London: Profile Books.

Sylvester, David. 1954. "The Kitchen Sink." *Encounter* 3 (6): 61–3.

Tadié, Alexis. 2015. "Running for Freedom: The Politics of Long-Distance Running in Modern Fiction." *The International Journal of the History of Sport* 32 (2): 286–98. https://doi.org/10.1080/09523367.2014.967227.

Tally Jr., Robert T. 2013. *Spatiality*. London and New York, NY: Routledge.

Taylor, Christopher. 1986. "Realism and the Language of Realism in the Works of Alan Sillitoe." In *Four Fits of Anger: Essays on the Angry Young Men*, edited by Mark Brady, John Dodds, and Christopher Taylor, 100–49. Pasian di Prato, IT: Campanotto Editore.

Temple, Julien. 1986. *Absolute Beginners*. London: Palace Pictures.

Terris, Olwen. n.d. "Coronation Street (1960–)." BFI Screen Online. Accessed April 11, 2017. http://www.screenonline.org.uk/tv/id/460796/index.html.

Thompson, E. P. 1963. *The Making of the English Working Class*. New York, NY: Pantheon Books.

Thrift, Nigel, and Peter Williams. 2014 [1987]. *Class and Space (RLE Social Theory): The Making of Urban Society*. London: Routledge & Kegan Paul.

Todd, Selina. 2019. *Tastes of Honey: The Making of Shelagh Delaney and a Cultural Revolution*. London: Chatto & Windus.

Tynan, Kenneth. 1956. "The Voice of the Young." *The Observer*, May 13, 1956.

Tynan, Kenneth. 1961. *Curtains: Selections from the Drama Criticism and Related Writings*. New York, NY: Atheneum.

Vidler, Anthony. 2000. *Warped Space: Art, Architecture, and Anxiety in Modern Culture*. Cambridge, MA: The MIT Press.

Waal, Kit de, Ed. 2019. *Common People: An Anthology of Working-Class Writers*. London: Unbound.

Wain, John. 2013 [1953]. *Hurry on Down*. Richmond, VA: Valancourt Books.

Wake, Oliver. n.d. "Tynan, Kenneth." BFI Screen Online. Accessed February 14, 2021. http://www.screenonline.org.uk/tv/id/454700/.

Walker, J. Holland. 1928. "An Itinerary of Nottingham: Ilkeston Road, Alfreton Road, Talbot Street, Wollaton Street." *Transactions of the Thoroton Society* 32. http://www.nottshistory.org.uk/articles/tts/tts1930/itinerary1930p11.htm.

Warf, Barney, and Santa Arias, Eds. 2014. *The Spatial Turn: Interdisciplinary Perspectives*. London and New York, NY: Routledge.

Warren, Tony. 1960. *Coronation Street*. Manchester, UK: Granada Television.

Waterhouse, Keith. 2013 [1959]. *Billy Liar*. Richmond, VA: Valancourt Books.

Watt, Ian. 1952. "Realism and the Novel." *Essays in Criticism* 2 (4): 376–96.

Welsh, Irvine. 1993. *Trainspotting*. New York, NY: W. W. Norton & Company.

Westphal, Bertrand. 2011. *Geocriticism: Real and Fictional Spaces*. Translated by Robert T. Tally Jr. Basingstoke, UK: Palgrave Macmillan.

White, Edward. 2016. "Northern Powerhouse." *Paris Review Daily* (blog). February 11, 2016. http://www.theparisreview.org/blog/2016/02/11/northern-powerhouse/.

Whitehouse, Mary. 1967. *Cleaning up T.V.: From Protest to Participation*. London: Blandford Press.
Williams, Raymond. 1973. *The Country and the City*. London: Chatto & Windus.
Willis, Paul. 1981. *Learning to Labor: How Working Class Kids Get Working Class Jobs*. New York, NY: Columbia University Press.
Wilson, Colin. 1956. *The Outsider*. London: Victor Gollancz.
Wilson, Colin. 2007. *The Angry Years: The Rise and Fall of the Angry Young Men*. London: Robson Books.
Wilson, Nicola. 2015. *Home in British Working-Class Fiction*. London: Routledge.
Wintle, Angela. 2015. "Irvine Welsh: 'I Was a Heroin Addict—Then I Found Buy-To-Let.'" *The Telegraph*, June 7, 2015, sec. Finance. http://www.telegraph.co.uk/finance/personalfinance/fameandfortune/11653606/Irvine-Welsh-I-was-a-heroin-addict-then-I-found-buy-to-let.html.
Wood, Denis, and Robert J. Beck. 1994. *Home Rules*. Baltimore, MD: The Johns Hopkins University Press.
Woodroofe, Kathleen. 1975. "The Irascible Reverend Henry Solly and His Contribution to Working Men's Clubs, Charity Organization, and 'Industrial Villages' in Victorian England." *Social Service Review* 49 (1): 15–32. https://doi.org/10.1086/643207.
Woodward, Phil, 1989. *Out on Tuesday/Out*. London: Channel 4.

Index

Abbott, Paul 10
abortion 71, 105–6, 110, 137
Abortion Act, The (1967) 110
Absolute Beginners (Temple) 143, 155
Absolute Beginners (MacInnes) 63, 69, 127, 141–2, 144, 146, 155, 167
absolute space (Harvey) 120–1
acquiescence 39, 55, 59–60, 72, 97, 101, 111, 163, 167
   See also: resignation
Adams, Ann Marie 23
aesthetics
   spaces of transit 120
   class 40, 169–73, 188
   commodified 9–10, 175–6, 182–4
   housing 29, 34–7, 47–8, 66
   institutional 76, 82
   kitchen sink 5, 8, 11, 21, 64, 92, 99, 161–5, 167, 169–73, 182, 185, 187, 191, 195
   political 20, 24, 45, 69, 111, 135, 156–61, 175, 179, 186–7, 195, 197
   realist 3, 5, 116, 153, 156–61, 178, 187, 191, 196
   spatial 12, 20, 23–4, 42, 116, 125, 138, 169–73, 185
affluence, era of 5, 48, 55–6, 58–9, 90, 100, 103, 130
agency 17, 57, 92–3, 111, 113, 115, 137–8, 140, 148, 153, 191
   See also: autonomy
aggression 65, 100, 104, 137, 163, 175
aggro-effects 189, 198
Airey 32–3, 35
   See also: prefabs
AIROH 32–4, 67
   See also: prefabs
Alcalá, Roberto del Valle 11
alcohol 76–8, 127, 130, 178
alcoholism 7
Aldridge, Meryl 133
Alexander, Anthony 87

alienation 2, 4, 9–10, 18, 23–5, 27, 31, 36–7, 42, 47–8, 51, 53, 60, 83, 90, 96–7, 104, 119, 123, 132, 135, 186, 192–3
   See also: frustration
Allen, Trevor 126
Amis, Kingsley 4–7, 65, 161–2
Anderson, Lindsay 6, 8, 60, 64, 99, 164
Angry Young Man 4, 6–8, 11, 50, 60, 64, 66, 106, 137, 149, 162, 164, 166, 188
   See also: kitchen sink realism
antisocial behavior 10, 97, 128–9, 149–50
   See also: delinquency
anxiety
   class 1–2, 32, 36, 40, 49, 51, 54, 57, 61, 63, 71, 103, 143, 153, 136, 165, 181
   cultural 5–6, 36, 160
   precarity 35, 50, 53, 60, 98, 176, 178
   social 2, 28, 37, 56, 68, 73, 85, 160, 162, 183
   spatial 35, 43, 46–7, 50, 73, 74, 87, 133, 139, 147, 194–5
architectural uncanny (Vidler) 46–7, 125
architecture 82, 84, 86–7, 99
Arden, John 162
Arias, Santa 12–13
Artaud, Antonin 165
Atha, Christine 47–8
aspiration 27, 31, 52, 73, 161, 173, 184
   See also: social mobility
atomization 29–31, 38, 49, 66–7, 79, 98, 134
   See also: fragmentation
Augé, Marc 122–3, 135
austerity, era of 5, 25, 48, 60, 90, 110, 130
authenticity 10, 18, 55, 60, 64, 94, 99–100, 106, 108, 110, 153, 160–1, 165, 168–70
   See also: realism
autonomy 26–7, 33, 36, 38, 53, 55, 65, 88, 93, 98, 108, 111, 115, 134, 137, 180
   See also: agency

Bacchanal (Skilton) 180
Bachelard, Gaston 45–6
back-to-backs 39, 148
    See also: housing
Bakhtin, Mikhail 13
Bandung File (Cohen, Lanning, Thomas) 180
Barker, Pat 66, 191
Barstow, Stan 5, 44, 83, 133, 162
Barthes, Roland 158–60, 167, 172
Barwise, Patrick 197
Bates, Alan 6
Battersea Power Station 109, 112, 136
Beaven, Brad 77, 129, 131
Beck, Robert J. 45–6
beer 68, 75, 95
behavioral sink (Calhoun) 18, 25, 43–5, 78, 128, 193
Benefits Street (McKerrow) 2, 182, 184–5, 187, 195
Bentley, Nick 141, 143
Beveridge Report, The (1942) 5, 21, 24, 67, 80, 165
    See also: Social Insurance and Allied Services Act (1942)
Beveridge, William 80
Bevin, Aneurin 65–6
    See also: Housing Act (1949)
Billy Liar (Waterhouse) 4, 74, 89, 162–3
Binns, David 73
BISF 32–5
    See also: prefabs
Black on Black (Hampton) 180
Blasted (Kane) 189
Blishen, Edward 23
Blitz, The 25, 27, 35, 73, 83, 86, 124
bombing 38, 88, 164, 189
    See also: Blitz, The
bomb sites 20, 73, 108–9, 115, 124–7, 138, 168
Bond, Edward 5, 162, 189, 197
Borsay, Peter 130–1
borstal 84, 94, 97–8, 102, 107, 131–2, 148–53
Borthwick, Stuart 183
Bottomley, Maurice 127
Bourdieu, Pierre 16, 111
Bourke, Joanna 30–1
Bowie, David 155
Brady, Mark 7, 10
Braine, John 5–7, 73, 125–6, 162, 170

Braithewaite, E. R. 6
Bratby, John 3, 106
Brien, Alan 64
Briggs, Raymond 181
Brighouse, Harold 68
Britain, Janie 183
British New Wave, The 6, 8, 9, 167–8, 175–6, 179, 197
Broadcasting Act, The (1981) 180
Brooke, Stephen 110, 136
Brooks, Gillian 197
Brookside (Redmond and McKeown) 180–3
brutalism 66, 188
Bullock, Nicholas 124
Butler, Judith 45
byelaws 29–31, 36, 47, 184
Byelaws Act, The 28–9
    See also: Public Health Act, The (1875)

Calhoun, John B 18, 25, 43–5, 47, 78
capitalism 16–17, 87, 119–20, 123
Carpenter, Humphrey 7
cartography 13–14, 95
Castronovo, David 7, 163
Cathy Come Home (Loach) 154
Cathy Come Home (Sandford) 154
censorship 71, 112, 164
Channel 4, 113, 179–87, 197
Chansky, Dorothy 8
Chaplin, Sid 162
Chapman, Stanley D., 68
chav 2, 10, 196
Cherrington, Ruth 77
Churchill, Winston 25
City of Spades (MacInnes) 20, 115, 127, 141–7, 149–50, 153, 155
    class in 144–7
    immigration 141–2, 154–5, 184
    space in 127, 143–6
Clarke, Alan 181
class
    anxiety 1–2, 32, 36, 40, 49, 51, 54, 57, 61, 63, 71, 103, 143, 153, 136, 165, 181
    articulation 18, 24, 31, 47, 45–51, 55, 60, 72, 79–80, 89, 92–3, 111, 115, 122, 141, 153, 156, 175, 196
    consciousness 4, 11, 15, 18–19, 24–5, 28, 38, 45, 49–50, 54–5, 60, 62–3,

72, 75, 80, 92–3, 110–11, 115, 131, 135, 140–1, 162
fetishism 4, 18, 21, 26, 28, 115, 154, 156, 169, 195, 198
fragmentation 5, 18, 29–30, 38, 49, 54, 66–7, 70, 79, 98, 134, 140
monolith 2, 18, 24–5, 30, 50, 72, 136, 195–6
solidarity 25, 30–3, 53–4, 63, 67, 90, 98, 110–11, 178
status 16, 20, 30, 49, 59, 78, 91, 100, 103, 114, 118, 140, 144, 170
stratification 13, 18, 20, 24, 53–4, 57, 60, 75, 79, 90, 111, 115, 163, 189
tourism 21, 92, 105–6, 110, 114, 156, 198
Clayton, Jack 6, 126
clubs 55, 76–80, 95–6, 109, 124, 126–8, 131, 135, 138, 146, 147
collective
  action 120, 122, 136, 153
  shared affect 7, 140
  as social body 19, 30–1, 37, 50
collective consciousness (Durkheim) 72, 92–3, 95
Collins, Tony 113
Collinson, Peter 6, 89, 105, 154
colonialism 6, 75, 141–3, 145
Colquhoun, Ian 66
commodities 46, 85, 90, 176, 178, 190
commodity culture 48, 103, 110, 130
community
  as homogenizing 29, 92, 96, 167, 175, 177
  as identity 19, 27, 29, 30–1, 34, 36, 56, 69, 128, 136, 140
  ideological effects of 58, 77, 81, 98, 107, 108, 120, 147
  neglect 132, 138, 141, 149, 184
  representations of 72, 78, 102–3, 136, 173–4
  separation from 30, 37, 42, 73, 75, 93, 103, 168, 186
  spirit 28, 54, 58, 61, 67, 89–90, 95–6, 114, 131, 134, 138–9, 178, 184
  transformations of 118, 119, 134, 139, 146, 176
  wellbeing 27, 89–90, 109–10, 130, 132
conceived space (Lefebvre) 118, 120–1
Connolly, Nathan 196

construction
  appeal of 47
  corner cutting 27, 32, 36, 67
  expediency 27, 36
  factory 86
  high-rise 27, 36, 42, 66
  ideology 90–2, 143
  resistance to 119
  school 81–2
consumerism 32, 46, 48–9, 90, 109, 118, 149, 179, 190
Cordeaux, J. K. 71
Coronation Street (Warren) 173–9
Couldry, Nick 174
Countdown (Goodall) 180
counterhegemonic space 145
  See also: spatial production
Country and the City, The (Williams) 13, 22
Coupe, Bernice 23
Courtenay, Tom 6
Coward, Noël 52
crime 1, 36, 94–5, 97, 143, 147–50, 153, 180
  See also: delinquency

Daniels, Anthony 147
Darley, Gillian 86
Davies, Colin 33
Day of the Sardine, The (Chaplin) 162
Declaration (Maschler) 8, 57, 164
decor 46–9, 66, 75–7, 80, 138, 177, 190
defensible space (Calhoun) 19, 25, 43–4, 46–8, 52
deindustrialization 2, 184, 185
Delaney, Shelagh 5, 7, 11, 16, 18, 22, 25–6, 38, 41–3, 50, 60–5, 68–9, 74, 82–5, 99, 107,112, 137, 141, 166, 170, 184, 191
  development as writer 82–3, 166
  education 60, 83, 112
  home life 41–3, 170
delinquency 36, 40, 44, 59, 96–7, 128–30, 161, 193
Dell, Edmund 181–2
demolition 29–30, 87, 106, 139–40
  See also: slum clearance
dereliction 18, 25, 28, 42, 45, 61, 74, 125–6, 139, 187
Deserters, The (Sillitoe) 94, 113, 155

dialectical tension 16, 17, 92, 118, 120–1
  See also: spatial production
diaspora 12, 20, 187
Dickson, Paul 32
differential space (Lefebvre) 19, 118–20
disenfranchisement 2, 7, 51, 55, 63,
    149–50, 164, 193
  See also: frustration
documentary
  films 9, 41–2, 88, 135, 181, 184, 193
  style 3, 17, 62, 64, 93, 105–6, 154, 158,
    166, 168, 170, 172
Downes, David 132
Doxa (Bourdieu) 16
Drabble, Margaret 105
drinking 55, 58, 75–80, 96, 130, 177
drugs 142, 192–3, 195
Dugan, Emily 37
Dunn, Nell 5, 7, 11, 19–20, 26, 72, 74, 78,
    89–90, 93, 105–10, 112, 114–15,
    135–41, 145–7, 154, 161–2, 171
  development as writer 105
  home life 89–90
  work 108
Durkheim, Émile 72, 91, 93, 95, 111

Ear to the Ground (Ravenscroft) 181
Eastern Eye (Morgan and Toppin)
    180
Education Act, The (1944) 80, 82–3, 85,
    162
Eliot, George 112
Elliot, Claire 193
Ellis, Samantha 166
Elsley, Bryan 183
emasculation 57, 65, 68
  See also: masculinity
embourgeoisement 55
Emecheta, Buchi 6
Engelhart, Katie 77
entertainment 77, 102, 131–2, 179, 183
entrepreneurialism 55, 88, 98, 107–8, 187
environmental ethology (Wood and Beck)
    48
Essential Work Order, The (1941) 88
estates 10, 26, 27, 31, 34, 37, 39, 42, 78,
    112, 117, 123, 133–4, 139, 192,
    193
  See also: housing

ethnicity 1, 12, 20–1, 143, 187
ethics
  and social policy 37
  as technical device 21, 23–4, 45, 111,
    116, 153, 156, 160, 169, 172, 175–6,
    178–9, 182, 187, 195–7
ethnography 14, 40, 42, 54, 58, 183
existential crisis 16–17, 19, 55, 59, 60, 65,
    69, 115, 163
exploitation
  of identity 3, 21, 90, 105, 156–7, 173,
    184, 194–6
  of labor 39, 100–2, 148, 172
  of social division 1–2
Everybody's Child (Fraser) 193

factories
  acts 88
  architecture 86
  authors and 38–40, 71, 84, 106, 112
  cultural role 90, 167
  identity 65, 71, 88–9, 96, 99, 106–8,
    110, 115, 137
  omnipresence of 98, 102, 104, 192
  problems with 87, 102, 111, 124, 160
  representations of 55–9, 67–9, 87,
    89–90, 93, 96–9, 101, 137–40, 148,
    168–9, 171–2, 176
fashion 48–9, 79, 109
fathers 39–40, 50–1, 53–4, 56–9, 67–9, 83,
    87, 89, 98–9, 139, 148–9, 152, 167
Feldman, Gene 8
Female Eunuch, The (Greer) 137
Feminine Mystique, The (Freidan) 137
fetishism 4, 18, 21, 26, 28, 115, 154, 156,
    169, 195, 198
  See also: class
Finney, Albert 6
Finnimore, Brian 33
Firstspace (Soja) 121
Foucault, Michel 12–14, 19, 62, 115,
    120–3, 135, 146
fragmentation
  of collective 18, 29–30, 38, 49, 54,
    66–7, 70, 79, 98, 134, 140
  as literary device 106, 108, 110–11,
    171
Fraser, Garry 193
Frears, Stephen 181, 185–7

Freidan, Betty 137
frustration 2, 4, 7, 10, 17, 24, 55, 60, 70, 72, 88, 97, 143, 149–50, 162, 175, 185

Garden City Movement (Howard) 132–3
Gardner, Colin 197
gender
    gendered labor 25, 49–50, 65, 74, 106–7, 135
    shifts in culture 50, 104–5, 110, 113, 137, 140, 146, 196
    spatial dynamics 35, 53, 75–6, 95, 136–41, 157, 178, 197
generational divides 46, 49–51, 74, 79, 96, 128, 164, 177, 183
gentrification 37, 42, 87, 108–10, 139, 141, 143, 176
geocriticism (Westphal) 14–15, 17, 116–17, 153–4
geographical imaginary 117
geography 12–13, 15, 17, 43, 48, 66, 75, 92, 94, 110–11, 116–17, 122, 131, 136, 167, 193
Georgian housing 28, 76, 114
Geraghty, Christine 174–5
Gibson, Tony 129–30
Gidley, Ben 66
Gilleman, Luc 23
Gilroy, Paul 1
Gindin, James 79, 95
Gissing, George 160
Gössel, Peter 86
Graves, Robert 93–4, 113
Great Depression, The 38
Great Fire of London, The 28
Greaves, Derrick 3
Greer, Germaine 137
Grenfell Fire, The 67
gritty
    aesthetics 106, 114, 164, 166, 168–70, 183–6, 188
    identities 4, 21, 156, 182, 190–1, 197
Gropius, Walter 86
Gunn, Thom 6
Guyan, Kevin 45

Habitus (Bourdieu) 16, 111
Hammond, Matthew Brown 103, 107
Hanley, Lynsey 10, 37
Hanson, Gillian Mary 38, 55, 87, 149
Hardy, Thomas 160–1
Harris, Richard 6
Harvey, Andy 104
Harvey, David 13, 16–17, 19, 104, 115, 117, 119–23, 125, 135, 142–3, 146, 152, 154
Harwood, Elain 81–2
Haslam, Dave 126
Hastings, Michael 5
Heath, Edward 1
Heilpern, John 40, 68
Hemingway, Judy 193–4
Henri, Adrian 106, 109–10, 140
heterodoxy 130
    See also: status quo
heterotopic space (Foucault) 12, 19, 62, 104, 115, 121–2, 125–6, 135–6, 146, 172
Hierarchies 82–3, 96, 103, 151, 153
Higson, Andrew 8, 168
Hines, Barry 191
Hobson, Dorothy 179–80
Hoggart, Richard 5, 11, 24, 30–1, 49–50, 54, 57–8, 64, 85, 109, 161, 175, 177
Holdsworth, Nadine 165
Holroyd, Stuart 6
homogeneity 27, 28, 24, 49, 59, 118, 119, 142, 146, 157–8, 167, 175, 177, 182, 183
    See also: sameness
Hopkins, Bill 5–8, 164
Houghton, Stanley 68
housing
    acts 25–6, 28–9, 33–4, 65–7
    back-to-backs 39, 148
    byelaws 29–31, 36, 47, 184
    crisis 27, 29, 37, 42, 46, 50, 61, 123, 133, 143, 163
    estates 10, 26–7, 30–1, 34, 37, 39, 42, 78, 112, 117, 123, 133–4, 139, 192–3
    Georgian housing 28, 76, 114
    high rise 26–7, 34, 36–7, 42, 66–7, 91, 142
    mass housing 27, 56, 82, 123, 193
    prefabs 26–7, 32–6, 42, 66–7, 109
    slums 26, 30, 42, 114
    tenements 26, 29, 39, 61

terraces 26–34, 36, 39–40, 42, 56, 67, 101, 114, 150, 176–7, 184
two-up two-down 26, 29, 34, 57
Housing Act, The (1949) 25–6, 65
Housing Act, The (1980) 66
Housing Defects Act, The (1984) 33
Housing Subsidies Act, The (1956) 67
Housing (Temporary Accommodation) Act, The (1944) 25, 34
Howard, Ebeneezer 132–3
Hurry on Down (Wain) 163
Hutchings, William 19, 22, 28, 64, 100, 102

Iball, Helen 190
idealization 44, 114, 145–6, 170, 178
See also: romanticism
identity
articulated 18, 60, 65, 79–80, 92, 111, 128, 143–4, 160, 196
classed identity 4, 16, 21, 24, 30, 41, 61, 72, 91, 111, 134, 144, 153, 172
crisis 16–17, 19, 47, 60, 84, 115
fetishized 4, 18, 21, 26, 28, 115, 154, 156, 169, 195, 198
informed 10–12, 72, 91, 93, 103, 115–16, 118, 122, 129, 135, 139, 141, 166–7, 175, 191
insubordinate 8, 10, 22, 40, 55, 57, 59, 71, 97–8, 131, 153, 179
monolithic 2, 18, 24–5, 30, 50, 72, 136, 195–6
renegotiated 4, 11, 17, 25, 65, 73, 75, 78, 80, 92, 99, 107, 111, 120, 125, 128, 141, 143–4, 160, 166–7, 172, 195
ideology 24, 28, 47, 50, 53–4, 57, 63, 73–4, 91, 111, 121, 124, 136, 143, 151, 160, 176, 190
immigrants 1, 12, 60, 74, 127, 141–3, 145–7, 154, 184
imperialism 1, 26, 74, 141, 146
See also: colonialism
imprisonment 35, 51, 63, 94, 98, 150, 151
See also: borstal
Imrie, Rob 73
industrial romanticism (Manvell) 168
industry
impact on identity 56, 160, 169
postwar 38, 79, 107, 109
production 33, 170
regions of 13, 25, 27–8, 68, 77, 86–8, 124, 128, 136, 171, 158, 184, 189
institutions
environments 43, 72, 75, 77–81, 91, 95, 101, 107, 109, 124, 145–7, 151, 171–2, 177
ideological 19, 72, 76, 78, 85, 102–3, 111, 163
social and cultural 53–4, 74, 79, 80, 93, 97, 143
insubordination 40, 71, 97, 131, 153
See also: rebellion
In-Yer-Face (Sierz) 165, 188–91
Ironside, Virginia 89, 112

James, Henry 47
Jarman, Derek 181
Jeffries, Stuart 181
Jennings, Elizabeth 6
Jennings, Paul 75–6, 78–9, 112
Joby (Barstow) 44
John, Augustus 127
Jones-Davies, Sue 180
Jones, Judith 173
Jones, Owen 2, 10, 196
Jordan, Neil 181

Kaika, Maria 46–7
Kalliney, Peter J., 50, 54, 161–3, 167
Kane, Sarah 189–90
Kestrel for a Knave, A (Hines) 191
Kind of Loving, A (Barstow) 133–4
kitchen sink realism
aesthetics 9–10, 15, 23, 64–5, 156
audience 10–11, 23, 50–1, 63, 69, 74, 159, 170–1
censorship 71–2, 112
commodification of aesthetics 173–9, 184–5
critical approaches to 5–11, 161–4
cult classics 9, 195
as elevated realism 5, 38, 67, 157–61, 170
emphasis on space 11, 24, 38, 44, 51, 64–5, 74, 111–12, 115, 169–73, 195–7
extension of aesthetics 173, 179–80, 187

legacy of 10, 17, 21, 71, 187–8, 195–7
motifs 74–5, 87, 164–9
origins of label 3–4, 106, 175
outsider motif 5, 8, 19, 22, 40, 69, 72, 93, 162
painters 3–4, 106
rejection of label 4, 6–7, 21
taboo topics 60, 113, 164, 167, 169, 180–1, 188–9
Kitchin, Laurence 60
knowable communities (Williams) 15, 17, 22, 74, 117
Kops, Bernard 5
Kureishi, Hanif 186–7

Lacey, Stephen 8–9, 100, 165
Lady Chatterley Trial 10
Laing, Stuart 64, 166
Lambert, Richard 39
Larkin, Philip 6–7
Lay, Samantha 8, 161, 167–8
Lefebvre, Henri 13, 15–17, 19, 44, 91, 111, 115, 118–23, 132, 135–6, 142–3, 146, 150–4, 171
Leigh, Mike 181, 185–6
Lessing, Doris 164
Leuthäuser, Gabriele 86
Lichtenstein, Claude 60, 163
Life Is Sweet (Leigh) 185–6
limitations (Willis) 59
limits
　social 11, 19, 24, 55, 60, 69, 72, 79, 99, 152–3
　spatial 11, 16, 44, 47, 53, 57, 75, 79, 100, 119, 133, 136, 140–1, 143, 145–6, 147–8, 191
Linkon, Sherry Lee 196
Littlewood, Joan 41, 82–3, 165–6
lived experience 5, 10–11, 13–15, 17, 31, 38, 41–3, 45, 55, 64, 74, 83, 85, 90, 92, 117, 120, 136, 141, 174
lived space (Lefebvre) 15, 118
Loach, Ken 6, 89, 105, 108, 110, 137, 154, 171, 181
London 2, 6, 14, 27–8, 41, 67–8, 81, 83, 89, 106, 108–9, 112, 114, 124, 127–8, 136, 141–3, 145–6, 154, 163–4, 166, 185–7

Loneliness of the Long Distance Runner, The (Richardson) 67, 147
Loneliness of the Long Distance Runner, The (Sillitoe) 20, 67, 69, 84, 94, 97, 102, 107, 113, 115, 132, 147–55, 167
　development of 150
　identity negotiation in 97, 149, 151
　spatial negotiation in 149–2
Look Back in Anger (Osborne) 4, 8, 10, 17–18, 23–5, 40–1, 47, 51–6, 62–3, 65, 68–9,73, 83, 138, 143, 162–3, 165, 171, 174, 189–90, 197
　as blueprint 165
　identity negotiation in 52–4, 60, 62, 64–5
　spatial negotiation in 23–4, 52–3
Look Back in Anger (Richardson) 197
Lucky Jim (Amis) 4, 65, 162
Lukács, György 91

MacInnes, Colin 6, 8, 20, 26, 60, 63, 74, 109, 115, 126–8, 141–7, 154–5, 162, 167, 184
　on Delaney 60, 63
　immigration 127, 141–3
　on London 110–11
MacLeod, Lewis 78, 194
making do 30–1, 52, 61
Mansfield, Jane 104
Manvell, Roger 168
marginalization 3, 44–5, 115, 127–8, 141–2, 147, 168, 193, 197
Marwick, Arthur 70
Marx, Karl 16, 102
Maschler, Tom 6, 164
masculinity 8, 45, 100, 104, 108, 142, 162–3, 190, 196
　See also: emasculation
Mass Observation 30–1, 35–6
McKellan, Ian 181
McKinney, Devin 145, 147
mechanical solidarity (Durkheim) 91, 111
Mellor, Leo 12, 116, 125–6
Mills, C Wright 117
mimeticism 3, 94, 135, 153
　See also: verisimilitude
Ministry of Reconstruction, The 25
Mitchell, Dennis 135
modern architecture 36, 48, 82
modernist literature 125, 162

Mona Lisa (Jordan) 181
Monkhouse, Allan 68
mothers 39–40, 60–1, 63, 69, 89, 177
motifs 5–7, 10, 15, 18, 21, 23, 72, 75, 83, 94, 115, 154, 157, 162, 164–6, 168–70, 172, 177–9, 187–8, 191–2, 196–7
 See also: thematics
Mr Love and Justice (MacInnes) 127, 141–2, 155
Mucignat, Rosa 157–9
multigenerational housing 46, 49–50, 74, 177, 183
 See also: generational divide
Murray, Jenni 105
My Beautiful Laundrette (Frears) 181, 186
My Beautiful Laundrette (Kureishi) 186–7

Naked (Leigh) 185–6
nationalism 12, 17, 27, 86, 90, 132, 148, 163, 186
Neaverson, Peter 39
Neilson, Anthony 190
Nethersole, Reingard 13–14
New Towns Act, The (1946) 34
New Towns Movement, The 87, 133
nine-way matrix (Harvey) 120–1
non-place (Augé) 122–3
nostalgia 2, 5, 24, 26, 64, 76, 170, 175–6, 178

oppression 2, 29, 39, 55, 60, 63, 105, 145, 162, 165, 191, 194, 196
 See also: disenfranchisement
Orr, Dee 180
Orwell, George 5, 64, 175
Osborn, Frederic J., 133
Osborne, John 4–8, 10–11, 16, 18, 23–6, 38, 40–1, 47, 51–5, 59–60, 62–5, 67, 69, 83, 99, 105, 142–3, 145, 149, 161–5, 190–1
 class position 41, 161–2
 education 41, 83
 home life 40–1, 67
Osmond, Humphry 43, 68
Our Lives (Perks) 181
Out on Tuesday / Out (Woodward) 180–1
Outsider, The (Wilson) 5, 8
 as kitchen sink motif 5, 8, 19, 40, 69, 72, 93, 162

Palmer, Marilyn 39
paralogical discourse (Westphal) 14, 117
parks 128, 132–4, 144
Patterson, Michael 8
Paul, Ronald 44–5
Penetrations (Willis) 59
Penetrator (Neilson) 189–91
People to People (Robertson and Tammes) 181
perceived space (Lefebvre) 16–17, 44, 92, 118, 120–1
persistence 28, 83–4, 91, 170
 See also: tenacity
Phillips, Lawrence 155
In the Pink (Derkow) 180
Pinter, Harold 6
Pittock, Malcolm 104
place identity (Proshansky) 44
policies 1–2, 79, 83, 109, 164, 184, 187
Poor Cow (Dunn) 171
Poor Cow (Loach) 171
poverty 23, 26, 37, 38, 52, 54, 62, 73, 75, 81, 109, 114, 126, 130, 132–3, 146, 165–6, 170, 184–5, 197
Powell, Enoch 1–2, 4
prefabs 26–7, 32–5, 42, 66–7, 109
Price, Cedric 166
Prieto, Eric 15, 17, 117
 privilege 84, 90, 114, 183
Production of Space, The (Lefebvre) 13, 118
proletarian Byronism (Hutchings) 19, 28, 64
propaganda 26, 32, 67, 90, 148, 155, 172
Proshansky, Harold M., 43–4
Prunetti, Alberto 2–3, 195–6
Public Health Act, The (1875) 28–9
pubs
 See also: clubs
 aesthetics 76
 class demarcation 75, 76
 community 77, 79
 gender demarcation 76
 history 76
 ideology 77–9
 "local", 76, 79
 working-men's clubs 76–7

Race Relations Act, The (1965) 1, 21
Race Relations Act, The (1968) 21
racism 1, 143, 186, 196

Radcliffe (Storey) 84
Ramsay, Lynne 181
Rattigan, Terrence 52, 190
Ravenhill, Mark 190–1
Raving Beauties, The 180
realism
　See also: kitchen sink realism
　documentary-style 3, 17, 62, 64, 93, 104–5, 154, 158, 166, 170, 172
　ethnography 14, 40, 42, 54, 58, 183
　genealogy of 157–61
　naturalism 160–1, 172
　social realism 3, 8, 40, 64, 153, 160–2, 166, 168, 170, 193
reality effect, the (Barthes) 158–9
rebellion 10, 22, 55, 57, 59, 97–8, 149
　See also: insubordination
recreational space 132–4
redevelopment 18–19, 24–7, 29–30, 35, 37, 42, 67, 90, 134, 140, 144–5
　See also: renovation
Redhead, Steve 101
Redmond, Phil 181–2
reimagining
　of identity 163
　of space 110, 121, 128
Reisz, Karel 6, 69, 71, 98, 112
relational space (Harvey) 120
relative space (Harvey) 120
renovation 27–8, 31, 33, 76, 184
representation
　authenticity 10, 18, 51, 55, 64, 94, 99–100, 108, 110, 153, 161, 165, 168, 169–70
　literary 13–14, 19, 25, 79, 116–17, 125, 145–6, 153–4, 156–59, 162, 183
　lived experience 5, 10–11, 13–15, 31, 38, 41–3, 45, 74, 83, 85, 90, 92, 117, 141, 174
　marginalized voices 3, 40, 100, 141–2, 147, 166–8, 179, 181, 187, 197
　media stereotypes 2, 40, 100, 128, 143, 184–5, 196
　working-class 3, 5, 8, 11, 18, 20–1, 24, 45, 55, 58, 72, 74, 93, 112, 139, 170, 172–3, 178, 185, 188, 192, 195–7
resignation 31, 39, 50, 55, 57, 59, 69, 72, 79, 96, 119, 145, 163, 192
　See also: acquiescence

Richardson, Tony 6, 62, 67, 69, 147, 149, 197
Rita, Sue, and Bob Too (Clarke) 181
Roache, William Patrick 177
Road to Wigan Pier, The (Orwell) 5, 64
Romanticism 159–60, 167
romanticization 2, 18, 24–5, 42, 44, 62, 64, 73, 114, 168, 170, 175, 177–8, 197
　See also: idealization
Rooke, Alison 66
Room at the Top (Braine) 7, 125–6, 170
Room at the Top (Clayton) 126
Rosen, Andrew 49
Rosenfield, Orna 66
Rugby 89, 100–3, 106, 113, 119, 168
Russell, Ken 41–2

Salwak, Dale 6–7
sameness 27, 28, 34, 49, 158, 167, 177
　See also: homogeneity
sanctuary 19, 49, 53–4, 56, 58, 72–4, 127, 138, 167, 176, 190
Sandford, Jeremy 106, 114, 154
Saturday Night and Sunday Morning (Reisz) 69, 70, 98, 112
Saturday Night and Sunday Morning (Sillitoe) 4, 10, 18–19, 25, 39–40, 46, 50, 55–9, 65, 71–2, 76, 78, 80, 84, 93–9, 108, 111–13, 130, 139, 147, 149–50, 153, 155, 163, 168, 177, 190, 196
　censorship 71, 112
　development of 93–5, 150
　identity negotiation in 22, 55, 59, 69, 76, 89, 96, 130
　spatial negotiation in 26, 56–8, 65, 67, 76, 95, 98–9
Saved (Bond) 90
Saville (Storey) 191
Schlesinger, John 6
Schofield, Camilla 1
schools 80–5
　acts 80–1
　architecture 81–2, 84, 86
　authors and 41, 60, 82–5, 88, 97–8, 101, 112, 114
　identity 82–5
　problems with 82
　representations of 62, 83, 97–8, 124, 132, 184

Schregenberger, Thomas 60, 163–4
secondspace (Soja) 121
Selvon, Sam 6
Sex Disqualification (Removal) Act (1919) 25
Sexuality 22, 60–1, 113, 138, 142, 154, 183, 187
Shameless (Abbott) 2, 10
Shelagh Delaney's Salford (Russell) 41–2
Shopping and Fucking (Ravenhill) 189–90
Sierz, Aleks 5, 188–91
Sillitoe, Alan 4–5, 7, 10, 16, 18–20, 22, 25–6, 38–42, 48, 50–1, 55–60, 62–5, 67–9, 71–2, 74, 76, 78, 83–5, 87–9, 93–9, 101–2, 107–9, 112–13, 115, 130, 132, 142, 145, 147–53, 162–3, 167–70, 177, 190, 192
   education 83–6, 88, 97–8
   home life 38–40, 68–9, 78, 94
   work life 39–40, 87–8
Sillitoe, Christopher 39
Sillitoe, Sabina 39
Situationist International, The 13, 119
Skeggs, Beverley 66
Skins (Gay) 182–4
Skovmand, Michael 7
Skovmand, Steffen 7
slums
   clearance 25, 29, 34, 37, 39, 42, 44, 47–8, 73, 87, 125, 133, 138, 176, 181
   conditions 26, 30, 37, 39, 61, 106, 139
   prewar 26, 30, 42, 114
Smith, Jack 3
Smithson, Norman 44
Smithson, Peter 44
Snowman, The (Briggs) 181
social field (Bourdieu) 16
Social Insurance and Allied Services Act, The (1942) 21
   See also: Beveridge Report, The
social mobility 2, 48, 52–4, 68, 73, 89, 92, 101, 103–4, 131, 162, 182–3, 187
social status 10, 16, 20, 28, 49, 56, 65, 78, 97, 100, 103–4, 109, 114, 118, 140, 142, 144, 162, 170
   See also: stratification
Soja, Edward 12–13, 19, 115–16, 121–3, 135, 143
Solly, Reverend Henry 77

spatial production (Lefebvre) 13, 16–17, 20, 111, 117–20, 123, 126, 135, 142, 145, 147, 151–3
spatial triad (Lefebvre) 19, 91–2, 118, 120–1, 153, 171
spatial turn, the 12–13, 115–17, 121, 124
Spear, Eric 176
squats 63, 117, 184, 187
status quo 19, 45, 55, 59, 72, 92, 130, 139, 141, 167
   See also: heterodoxy
stereotypes 2–3, 100, 128, 137, 155, 184–5, 197
Storey, David 5, 19, 72, 78, 83–4, 85, 87, 89–90, 93, 99–105, 119, 132, 162, 168, 191
   education 83–5, 101
   home life 84, 89
   work life 89
stratification 13, 18, 20, 24, 53–4, 57, 60, 75, 79, 90, 111, 115, 163, 189–90
subculture 4, 17, 46, 48, 128, 141, 143, 145, 154, 192
subterranean 146
   See also: underground clubs
subversion 10, 21, 72, 78, 88, 98, 115, 119–20, 122–4, 126, 132, 135–6, 157, 159, 184, 197
Sutherland, John 84
Sylvester, David 3–4, 106, 175

taboo 60, 113, 164, 169, 169, 180–1, 188
Tadié, Alexis 147
Tally Jr, Robert T., 12–13
taste 47–9, 177, 180
Taste of Honey, A (Delaney) 4, 18, 22, 25, 41–2, 50, 60–5, 69, 84, 137, 141, 163, 184, 191
   identity negotiation in 42, 50, 63, 84
   spatial negotiation in 41, 61–3, 141, 163, 191
   taboo content 60–1
Taste of Honey, A (Richardson) 62, 69
Taylor, Christopher 10
technology 38, 48–50
television 2, 10, 21, 58, 113, 149, 155, 173–174, 179, 181, 186
Temple, Julien 143
tenacity 91, 96, 170
   See also: persistence

terraces 26–34, 36, 39–40, 42, 56, 67, 98, 101, 114, 150, 176–7, 184
  See also: housing
Terris, Olwen 175
territory 17, 56, 95, 110, 130, 136, 143–4
Thatcher, Margaret 2, 66, 181, 183, 186–8, 194
Theatre of Cruelty (Artaud) 165
thematics 23, 94, 122, 134, 149, 188–89, 195
  See also: kitchen sink realism
thirdpace (Soja) 116, 121–2
This Sporting Life (Anderson) 99
This Sporting Life (Storey) 19, 72, 78, 80, 87, 89, 93, 99–112, 119, 132, 168
  development of 100
  identity negotiation in 99–100, 102–5
  spatial negotiation in 89, 101–3
Thomas, Roger 160, 183–4
Thompson, E. P., 85
Thrift, Nigel 15, 17
Todd, Selina 41
tradition
  historical 14, 28, 37, 46, 48, 50, 53, 56–7, 74, 102–3, 130, 138
  housing 27, 32, 34, 61, 188
  institutions 76–8, 82, 84–5, 137, 145, 162–3
  literary 111, 148, 159–61, 168, 171, 190
  working-class 5, 25, 31, 38, 51, 60, 75, 79, 92–3, 110
Trainspotting (Welsh) 191–5
transgressive space 123–4, 133, 135, 153, 172, 184, 191
transitory space (Augé) 121, 127, 129, 138
trauma 73–4
Tynan, Kenneth 5, 7–8, 17, 23, 51, 65, 68, 164–6, 174

Up the Junction (Collinson) 89, 105, 154
Up the Junction (Dunn) 19–20, 72, 74, 80, 89–90, 93, 105–11, 113, 114–15, 135–8, 140–4, 146–7, 149–50, 153–4, 163
  class tourism 105–6, 110
  development of 105–6, 108
  identity negotiation in 78, 109–10, 112
  spatial negotiation in 106–7, 109–10, 112

underground 9, 78, 124, 126–8, 135, 138, 146–7
  See also: subterranean
Up the Junction (Loach) 89, 105, 108, 110, 137
upheaval 30, 35, 40, 47, 74, 77
  See also: gentrification
Union Street (Barker) 66, 191
unions 77, 88
urban
  centers 1, 28, 36, 136, 143
  experience 12, 116, 125, 129, 146, 167–8, 188
  periphery 34, 37, 56, 81, 124, 132–3
  planning 43, 66, 74–5, 77, 87, 91–2, 119, 132–3, 158
  renewal 26–7, 30, 42–3, 81, 87, 138–9, 141, 142–3, 150, 176
Uses of Literacy, The (Hoggart) 5, 54, 64, 85, 109

verisimilitude 3, 17, 24, 67, 100, 140, 168, 172, 182–3
  See also: realism
vernacular 7, 106, 109–10, 135, 137, 140–1, 159, 166, 194
Veronica 4 Rose (Chait) 181
Victorian era 23, 27–8, 32, 39–40, 42, 48–9, 51–2, 68, 75–6, 84, 158–60, 177, 184
Vidler, Anthony 47
vignettes 94, 96, 106, 111, 135, 138, 147, 155, 159, 192
Viner, Fan 180
violence
  behavior 130
  depictions of 71, 89, 101–2, 105, 175, 185–6, 188, 190, 192, 198
  social forces 46, 125, 193, 195

Waal, Kit de 196
Wain, John 5, 163
Walker, J. Holland 39
Walter (Frears) 181
war damage 124, 127, 133, 144–5, 149, 170
Warf, Barney 12–13
Warren, Tony 173
waste 73, 184, 190, 194
Watchers and the Watched, The (Chaplin) 162

Waterhouse, Keith 4–5, 74, 83, 89, 162
Watt, Ian 85
We Loved in Bohemia (Allen) 126
Welfare State, The 5, 7, 18, 20–1, 24, 27, 52, 55, 58, 60, 68, 70, 80, 83, 85, 98, 103, 116, 123, 162
Welsh, Irvine 191–5
Wesker, Arnold 5, 26, 83, 162
Westphal, Bertrand 13–15, 17, 116–17, 153–4
Wheatley, Ben 181
Whitehouse, Mary 137
Whitelaw, William 180
Whitread, Rachel 46–7
Wigley, Mark 46
Williams, Peter 15, 17
Williams, Raymond 11, 13, 15, 17, 22, 74
Williams, Vaughan 47
Willis, Paul 59, 119, 130–1
Wilson, Colin 5–8, 164
Wilson, Nicola 11, 137, 176
Wimpey no-fines 32–5, 41
  See also: prefabs
Wintle, Angela 193
Wood, Denis 45–6
Woodroofe, Kathleen 77
Woolton, Lord 25
Wordsworth, William 159
Working-class
  See also: class
  alienation 2, 4, 10, 18, 23–5, 31, 37, 42, 47–8, 51, 60, 83, 97, 104, 135, 192–3
  aspirations of 27, 31, 52, 161, 173, 174
  audience 5, 67, 99, 105, 159
  concerns 61, 63, 181
  culture 2, 18, 49, 65–6, 72, 75, 94, 131, 168, 175, 178, 191
  formation of 85–6
  identity 2, 4, 26, 30, 37, 41, 61, 79, 91, 93, 111, 124, 134, 136, 153, 172, 175, 179
  literature 3, 5, 15, 40, 51, 95, 158, 159, 172, 188, 194, 196
  regions 5, 15–16, 28, 94, 100, 105, 108, 124, 128–9, 142, 171, 184
  representation 3, 5, 8, 11, 18, 20–1, 24, 45, 55, 58, 72, 74, 93, 112, 139, 170, 172–3, 178, 185, 188, 192, 195–7
  space 11, 14, 19, 33, 44, 49–50, 69, 72–3, 75, 78, 80, 90–3, 95–6, 99, 101, 105, 107, 118, 123, 132, 134–6, 139, 146–7, 149, 162, 167, 169–70, 172, 175 195
  tastes 47–9, 52, 177, 180
  them and us 24, 54, 83, 103, 151
  values 1, 5–6, 79, 91–2, 138
  voices 85, 105–6, 108, 143, 164, 166–7, 187, 190
working-class imaginary 20, 42, 61, 115–16, 143, 152
World of Little Foxy, The (Smithson) 44
WWI 35, 107, 112, 131
WWII 2, 13, 24–6, 28–9, 38, 73, 86, 88, 90, 127, 133, 166

youth 4, 65, 77, 129, 143
youth subculture 17, 46, 48, 127, 141, 145, 154
  See also: subculture

Zola, Émile 160

www.ingramcontent.com/pod-product-compliance
Lightning Source LLC
Chambersburg PA
CBHW062218300426
44115CB00012BA/2120